YALE AGRARIAN STUDIES

JAMES C. SCOTT, SERIES EDITOR

Issues of "Legibility"

- The expansion of regional road networks finally domesticated these mountains; they were increasingly tamed by the automobiles and turned into a vacctioner's retreat. p 3

The Agrarian Studies Series at Yale University Press seeks to publish outstanding and original interdisciplinary work on agriculture and rural society—for any period, in any location. Works of daring that question existing paradigms and fill abstract categories with the lived-experience of rural people are especially encouraged.

—James C. Scott, *Series Editor*

James C. Scott, *Seeing Like a State: How Certain Schemes to Improve the Human Condition Have Failed*

Brian Donahue, *The Great Meadow: Farmers and the Land in Colonial Concord*

J. Gary Taylor and Patricia J. Scharlin, *Smart Alliance: How a Global Corporation and Environmental Activists Transformed a Tarnished Brand*

Michael Goldman, *Imperial Nature: The World Bank and Struggles for Social Justice in the Age of Globalization*

Arvid Nelson, *Cold War Ecology: Forests, Farms, and People in the East German Landscape, 1945–1989*

Steve Striffler, *Chicken: The Dangerous Transformation of America's Favorite Food*

Parker Shipton, *The Nature of Entrustment: Intimacy, Exchange, and the Sacred in Africa*

Alissa Hamilton, *Squeezed: What You Don't Know About Orange Juice*

Parker Shipton, *Mortgaging the Ancestors: Ideologies of Attachment in Africa*

Bill Winders, *The Politics of Food Supply: U.S. Agricultural Policy in the World Economy*

James C. Scott, *The Art of Not Being Governed: An Anarchist History of Upland Southeast Asia*

Stephen K. Wegren, *Land Reform in Russia: Institutional Design and Behavioral Responses*

Benjamin R. Cohen, *Notes from the Ground: Science, Soil, and Society in the American Countryside*

Parker Shipton, *Credit Between Cultures: Farmers, Financiers, and Misunderstanding in Africa*

Paul Sillitoe, *From Land to Mouth: The Agricultural "Economy" of the Wola of the New Guinea Highlands*

For a complete list of titles in the Yale Agrarian Studies Series, visit www.yalebooks.com.

Sara M. Gregg

Managing
the Mountains

LAND USE PLANNING, THE NEW DEAL,

AND THE CREATION OF A FEDERAL LANDSCAPE

IN APPALACHIA

Yale UNIVERSITY PRESS

NEW HAVEN AND LONDON

Published with assistance from the Mary Cady Tew Memorial Fund.

Yale University Press books may be purchased in quantity for educational, business, or promotional use. For information, please e-mail sales.press@yale.edu (U.S. office) or sales@yaleup.co.uk (U.K. office).

Set in Scala and Scala Sans type by Westchester Book Group, Danbury, Connecticut.

Printed in the United States of America by Sheridan Books, Ann Arbor, Michigan.

Library of Congress Control Number: 2010929597
ISBN 978-0-300-14219-8

A catalogue record for this book is available from the British Library.

This paper meets the requirements of ANSI/NISO Z39.48-1992 (Permanence of Paper).

10 9 8 7 6 5 4 3 2 1

For my parents

CONTENTS

A typical Blue Ridge Mountain farm. Arthur Rothstein, *Home of Fannie Corbin, Shenandoah National Park, Virginia. House on Corbin Hollow farm,* October 1935. Farm Security Administration, Office of War Information Photograph Collection, Library of Congress. LC-USF33-002167-M2

IN 1935, Resettlement Administration photographer Arthur Rothstein captured this image of a mountain farmstead, using the scene to evoke the Appalachian Mountains' hardscrabble, poignant beauty. This farm represents the more than 150,000 households that eked out a subsistence from the rocky soils of this region during the early twentieth century. In the preceding decades, economic depression, erosion, drought, and government policies had undermined the already tenuous hold of these farmers on their land. In some areas, these forces brought the mountain way of life to an end, transforming stretches of the Appalachian Mountains from a vernacular agrarian landscape to federally managed forest. This book tells the story of that conversion using the experience of communities in Northern and Southern Appalachia: in the Green Mountains of Vermont and the Blue Ridge Mountains of northwestern Virginia.

At the dawn of the twenty-first century, visitors to Appalachia's forested lands encounter few visible reminders of the households that populated the mountains a century ago. As a consequence, it is easy to envision a landscape with a long and uncomplicated history; the dense forests appear untouched, except for the occasional mountain resort or ski area. Today much of the region is dedicated to recreation and forestry, *Tourism* and the Blue Ridge and Green Mountains are tourist meccas that offer rugged beauty and solitude within an easy drive of some of the nation's largest cities. These upcountry areas exemplify how we have implemented conservation policies in the United States and remind us of the compromises that have been made to open public access to natural areas.

Beginning in the early twentieth century, federal land use planning was implemented on a regional level, which tells a story integral to the history of conservation planning in both Northern and Southern Appalachia. Today's reforested landscape is the product of almost a century of land use change. This process began early in the twentieth century, as local people and regional planners began to recognize the limits of mountain agriculture. In the intervening decades, plans to convert marginal farms to managed forests were complicated by a process of negotiations with local realities, tempered by markets, ecology, and political conditions. This middle period raises as many questions about American land policy and political reform as it answers, as the path to conservation planning demonstrated the contingencies of the federal system.

This book addresses the regional scale of land use change alongside the impact of local interests upon the national scene. By chronicling the collaborations between the states and the federal government, as well as how experts imported from afar brought a program for land use planning to the Appalachian environment that was at odds with local perceptions of best use, this book mediates between the top-down political histories of Progressive reform and the New Deal and the local purview of many environmental histories. Furthermore, it surveys those farms at the margins of production, branching off from the "cows and plows" approach that has often characterized histories of agriculture.

The twentieth-century history of the Appalachian Mountains demands a deeper look behind their sylvan façade. These decades were full of powerful personalities, competing visions, and ecological nuance, and even though no single book could ever address them in their entirety, this study mediates among disparate local histories in order to tell a cohesive story about the region. From the 1910s through the 1930s, reformist ideologies, economic dislocations, and government expansion converged, and as a consequence the Appalachian landscape began to reassume a primeval aspect. The process of restoration begs several questions about the federal role in promoting a conversion from farms to forests in the Appalachian region. How and why did the Appalachian Mountains of Virginia and Vermont become a recreational escape for American tourists and hikers? What prompted the great shift in land use that occurred between the 1910s and the 1940s, as millions of acres of the mountains were placed under federal management with farms and private forests converted to public lands? *Managing the Mountains* explains how the evolution of conservation policy in Appalachia redefined national land use planning and led to an expanded, interventionist federal government. In the end, we must ask who benefited most from this new phase of state planning: the people moved out of the mountains, the expanding federal bureaucracy, or those to whom access to new recreational areas was opened? Some had to give up their land for the larger national cause, others were forced to confront the rejection of their vision for an improved natural landscape, and still others benefited from newfound access to the mountains. The creation of national parks and forests in the East, along with the expansive land reform projects of the New Deal, represent an enormous societal gamble made by conservationists and land use planners on behalf of the greater good. During the 1920s and 1930s the federal government took unprecedented steps to conserve the natural landscapes remaining in the Appalachian Mountains, and in the process it reshaped the recreational and cultural inheritance of the region. This was no small step for the expanding national government, and the planners at the helm faced many challenges from the communities they sought to change.

The twentieth-century history of these mountain landscapes is rife with tensions between professional land use planners' promotion of conservation and the historic sway of local practices. The vision of Appalachia as a forested commons came into conflict with Progressive plans for expert management and land use reform; the debate over the future of the mountain landscape reintroduced many of the issues first raised about government conservation policy in the late nineteenth century. The regulation of agriculture and forestry provided a particularly acute point of conflict between local people and federal officials. Because of the long legacy of land use in the Appalachian region, local people and their private property rights were a critical impediment to the implementation of conservation policy in the eastern United States.

Land use planning underwent a transformation in the early twentieth century. First, during the 1910s and 1920s, the federal government assumed a new objective: conservation through land acquisition. Congress'

Congress' decision to return private land to the public domain represented a dramatic break with centuries of American precedent, and this action prepared the way for a paradigm shift in federal and state policies. In Appalachia, this change meant that small subsistence farms were targeted for conversion to federally managed forests. The implementation of this policy led to some of the earliest environmental consequences of state planning and signaled the expansion of government through a new approach to land management. The consequent removal of agricultural uses and the proliferation of new forests and recreation areas in the mountains had a significant ecological impact on the region's natural landscape.

Second, the recreation and conservation initiatives of the 1910s and 1920s were the predecessors of the land use programs of the New Deal. While many scholars agree that New Deal planning had its roots in the conservationist ideals of the Progressive Era, too few acknowledge the policy precedents established within agriculture and forestry. Moreover, the federal development of recreation areas during the 1920s established a model for intervention in land use that paved the way for the landscape planning of the 1930s. Because of the progress of land acquisition and recreation projects already under way in Appalachia, New Deal planners had models of how to manage ambitious new conservation projects nationwide. Although these antecedents did not ensure federal success, the legacy of early conservation programs helped to cultivate a greater receptiveness toward many New Deal initiatives.

Third, the experiences of Virginia and Vermont in the 1930s demonstrate how the success of the New Deal was tempered by local reactions to federal initiatives as much as by the better-chronicled clashes between liberals and conservatives in Congress. The New Deal era also illustrates how local responses to federal planning were tempered by the land use policies of the preceding decades. As plans for federal recreation and conservation areas proliferated, the people threatened with displacement responded—addressing their complaints to state officials, federal agents, the President, and the Supreme Court. While some of these protests were received at the highest levels of power, many others went unheeded, and consequently the impact of political pressure on land use planning proved to be an important component of the history of the region. Conflicts over who would control the land raised alarm about the future of local autonomy and government power, resonating from small hollow communities through the offices of federal policymakers in Washington, DC. The stories from Virginia and Vermont complicate the traditional analysis of Appalachian oppression by allowing residents' vision to stand alongside the ambitions of those planners who sought to improve conditions in the mountains according to experts' principles of best use.

Federal land use planning and conservation policy during the first three decades of the twentieth century led to fundamental changes in the approach of government to private lands, and spurred the expansion of the federal government. The transition from subsistence landscapes to federally managed public spaces reflects the intersection of Progressive Era planners' ambitions to promote recreation and consumption with conservationists' efforts to monitor forest protection and production. Although these projects culminated in the massive public works programs of the New Deal, their primary impact began to be expressed a decade earlier, during the quiet ascendance of federal land use planning in the eastern United States.

Thesis
Conservation Policy as an Extension of federal Governance

Three early-twentieth-century Land Use planning transformations

1| Conservation through land acquisition: Eminent Domain
- Appropriation & Expropriation

2) Shifts in Conservation initiatives 1910s + 1920s that "cultivate a greater receptiveness toward New Deal initiatives."

3) New Deal was tempered by local reactions to federal initiatives

ACKNOWLEDGMENTS

WRITING HAS BEEN IN MANY WAYS a solitary process, yet this book is the culmination of a wide range of collaborations that have made research and the act of writing so much more fulfilling. Over the years I have benefited from the insights of people who have read this book in its entirety, including my graduate advisor, Betsy Blackmar; members of my dissertation committee, Ellen Baker, Alan Brinkley, Pete Daniel, William Leach, and Steven Stoll; the anonymous readers at Yale University Press; and several friends, including Anne Effland, Travis Jacobs, and Neil Maher, along with many others who read parts of the manuscript. The shortcomings and oversights are my own, of course, but each of these readers has contributed to strengthening the final version, and to them I am most grateful.

My colleagues in environmental and agricultural history have been gracious in welcoming me to present parts of this work at seminars and colloquia across the country, and I am especially thankful to Pete Daniel and Jeffrey Stine at the National Museum of American History; Shane Hamilton and Paul Sutter at the University of Georgia; Karl Brooks, Gregory Cushman, and Don Worster at the University of Kansas; Dona Brown at the Center for Research on Vermont; and Jim Scott at Yale University's Program in Agrarian Studies both for welcoming me to their institutions and for the wonderful conversations and keen insights of the curators and faculty as well as the excellent graduate students who populate these institutions.

I conducted the research for this project at a number of state and federal libraries and archives, where I was hosted by some of the most knowledgeable specialists in their fields. It was with particular pleasure that I visited the Vermont State Archives, where Gregory Sanford was always a source of insight and good conversation; the Special Collections Department at the University of Vermont, where Connie Gallagher, Jeffrey Marshall, and the excellent staff were ever ready to answer the most arcane question; the Vermont Historical Society library, where librarian Paul Carnahan performed a last-minute miracle, supplying a wonderful photograph; the Shenandoah National Park Archives, during its brief open era, where Harry Henderson, Reed Engle, John Amberson, and Carrie Janney were endlessly patient, and later as Kandace Muller helped resolve some questions as the book was going to press; the Forest History Society Archives, where Cheryl Oakes was a particularly valuable source of suggestions; the National Archives in College Park; the file cabinet collection of the Green Mountain National Forest at Rutland, which David Lacy was kind enough to share and which proved to be a remarkable resource for material on the regional history of the national forest program; and the Potomac Appalachian Trail Club library in Vienna, Virginia. Of course, it almost goes without saying that I could not have asked for more enjoyable scenery to visit while conducting my research.

Over the past several years I have enjoyed the benefits of life as a postdoctoral fellow at the Woodrow Wilson Presidential Library, expanding my credentials in political and agricultural history as I have researched a new dimension of American history far removed from the subsistence farms of Appalachia. I am grateful to have had the opportunity to dedicate myself so fully to research over these years. I am particularly indebted to Ken Auer of the Farm Credit Council and Eric Vettel, formerly of the Wilson Library, for having made this fellowship possible.

[margin note: Wilsonian domestic Moment?]

Before I returned to Virginia and Washington, DC, my colleagues at Iowa State contributed to a wonderful intellectual community and a great network of comrades. First among them are Mike Bailey and Leonard Sadosky; our friendship has been an endless source of inspiration and amusement, and I am grateful to ISU for bringing them into my life.

A wide range of other colleagues in Ames offered a warm intellectual climate and good company: historians Patrick Barr-Melej, Kat Charron, David Hollander, John Munroe, and Matt Stanley were all certain to provide stimulating conversation; while Carla Fehr, Whitney Sanford, Emily Godbey, and the Sustainable Agriculture crowd made life outside the classroom both engaging and inspiring. The Center for Excellence in the Arts and Humanities and the Bioethics Program both welcomed me into their vibrant communities, and they offered regular opportunities to enjoy the best minds that ISU brought to campus—often around the dinner table, and those evenings will forever inform my teaching and scholarship. To Sheryl St. Germain, Brenda Daly, and Clark Wolf I am particularly indebted for making a junior professor so involved in the intellectual life of the university.

This project was supported at Iowa State University by money from the Center for Excellence in the Arts and Humanities, the College of Arts and Sciences Special Projects Research Initiation Grants, and the Big XII Faculty Fellowship; at Columbia University by various graduate fellowships; by a predoctoral fellowship at the Smithsonian Institution's National Museum of American History; by the Franklin and Eleanor Roosevelt Institute's Lubin-Winant Research Fellowship; by the Organization of American Historians' Horace Samuel & Marion Galbraith Merrill Travel Grant; and by the Vermont Historical Society's Weston A. Cate Award, a research award that funded the question that drove the project from its inception.

Without my professors at Middlebury College I would have entered life as a historian infinitely less prepared. Each of them has contributed to my intellectual development in ways that they can certainly recognize: in particular, historians Travis Jacobs, Jim Ralph, Tyler Priest, and Bill Hart made me aware of how much influence a teacher can have—both inside the classroom and in the larger world beyond. Just after graduation I had the good fortune to begin a great job working with Jan Albers, and this research assistantship provided me with a model of how to be a better scholar. It is in no small part due to the questions posed by Jan's *Hands on the Land* that I had the background and the insight to pursue this project. In the years since, Jan and her husband Paul Monod have been great friends and advocates, and I will always look back upon that year of research with pleasure.

Finally, my family and friends have endured this project as long as I have. Some have played an integral role in the academic career that brought me to this point, among them Columbia colleagues Jung Pak, Dan Maksymiuk, Kim Phillips-Fein, Reiko Hillyer, Jeffrey Trask, Ellen Stroud, Zach Schrag, and Ashli White. Others have become valued friends through the remarkable community of the American Society for Environmental History, especially Brian Donahue, Kathy Morse, Paul Sutter, Deborah Fitzgerald, Lynne Heasley, Ari Kelman, Louis Warren, Neil Maher, Emily Greenwald, and Cindy Ott, with whom I have shared many memorable meals. I feel fortunate to have such an inspiring network of supportive colleagues.

My extended family has always welcomed this somewhat peripatetic researcher and adventurer, and in particular Bill Maris, Ann Drennan, Faith and Roger Evans, Rob and Ginny Gregg, Louise and John Keenan, and Ann Mittelstadt and John Hartigan have provided delightful company, good food, and a warm bed.

I am convinced that there is no sufficient way to thank my parents, Ben and Susan Gregg, for everything they have done for me. Their homes, friendship, and unremitting support have provided me with a jumping-off point for a rich life, and I am grateful for all of it. This book is dedicated to them because not only did they make all of the work that went into it possible, but also because they have been a constant inspiration during its production. My father has provided unflinching (if endearingly biased) enthusiasm for all of my endeavors, and my mother has reminded me many times over the years of the value of hard work and commitment. It is in large part due to her model of dedication and determination—and her pinch babysitting skills during the past year—that I was able to complete this book.

My husband, Ben Hayes, has brought a sharp mind and keen insight into questions of life and history, and has been my companion in both work and adventure since we first connected while talking about the Appalachian landscape. I look forward to our future projects in writing, design, and child rearing as much as I enjoy looking back on the time we have spent together. The places we have been, the mountains we have climbed, and the waterfalls you have encouraged me to swim behind have shown me parts of myself I did not recognize before. Our dogs Aiken and Turtle have enthusiastically helped us explore the mountains of

both Virginia and Vermont, while Camille always helped to make light
of the many piles of paper forever surrounding my desk. Finally, to our
son, Alden, who arrived as I was finishing revisions on the manuscript,
I wish for you all of the adventures beautiful forests can offer—and so
much more. I look forward to teaching you the ways of the world on our
very own hill farm in Vermont.

Introduction

FARMS AND FORESTS: AN APPALACHIAN PORTRAIT

THE APPALACHIAN MOUNTAINS STRETCH from northern Alabama to Quebec, moving from the Deep South through New England and encompassing a diversity of cultural and political landscapes. In spite of the range's geological and topographical continuity, the Northern and Southern Appalachians have rarely been studied together. Yet it is worth reconsidering Appalachia as a whole because the northern and southern mountains share a number of important characteristics. They boast a moderately rugged terrain; have historically been covered in forest and are ideally suited to growing trees; proved viable for small-scale farming and husbandry; and are proximate to important agricultural areas. Most important, the mountains have remained a place apart for much of the nation's history. During the early twentieth century the mountains remained largely detached from expanding regional markets, even as road networks and rail lines bisected their ranges and visitors increasingly found easy access into the quiet recesses of the upcountry. Appalachia was, moreover, repeatedly caricatured by visitors and the press, and it came to represent in the public imagination a particular bygone and unsustainable way of life. These caricatures developed into a critical component of the rhetoric of poverty and backwardness that eventually facilitated the transformation of private property into federal lands.

1

In Virginia and Vermont (as well as throughout Appalachia), the dynamism of the mountain landscape necessitated that local people constantly adapt to changing environmental conditions. This book offers a critical reevaluation of mountain ecology and land use practices, and it places into context the environmental and economic challenges that faced residents and policymakers during the early twentieth century. In this period new state prerogatives led to the push for federal oversight of local land policy, and the environmental impacts of the new purview of government eventually reshaped the Appalachian landscape. As land use planners committed to creating a new management paradigm in parts of the mountains, the American nation-state assumed an increasingly active role in mediating interactions with the nature of the region. Government (within both state and federal agencies and the U.S. Congress) embraced a new role, embarking on the conversion of private land into national parks and forests. This project not only contradicted three centuries of precedent but also required a significant revision of federal and state property law. For the first time, the state exercised the right of eminent domain for conservation and recreational development, thus redefining the scope of takings in the public interest. This book chronicles the reformist vision behind state and federal land use initiatives alongside their environmental impacts, supplementing the "hidden history" of American conservation that has been uncovered in the opposition of local people to the institutionalization of an externally conceived system of land use and land management.[1]

A regional approach to the expansion of the nation-state allows local nuance to mediate the traditionally top-down approach to federal land use planning. Like any region, Appalachia is far more diverse than it is frequently portrayed. This book looks past the oft-depicted coalfields of West Virginia or the rugged White Mountains of New Hampshire and examines the more typical agricultural and forested landscapes that blanketed most of the region. Although some sections of the Appalachian Mountains had been ravaged by natural resource extraction during the late nineteenth century, many others (including northwestern Virginia and Vermont) remained largely untouched by industrial forces. In the early twentieth century, therefore, the majority of the region remained in small farms. These areas were not part of an extractive economy in which outside landowners exercised a dominant influence on land use decisions and, thus, did not fulfill the preconditions for a colonial economy like those described by Appalachian scholars. In fact, land use in the 1920s in Virginia and Vermont looked similar to that in the 1880s, with all of the attendant advantages and disadvantages.[2]

Appalachian culture has long been portrayed as a symbol of independence, challenge, and rugged survival. Folklorists and vacationers rediscovered the region as a repository of folk culture in the late nineteenth century; shortly thereafter it was reinvented as a landscape of leisure through private ventures and, later, state and federal resources. Initially, the moderate mountain summers lured urban elites into the region's cool hollows and coves, and by the early 1920s the federal government started to take the initiative to expand access into mountain areas for all Americans. To a new class of tourists, the temperate Appalachian range appeared an ideal site for the development of national recreation lands. The expansion of regional road networks finally domesticated these mountains; they were increasingly tamed by the automobile and turned into a vacationer's retreat. In many important respects, Appalachia embodied the democratization of recreation, offering accessible, low-cost vacations for people from the eastern cities.

During the first decades of the twentieth century, recreation and conservation emerged as interwoven threads of federal land policy. Appalachia's Progressive Era projects built upon a framework of federal spending that had begun in the West with investments in transportation, park infrastructure, and reclamation during the nineteenth century. Virginia and Vermont, among other rural states, increasingly began to stake a claim to federal assistance in developing new industries, notably forestry and tourism, as a means of combating declining agricultural markets and economic uncertainty. Although the New Deal programs of the 1930s were the most obvious example of this quest for federal assistance, abundant precedents from the 1910s and 1920s demonstrate the continuity of federal-state cooperation.

These transitional decades also saw the maturation of a new cadre of experts working to reform American society; the expansion of a national government that embraced innovation and efficiency; and the emergence of an economically intertwined civil society that allowed for the state to enter a new phase of influence in the daily life of its citizens.[3] Policymakers aspired to ensure the most productive distribution of resources and energies for the entire nation and deployed researchers in agricultural economics, rural sociology, soil science, and forestry to bolster nascent conservation policies.

Appalachia in particular became a laboratory for planners during the 1910s and 1920s, as experts mobilized an innovative research apparatus, ideas about social uplift, and a focus on the protection of natural resources. At the same time, federal policy shifted from prioritizing land distribution to encouraging conservation. The first stage of government intervention in the region began in the forests, where overharvesting and destruction initially attracted the attention of conservationists. Conservation planning during this era began to include the protection of natural resources and scenic areas on private property, which led to an unprecedented land acquisition program and the creation of new federal parks and forests on formerly private land. Because there had previously been no formal regulation of forestry on private property, and no avenue for federal forestry experts to offer assistance to landowners, the first step toward forest protection occurred with the passage of the 1911 Weeks Act, which enabled the creation of eastern national forests on formerly private lands. This legislation implemented Progressive ideas about efficiency, best use, and the value of public improvements as the basis for reacquiring private land and regulating land use. The focus on resource management and the professionalization of a new class of experts laid the groundwork for a new land use program in the eastern mountains. These developments signaled the emergence of the modern state, which later expanded during the New Deal with federal land and soil surveys, planning programs, welfare initiatives, and infrastructural developments. These New Deal conservation programs should be considered as a critical part of the larger state transformation that occurred between the 1910s and 1930s.

This book surveys the three decades during which the Appalachian Mountains were transformed from a landscape dotted with small subsistence farms into a patchwork of federal landscapes. Beginning in the early 1910s, foresters spread out to assess the health of the Appalachian woodlands, while agricultural economists deployed their expertise to analyze the viability of mountain farms. Social reformers and local boosters joined together in the early 1920s to investigate conditions in the mountains, spurred by what they saw as a social and economic declension that hindered the development of the region. The efforts of these disparate groups culminated in the mid-1920s when local and state governments sought to collaborate with federal agencies in an ambitious plan to preserve wide swaths of the mountain forests. This confluence of events swept the Appalachian Mountains into national life in a new way, and as a result the federal government began to assert a greater influence on the economic and political landscapes of the Blue Ridge and Green Mountains. In the process, the tension between the locals' vision of the mountains as an open commons and the planners' ethos of conservation and reform ricocheted across the region, and the resultant conflicts over local autonomy and power continue to resonate in many areas of Appalachia today.

In both Virginia and Vermont the culmination of these planning initiatives came during the 1930s, as the expanded federal government sought to redevelop the American landscape. In the end, the success of individual New Deal programs was linked to the local traditions of land use planning and federal-state cooperation dating from the 1910s and the 1920s. The principal distinction between Virginia and Vermont was the organization of local political systems, and in particular the difference between county and township governments. Significant geographic and cultural differences distinguish these two systems, influenced primarily by the scale of government. Most of Southern Appalachia operates its local governments at the county level. By contrast, Vermont, like the rest of New England, is organized by township.[4] Towns commonly have a small population and relatively democratic representation, whereas counties tend to be larger and more dispersed. In contrast to Vermont townships, which range in size between 36 and 40 square miles, the average area of the counties in the northern Blue Ridge of Virginia is 425 square miles.[5] The small scale of local government in Vermont tended to encourage the participation of local people, whereas the diffuseness of political power in Virginia meant that individuals had a limited mechanism for influencing local politics. As a consequence, Vermont communities were routinely more effective in their attempts to maintain an influence over the course of regional planning decisions than those in Virginia. Local reactions to outside planners and land use change were strongly influenced by local democratic traditions and community agendas.

This book offers a sustained evaluation of conditions in Appalachia alongside those in academia during the early twentieth century—the

"Origins" of land use reform discussed in part one. The first two chapters frame the vernacular, subsistence culture of the Appalachian economy at the beginning of the twentieth century through an agro-ecological investigation of individual and communal land use in the Blue Ridge and Green Mountains. These regions were geologically and economically similar, and yet cultural and political circumstances in each diverged sharply, and their portrayal by contemporary experts influenced the way policymakers approached land use reform. The first chapter chronicles the hollow communities scattered throughout the Blue Ridge Mountains of Virginia, where clusters of self-sufficient households hugged the narrow streambeds. The mountains created a physical distance from markets and divided the counties representing these communities' political and economic interests, so that many of the people who lived the Blue Ridge had only a tenuous connection to local politics or the regional economy. The second chapter explores upcountry Vermont, where the rivers wending through the mountains left wider areas for settlement, and farms were oriented around small village centers that served as the nexus of local politics and trade. Moreover, the denser scale of Vermont towns engendered a tradition of local involvement in politics and state affairs and a sense of regional pride that celebrated local resources. These landscapes and local histories laid the foundation for the changes that were to come during the 1920s and 1930s. The third chapter visits a very different cultural landscape: the intellectual milieu that spawned Progressive Era land use planning in regional academic centers during the first decades of the century. Land grant colleges, and in particular their nascent agricultural economics programs, gave rise to a new generation of scholars who formulated a complex regional plan for reforming land use. Many of these experts moved into the federal government during the 1910s and 1920s; with the funding of federal conservation initiatives they were able to convert their ideas from paper into policy. These chapters lay the foundation for the land use changes that ensued during the 1920s and 30s.

The second part of this book, "Projects," follows Virginia and Vermont into the 1930s, surveying three trajectories of conservation planning and the negotiations over their implementation. Chapter four chronicles the creation of the Shenandoah National Park, which encompasses Virginia's Blue Ridge Mountain hollows, a site targeted in 1924 as ideal for a new national park to serve the nation's growing urban constituencies. Initially, local officials and federal policymakers promoted an innovative plan for recreation and conservation on what they perceived to be an uninhabited stretch of mountains. Only belatedly did they discover the deeply rooted communities that had already claimed the mountain forests and their resources. In spite of sustained local resistance, federal and state commitments to the park agenda meant that the project eventually culminated in the removal of mountain landowners and the dedication of a new national park. Chapter five examines a different trajectory of state-federal cooperation, as during the 1920s the State of Vermont and the U.S. government collaborated on disaster relief, the development of infrastructure, and a new national forest in the Green Mountains. In Vermont, the long tradition of local influence over state policy led to complex negotiations between local communities and federal planners. Chapter six examines Virginia's and Vermont's interactions with the New Deal. Land use planning was the primary ambition of the Resettlement Administration (RA), a Second New Deal measure that presented a comprehensive vision of land reform, moving beyond stopgap, temporary relief measures to a more universal, holistic approach to conservation, recreation, and social programs. In Virginia, the removal of mountain residents to create the Shenandoah National Park spurred federal plans for subsistence homestead communities, whereas Vermont state officials' discomfort with social planning led to the legislature's rejection of RA funding for conservation projects.

Disaster Relief? (handwritten marginal note)

Variations in the responses of these states to the proposed modification of the mountain landscape suggest the importance of tempering the blunt instrument of federal policy with local knowledge. The experiences of land use planners in Appalachia reinforce the necessity of taking a flexible, dynamic approach to land policy, because ultimately both human and natural communities displayed more local variation and greater independence than objective, rational plans were able to anticipate.

The impact of the Progressive Era and New Deal on the American political system is indisputable. The reforms of the first four decades of the twentieth century transformed national culture, and had a particularly visible impact upon the Appalachian landscape. The dynamic planning vision of the 1910s and 1920s and its influence on the New Deal, when money and manpower became available to implement

Thesis

conservationists' and social reformers' ideas, combined to reshape the nation. This book demonstrates the interconnectedness of these decades, and the importance of looking more closely at landscapes that at first glance appear to have a static history. The reconsideration of the history of the mountain forests permits a better understanding of how the modern Appalachian landscape has attained its present form, and why the ideas that have driven land use planning continue to matter to contemporary policymakers.

PART ONE ORIGINS

CHAPTER ONE

A Harvest of Scarcity

SELF-SUFFICIENCY IN THE BLUE RIDGE MOUNTAINS

IN THE SUMMER OF 1929, a group on horseback rode into a small community in the Blue Ridge Mountains of northwestern Virginia carrying their notebooks, a stash of pennies and chewing gum, and a number of hypotheses about the families living in the mountain hollow. The party included psychologist Mandel Sherman, journalist Thomas R. Henry, and a local teacher, Miriam Sizer, the primary field worker for the research project that had inspired this journey. The researchers encountered a setting that confirmed their greatest hopes for the project. The shady mountain hollows were cool and quiet, "realms of enchantment" in which people who harkened back to a bygone era appeared to live simply, with few of the comforts of contemporary culture. More important, the people appeared different: in appearance, in speech, and in their expectations of what their lives would bring.[1]

Along with the principal investigators traveled a small group of experts who shared Sherman and Henry's ambition to study social and cultural environment within the mountains. The visitors represented an urban elite that was increasingly concerned about economic and social conditions in the poorest sections of the nation. The dust jacket of Sherman and Henry's book, *Hollow Folk*, conveyed the sense of importance surrounding this endeavor: "The story of these backward people, begun and carried out as a scientific research project, has a far broader field of interest than that of the social worker or psychologist . . . as they are both an indictment and a challenge to our much-vaunted civilization." These scholars sought to explain the complexity of modern civilization through this analysis of what they called the "backwash" of modern life, and they traveled to the Blue Ridge with a purpose at once analytical and journalistic. Eventually, their account of the development of local culture would temper public perceptions about mountain life. The research of scholars like Sherman and Henry provided the impetus for programs to uplift the people and protect the mountain landscape, and it spurred the entry of the federal government into new areas of American life.[2]

As Sherman and Henry discovered, the Blue Ridge Mountains were both culturally and economically distant from the contemporary United States. During the preceding decades large parts of the Appalachian upcountry had remained separate from the social and political influences of lowland communities, and as a consequence even people living in neighboring valleys perceived that the mountain environment was unfamiliar territory. Many Virginians saw this region as a static, unimproved remnant of bygone days. Yet the Blue Ridge Mountains were instead a landscape in flux. In the 1920s what appeared to be normative conditions were the product of significant dislocations in the mountain landscape, caused by steady population growth, the expansion of agriculture onto less fertile land, and ecologically devastating land cover changes. Most visitors overlooked those shifts, however, choosing to interpret the hollows as problem communities characterized by a simple narrative of ignorance, poverty, and maladjusted land uses.

The decline affecting these mountains reflected the conjuncture of a number of transformations within the local environment. Recent changes included the destruction of the chestnut trade; while what appeared as social regression was the consequence of unchecked population growth alongside county politicians' neglect of the economic and educational needs of the mountain people. Because the mountain area was beyond the purview of government, in reality rather than by law, no state or county agency attempted to confront the social and economic disadvantages faced by these communities. Local economic and social stressors perpetuated by blight, depression, drought, and federal conservation initiatives shook the foundations of the regional economy, contributing to a crisis by the early 1930s, when plans for a national park in the Blue Ridge were realized.

This was complex terrain, with considerable economic and social diversity, tempered by both the ecology of the mountains and a long history of land use. Residents employed all of the resources at their disposal to maintain themselves on their small farms, and they adapted both their agricultural practices and their expectations to the carrying capacity of the upcountry landscape. The contingency of mountain survival is best explained through an examination of local subsistence practices, modes of production, and the boundaries of community. Ultimately, this reappraisal of land use complicates Sherman and Henry's, and their successors', assessment that Blue Ridge communities were economically unviable.

SURVEYING THE LANDSCAPE

The hollows that Sherman and Henry entered in 1929 comprised part of a geographic and cultural region with a rich and storied history. The Blue Ridge Mountains of Virginia represent the northernmost sweep of the Southern Appalachian range and the transition to the northern section, which stretches across the Mid Atlantic and through New England. These mountains are narrower than the rest of the southern range, and while they share the region's topographic features, they never developed industrial patterns characteristic of the mining and lumbering communities to the south and west. While parts of the Blue Ridge were logged and grazed, most of the area remained forested and in the control of private owners, either mountain smallholders or valley cattlemen and other outside investors. This was the prototypical Appalachian landscape of small, self-sufficient farms.

The Blue Ridge, although considerably lower in elevation than the Appalachians to the south, offered abundant challenges to those who farmed their contours. Although railroads and state roads crossed the mountains at the lowest gaps, reaching settlements in the mountain hollows remained difficult in the early twentieth century; good wagon roads led to the mountains, but "few penetrate[d] far into it." Consequently, access to the hollows could only be gained along rocky paths that ran along the streams.[3] Land use centered on mountain streambeds, with farms clustered around the flatter terrain, where soils were enriched by centuries of humus and nutrients flowing down from the higher elevations. The topography of the mountains meant that each hollow was its own distinct community. As sociologist E. A. Ross described it: "Each settlement

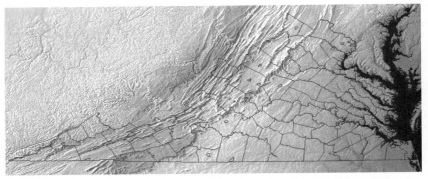

Virginia landforms. Note the significance of the Blue Ridge Mountains, the first tier of mountains moving west from the coast, as well as the location of county boundary lines. Map of Virginia from *U.S. State Images from 30 Second Topographic Data* (June 1999), http://www.ngdc.noaa.gov/mgg/topo/state2.pl?region=va.jpg, accessed on January 21, 2010.

is a shoestring along one of these water courses and constitutes a world within itself, for it is insulated from its neighbors by one or two thousand feet of steep wooded ridge."[4] The mountain terrain was highly variable; elevations varied considerably, from a low of 950 feet at Manassas Gap to a high of 4,049 feet at Hawksbill Mountain. The ridgeline averaged 3,000 feet, while the mountains covered a width of between one and thirteen miles—making for a narrow range, punctuated by steep inclines and descents.[5]

The mountain forests defined the region's ecology and its economy in 1920. In the preceding centuries an oak-chestnut forest dominated by red, chestnut, and white oaks and the American chestnut covered the northern Blue Ridge Mountains. Hardwood stands represented an estimated 85 percent of the forest between 1,200 and 4,000 feet in elevation, primarily along well-drained slopes with acidic soils composed of granite and schist. The American chestnut predominated, representing between 15 and 20 percent of the forest and, in some localities, up to 60 percent of the total tree cover.[6]

A biologically diverse mixed mesophytic forest populated the hollows and coves, where settlement was most dense. "From the standpoint of human geography the most important features of this whole region are its basins, gorges, and coves," Rupert Vance observed in his *Human*

Geography of the South. "It is these areas that make the region, for these comparatively small and scattered coves and valleys contain the population."[7] The alluvial soils of the streambeds combine the silty and sandy loams that descended with floodwaters and, as a consequence, were the most fertile parts of the mountains. Because of the combination of aspect and weather patterns, the hollow-cove hardwood forest predominated along the cooler, moister eastern and northern exposures of the mountains, areas cloaked with basswood, tulip trees, yellow birch, sugar maple, black gum, white ash, and American elm. Out of this landscape the people stitched together a patchwork of uses from farms and the mountain commons. The range of forest types in the mountains provided the essential elements for the production of food and shelter, and residents exploited their full benefit. Local resources offered some degree of independence from outside economic pressures, yet in years of drought or limited yields this insularity also meant uncertainty due to the fluctuations in local ecology. During the late 1920s and particularly during the 1930s, a number of changes coincided that threatened the viability of the mountain economy.

During the first decades of the twentieth century an expanding lumber industry targeted Southern Appalachia's remaining timber. While the northern Blue Ridge remained relatively isolated from large-scale logging, due in part to the limited extent of the forests in this region, some areas within the range were harvested repeatedly during the nineteenth and early twentieth centuries. Small-scale, local use dominated, employing portable mills to produce lumber, tanbark, and railroad cross ties.[8] In 1914, U.S. Forest Service examiner R. Clifford Hall studied the history of land use in the Blue Ridge as part of his survey of forest conditions in the region. This report paints a picture of the condition of the forested landscape: of the 80 percent of this region still forested in 1914, 50 percent was covered with "culled and cut over" trees in some stage of regrowth. The 30 percent remaining in old growth was located largely along the eastern side of the mountain ridges, in an area distant from rail lines and the Shenandoah River. Reflecting the Forest Service mandate for protecting vulnerable watersheds, Hall reported that this region was sustainably used by small farms and logging interests, unlike the Appalachians further south where a highly developed commercial timber industry threatened the forests; he recommended that the federal government focus its conservation efforts elsewhere.[9]

A national forest would have significantly altered local land use, because the forest operated as an open-access commons. Chestnuts, morels, berries, and herbs supplemented the diet and income of families who maintained themselves in part through the natural bounty of the landscape.[10] The American chestnut, in particular, sustained local communities through a multitude of products. The tree yielded nuts for consumption and sale, and a mature tree produced up to ten bushels of chestnuts each year. These were critical to the survival of squirrels, wild turkeys, white-tailed deer, bears, raccoons, and grouse, along with humans and their livestock. Local residents valued this free source of nutrients, which ensured a secure supply of protein for many households. The seasonal abundance of the chestnut crop, coupled with the practice of allowing hogs to browse on oak-chestnut mast, meant "the people had money and had meat on the table too."[11]

Into the twentieth century the plentiful and rot-resistant chestnut remained useful for a variety of purposes. The resource-rich chestnuts were seemingly inexhaustible. The species provided long-lasting and durable wood for construction, and its bark was used as a tanning agent for leather processing. Locals found that tanbark provided a valuable cash supplement to their farms, while the rail lines along the western edge of the mountains claimed a steady supply of crossties and wood for locomotive fuel.[12]

Abruptly, in the first decades of the twentieth century, natural cycles and the expanding national economy upended the chestnut economy. The catastrophic spread of an arboreal disease disrupted the ease with which residents lived in the mountains. In 1904 an Asian blight attacked New York City's chestnuts and spread quickly up and down the Atlantic Coast, killing trees with astonishing rapidity. By 1918 it had arrived in northwestern Virginia, and within a decade the blight had decimated the chestnuts in the Blue Ridge, summarily removing an important cash crop from the mountains and destroying the predominant species of the mid slope oak-chestnut forest. Once the centerpiece of the local economy for the poorest communities in the mountains, the chestnut's demise signaled a more systemic decline in the mountain ecology. The destruction of the chestnuts was the most dramatic example of landscape change, but markets for local forest products also shifted during this period as the lumber industry started to decline, in reflection of both the diminution of the most valuable timber and the conversion of railroads to coal power.[13] By 1930, hundreds of thousands of chestnut "ghost trees" stood sentinel over the Blue Ridge forests, precipitating the change in forest composition to an oak-hickory forest.[14] Animals and people were forced to adapt their survival strategies to the sudden absence of this important source of protein and cash. Even in the face of the loss of the chestnut, however, local residents' range of land use strategies permitted them to continue to extract a subsistence from the mountain landscape.

THE SELF-SUFFICIENT ECONOMY

For generations, farmers in the Blue Ridge Mountains lived comparably to other agriculturalists in the humid and temperate Southern Appalachian range, working small farms with livestock and a range of crops. Agricultural rhythms ordered daily life, and most of these farmers worked to maintain a competency rather than create a regular crop surplus for market. Households produced most of the goods needed for home use through a mixture of cultivation and gathering, and because there were only limited amounts of fertile land, small farms dominated the working landscape.[15]

Making a living posed a challenge: many mountain soils were not well suited to agriculture, and farmers practiced few of the labor-saving or yield-enhancing techniques employed by contemporary farmers in the lowlands. Moreover, the topography, combined with the effects of soil depletion, meant that farming had become progressively more difficult. Stories about the precariousness of mountain agriculture abounded, testaments to the ways in which this mountain landscape tested the ingenuity of its users. Locals observed that Blue Ridge farmers lived perched on the hillsides, in "steep patches where . . . a man has to hang on to a root with one hand while he hoes with the other and has to plant his corn by shooting it into the hill."[16] An early twentieth-century regional sketch evoked the challenges of mountain farming: "The oft-repeated tale of the man or boy who fell out of his field and broke his neck does not seem too exaggerated as one gazes at cultivated patches on steep mountain sides."[17]

Many Blue Ridge farms remained predominantly self-sufficient well into the 1930s, largely disengaged from market production and the cash economy. Unlike smallholders in industrialized Appalachia, they were not farming in order to supplement low wages from mining or lumbering. Many families cultivated their food on only a few acres of cropland, and the scale of Blue Ridge farms was significantly smaller than the national average. Mountain farms, like most others in this era, produced a wide variety of foods, and this diversification was especially important because mountain households remained both cash poor and physically distant from regional markets. Mountain paths were unsuited to transferring large quantities of produce, thus restricting market interactions, and families found few incentives to trade their small plots of essential foodstuffs for the challenges of cultivating and marketing large quantities of cash crops.[18]

The ability to harvest the full complement of local resources was critical to these farmers' survival. The Virginia researchers of the Writers' Program of the Work Projects Administration reported that the fact that some of the "mountaineers" can even "wrest a living from their steep and narrow fields" would surprise "even a student familiar with squalor," and yet, as federal and state agencies would eventually discover, the people "hold tenaciously to their small farms."[19] Contemporary agricultural economists classified most families in the Blue Ridge as "self-sufficing," as they depended primarily on the products of their farms to maintain themselves.[20] The 1930 census recorded 150,000 self-sufficing farms operating in Appalachia, and these households accounted for roughly one-third of the remaining self-sufficient farms in the United States (in a region that constitutes only 3 percent of the total land mass).[21]

Southern Appalachia boasted an unusually high density of self-sufficient farms in part because steady population growth pushed successive generations of families into the higher reaches of the mountains to cultivate smaller and more marginal farms. Virginia's mountain families grew at a disproportionately high rate; the average family size in the Blue Ridge was 5.01 persons, compared with the state average of 4.33 for white families of native parentage.[22] Farm size decreased as growing families divided their land, with offspring pushing onto smaller acreages upstream and deeper into the mountains. Federal censuses attest to the gradual pace of this change. The average Appalachian farm shrunk dramatically: from 187 acres in 1880 to 109 acres in 1900, down to fewer than 90 acres in 1910, and 86 acres in 1930.[23] This constriction considerably limited the range of opportunities available to mountain families,

Arthur Rothstein, *Home of a mountain family who will be resettled on new land, Shenandoah National Park, Virginia,* October 1935. Farm Security Administration, Office of War Information Photograph Collection, Library of Congress. LC-USF34-000389-D

which meant fewer acres of cultivable land, fewer acres in pasture, and less woodland to support the mixed economy of most mountain farms.[24] As elsewhere along the eastern seaboard, growing pressure on the land supply led to a more constricted existence for those families that remained in the mountains.[25] The coupled disadvantages of a perpetually increasing population and the limited economy of the mountains meant that more than half of all mountain farmers in Madison County, Virginia, did not own the land they worked. In 1932, 37 percent of mountain residents worked as caretakers or tenants with long-term usufruct arrangements but no clear title to the land, and squatters comprised another 23 percent.[26] Many tenants were related to the landowners from whom they rented, and kinship relationships frequently led landowners to impose few demands on their tenants. Moreover, the availability of farms for a nominal annual payment (often between $15 and $30 per year), or in exchange for services like salting cattle during the summer grazing season, meant that the mountains attracted people who possessed few resources to invest in property.[27]

The combination of increasing population and depleted soils generated a perpetual need for fresh land that brought less productive parts
of the mountains into production. By the 1930s, this system had begun
to show signs of strain. Erosion swept the nutrients from hilly fields when
drought threatened or heavy rains inundated the mountains.[28] Although
contemporary scholars argued that the Appalachian region was maladjusted to the agricultural needs of its inhabitants and better left unculti-
vated, few farm families left the region or altered their agricultural
practices. Agricultural economists repeatedly observed that the lack of
planning on mountain farms meant that "economic factors," or, to be
more explicit, the family's subsistence needs, "frequently exert a stronger influence on intensity of land use and on population density, than
does the quality of the land itself." Throughout the 1920s and 1930s,
these scholars suggested that farms would become increasingly unviable
without improvements through modern methods like fertilizing, mech-
anization, and contour plowing.[29] Nevertheless, research by government
agencies rarely translated into the practices of mountain farmers, who
often could not afford to heed their advice. Therefore, in spite of reams
of scholarly analysis of "marginal" and "submarginal" populations in the
mountains, the farmers themselves often continued to produce using
traditional methods. The disconnect between academic research and
farm practices was typical of the period, but the limited implementation
of new methods was particularly evident in Appalachia, where farmers
had the fewest resources to invest in improving their farms.

Gifford Pinchot, who began his career as a professional forester in
the Blue Ridge Mountains of North Carolina, commented on the consequences of a diversified economy for forest conservation. Pinchot recognized that much of the local need for forest resources resulted from the
poor quality of this land for farming: "They needed everything usable in
it—pasture, fish, and game—to supplement the meager living they were
able to scratch from the soil of their little clearings." Pinchot reported
that the local people, dependent on the full range of local resources,
"know nothing of game preserves and but little of property rights. On the
contrary, they regarded this country as their country, their common."
Pinchot, a perennial critic of haphazard private ownership, was concerned about the divergence between unregulated communal uses and
scientific management. Pinchot's observations about mountain farmers

in North Carolina foreshadowed other disagreements that were rooted in the cultural conflicts between the vernacular practices of subsistence farming and scientific managers' preference for carefully tended parks and forests.[30]

The disjuncture between local assessments of the viability of mountain communities and those of government officials laid the groundwork for additional disputes over the region's future. Because the researchers who studied the region believed that soil exhaustion, ecological change, and increasing population density all threatened the natural balance in the Blue Ridge, they mobilized the evidence to justify the creation of a new management regime. By contrast, mountain residents asserted their right to control local land use practices, defending the vernacular traditions of their communities.[31]

It was into this world of Madison County hollows that the researchers on horseback stepped in 1929, and their fieldwork left an extensive record of the economic and social interactions of people living in the hollows of the eastern Blue Ridge. The communities Sherman and Henry studied were typical of the Southern Appalachians during the early twentieth century—distant from railroads, largely untouched by improved roads, and socially distinct from the surrounding valley communities—and they appeared to represent a place apart from modern life. The product of Sherman and Henry's research was published as *Hollow Folk,* a 1933 book that chronicled the social and economic life of these mountain communities. This study, with its analysis of the historical and contemporary adaptations to local conditions, quickly emerged as the definitive treatment of Blue Ridge culture.

Central to Sherman and Henry's project was an examination of the "evolutionary" differences between communities: they graded the hollows according to access to schools, newspapers, and churches.[32] The researchers' agenda for evaluating these communities spoke to the concerns of the day: "Scattered about the mountains . . . were other hollows in various degrees of isolation from the outside world and, as it afterwards developed, approximately corresponding culture levels." Five communities were the target of deeper study: "one, a hollow of scattered families subsisting off the grudging, unaided bounty of nature; another, a community of primitive agriculturalists; another, one of small farmers; still another one in which were found in crude forms nearly all of the institutions of modern society; and finally, a small town at the foot of the mountains."[33] Although it is unique in its approach to cultural analyses, when paired with larger-scale studies of Appalachian agriculture Sherman and Henry's book offers both an evocative description of the economy of the Blue Ridge hollows and a provocative interpretation of mountain society, albeit one that is tinged with environmental determinism and social-scientific methodology.[34]

Miriam Sizer, a social worker and teacher, conducted fieldwork for the project by living among the mountain people of the hollows in the summer of 1929. She later marketed her expertise to the National Park Service, resurveying the families and compiling a 1932 report on conditions in the hollows that provided invaluable data on patterns of land use in the mountains.[35] Both of these studies focus on a small section, roughly 10,000 acres, of what would eventually become a 176,429-acre national park. Thus, these hundred and thirty-two families offer an intimate but unrepresentative perspective on some of the thousands of people who were relocated from the Blue Ridge because of national park development during the mid-1930s.[36]

The mountain landscape dominated the lives of hollow residents, as the quality and size of individual landholdings often determined the operation of the household economy. Farm management was cued to the terrain and extent of the land, and farmers located on the flattest, largest farms tended to produce for markets. As with other farms on difficult land, the Blue Ridge farmers adapted to the nature of their holdings and grew those crops most suitable for the terrain.[37] Significant differences in wealth and farming practices existed among neighbors within the hollows, just as there were differences between communities. While some farms were located closer to valley towns, along flatter alluvial land, others perched high in the mountains.[38] Those farming the highest elevations did not own adequate arable land or benefit from easy access to regional markets. Access to transportation also influenced the economic orientation of these communities. Many of the more affluent residents of the Blue Ridge lived along the country roads that crossed the mountains, or at the lowest elevations near valley communities. For example, Richards Hollow was located closest to a road, and it was the most market oriented. Corbin and Dark Hollows were situated at the highest elevations, along narrower riverbeds, and were consequently the most

Detailed topographic map of the four Blue Ridge hollows surveyed by Sherman and Henry's research team. The narrow flats of Corbin and Dark Hollows stand in contrast to the wider, lower lay of the land in Nicholson and Weakley (Old Rag) Hollows. *Stony Man, VA*, U.S. Geological Society topographic map, 1933 edition, surveyed 1927–1929.

economically independent and agriculturally vulnerable. By contrast, Nicholson and Weakley Hollows, wider, longer, and at lower elevations, had more diversified and prosperous households, with more tools and larger fields.[39]

Terrain exercised the greatest influence on the viability of farming in the mountains, and many areas had limited flat and fertile land.[40] Forest Service examiner Hall reported on the wide range of land types in 1914: "The soils are exceedingly variable, ranging from thin and sterile sands covered with a scrubby growth of timber to fertile clay loams well adapted to blue grass and suitable for cultivation where not too steep and stony."[41] Within the general patterns of mountain agriculture, however, consider-able variation characterized upcountry farms, and the mountains housed an economically varied population. The lay of the land created significant differences between neighboring communities, and a closer look at the terrain of two hollows, Corbin and Nicholson, permits further insight into the diversity among these hollows. Both were aligned along streambeds. Yet the Hughes River running through Nicholson Hollow had created a gently sloping flat that ranged in width from 2,000 to 5,000 feet before the hills rose from its edges, whereas the flat in Corbin Hollow was 800 feet at its widest, whereupon the mountains began to rise from the banks of Brokenback Run, one tributary of the Hughes River.[42] Nicholson Hol-low's terrain, and its proximity to valley communities, enabled its inhabit-ants to produce surpluses for market, as yields per acre were highest on the flat lands along the river. The range of farms within the hollows meant that some families prospered while others struggled in their attempt to make a living. The families with the fewest resources were literally "scrap-ing the bottom of the barrel" most years. In fact, some parts of Corbin Hollow had such poor soil that families gathered the majority of their income from wage work, depending less on crop yields than on local markets for labor and crafts.

Geographer Margaret Hitch reported on the appearance of agricul-ture in these adjoining communities in a 1931 article for the *Journal of Geography*. Hitch summarized the differences between Corbin Hollow and Nicholson Hollow, describing the typical farm in each. In Corbin Hollow: "On the steep slope above the cabin, in a semi-clearing where the underbrush gave way a little from the trail, we came unexpectedly upon four or five shocks of corn. This was the only corn 'field,' apparently, cul-tivated by the family living in this cabin. . . . A garden of sorts meandered among the boulders and fallen trees, a pumpkin vine and cabbages being most in evidence. Apples cut for drying were spread on one of the boul-ders altho we saw no fruit trees."[43] By contrast, the appearance of a more cultivated agriculture characterized Nicholson Hollow: "The greater por-tion of the lower slopes was occupied with orchards, corn fields with the corn now in the shock, hayfields or pastures, and here and there a cabin with a little group of farm sheds and a garden. The slopes, many of them, were quite as steep as the cultivated patches of Corbin Hollow (seemingly far too steep for soil maintenance); but this hollow was wider and more open than the smaller one, affording within it other slopes less steep." Hitch's descriptions suggest that the poorest families in Corbin Hollow lived on the margins of self-sufficiency on sloppy, poorly organized farms, and she contrasted their economic straits with the more productive farmers living in nearby Nicholson Hollow. The latter farmers more closely resembled the yeoman ideal of independent smallholders.[44]

This account of Nicholson Hollow's farms demonstrates the agricultural diversity of what Sherman and Henry called the more "advanced" hollows: at least a dozen crops filled the fields in Nicholson Hollow, including carrots, turnips, beets, peas, parsnips, and sweet corn, in addition to the staple corn, cabbage, potatoes, sweet potatoes, and beans that were also grown at higher elevations. Nicholson Hollow farmers cultivated grains, including corn, rye, oats, buckwheat, millet, and sorghum, as well as beans, cabbage, onions, apples, cherries, and pears.[45] In addition, families raised their own hogs, cows, and chickens, and they occasionally sold calves, milk, butter, eggs, and honey to the local stores, including one located just outside the mountains along the Hughes River. These farms provided abundant evidence of diversified, ample production, as Edwin White, an admirer of Appalachian culture, observed in 1937: "There are still many families who come as near as possible to being self-sustaining on their little farms. In a good year they will have plenty of corn for themselves and their stock; they have chickens and eggs, milk and butter, and plenty of meat from their own hogs; honey and sorghum provide sweetening." Families preserved fruits and vegetables by drying, canning, and burying (primarily cabbage, potatoes, and sweet potatoes) them for use later in the year. White continued: "A cellar or cave holds abundant supplies of potatoes, cabbages, turnips, possibly carrots and other vegetables; stored in stacks are large quantities of field peas and perhaps dried beans; and there is an abundance of dried and canned vegetables and fruits, sometimes tomato and fruit juices, preserves, pickles, kraut and the like."[46]

Corn and cabbage were the basis of the household diet, providing the essential nutrients that ensured the survival of even the poorest families. Geographer J. Russell Smith described the southern mountains as "the land of fried pork, fried squirrel and corn cakes or corn pone and beans. Corn is the mainstay. It is the chief crop, almost the only crop, of thousands of these mountain farms."[47] Corn was valued for its conve-

Arthur Rothstein, *Spreading apples out to dry, Nicholson Hollow, Shenandoah National Park, Virginia*, October 1935. Farm Security Administration, Office of War Information Photograph Collection, Library of Congress. LC-USF34 -000361-D

nience: it required a comparatively short growing season and relatively little maintenance until harvest. As a consequence, most bread was made from corn meal, and although a few families in the lowland hollows grew small quantities of buckwheat, rye, or oats, no one planted wheat. Corn was also the primary animal feed, supplementing the diet of farm livestock, particularly the horses, mules, milk cows, and chickens that remained near the farmstead.[48] The large mammals that once populated the mountains had been hunted out before the turn of the twentieth century, and consequently hogs provided mountain residents' staple meat. These animals roamed in the forest, thriving on chestnut and oak mast, and the prevalence of pork in the diet lies in part in the ease with which hogs grew themselves. In sum, mountain residents ate much like most other rural Southerners during the early twentieth century.[49]

Whereas some have seen Appalachian land use as a direct transference of Scots-Irish agricultural practices to the Americas, with a modified field, fallow, and forest landscape, others have interpreted the self-sufficient agricultural tradition as evidence of inefficient land use. These latter scholars have interpreted the disparity between trends in hollow agriculture and the technologies of the lowlands as evidence of a lack of sophistication and innovation, rather than a vernacular adaptation to the terrain. In fact, conditions in the mountains were such that self-sufficient farming represented one of the only ways for this region to remain in cultivation. Hollow farmers used tools that reflected the demanding terrain of the mountains. In spite of the limited technological advancement of mountain agriculture, local farmers had developed a range of effective techniques that permitted them to continue farming their mountain lands. For example, evidence of the alteration of the landscape through terracing occurs on several farms in Nicholson Hollow.[50]

Machinery that was becoming an important part of agriculture elsewhere, including tractors and threshing machines, was ill suited to this part of the Blue Ridge. In fact, many families did not even employ horse or mule power; instead, much of the labor in their fields was done by hand. Among the hollow families there were a total of forty-one horses and ten mules; as with the tools and other livestock, those communities with the least suitable land and the fewest resources possessed the fewest animals. In the more prosperous communities one of every two families owned work stock, whereas in the poorer communities roughly one in six families did.[51] Livestock significantly influenced farm management, and families who kept farm animals often were the most affluent in the mountain region.[52] Of course, the advantages of additional horsepower were balanced by the nutritional needs of horses and mules, and those farmers had to cultivate more grain to feed their horses, mules, and cattle, which boosted their acreage in cultivation. These figures mirrored a larger trend throughout Appalachia. A 1935 Bureau of Agricultural Economics study concluded that, although many farms included work stock, almost one-third of the farms in the region, "most of which were self-sufficing," owned no horses or mules. Thus, the hollows of the Blue Ridge were roughly equal to the broader region in the distribution of farm animals. The proportion of cattle in the Blue Ridge was also comparable to that for the region as a whole. Approximately 83 percent of the farms in Southern Appalachia reported milking cows, and farms with as few as one or two cows were often able to market some variety of their dairy surplus. There were 162 cows on the hollow farms, and the farm-by-farm breakdown indicates that although many farms kept two or more cows, another 20 percent owned none.[53] Households with several cows were almost certainly selling milk, cheese, or cream to local stores or, more informally, to their neighbors. As elsewhere, dairy and other crop surpluses provided an opportunity for earning cash to purchase other supplies that the families could not produce themselves. The balance between production and consumption determined each household's success.

PRODUCTION

Blue Ridge residents employed a range of modes of production as they managed their household economy, and they shifted their consumption patterns to reflect the opportunities presented by both the environment and local markets. Yet most accounts of the economy of the mountains tended to focus on the limited resources and constricted potential of upcountry farms. Researchers who studied the mountains perpetuated this perception, leading many Americans to envision the Southern Appalachians as a place apart, a remnant of the nation's pioneer past. The historical geographer J. Russell Smith, in his exhaustive *North America*, evoked the same imagery as many of his contemporaries: "The mountaineer has remained in the primitive stage where farming yields a bare subsistence and condemns the people to a life of poverty. The poorer mountain farmer usually has woodland, a steep field or two, fenced with rails, a cabin to live in, a gun, an axe, a home-made plow, a rude wagon, or, if the ground is too steep for wheels, a sled. The usual farm animals consist of one or two oxen, a cow, some pigs and sheep that run in the forest." With these limited assets many mountain families maintained themselves on the land, providing material for the economists, sociologists, and social workers who studied mountain communities who observed them with the utmost interest.[54]

By the 1920s experts in land utilization argued that experience had proven the futility of agricultural production on thin mountain soils. Agricultural economists, rural sociologists, and conservationists all described maladjusted land uses in the mountains, bemoaning what seemed to be an inevitable deterioration within mountain agriculture. These scholars used the amount of land in crops to demonstrate the limited prospects for agricultural production in much of this region: in the mid-1930s

Blue Ridge families were cultivating an average of 5.27 acres in crops, and over three-quarters of families lived off small fields of vegetables and grains.[55] Most of these farmers were not likely to have marketed significant produce from their gardens and fields, and 47 percent earned less than $200 a year from all of their efforts.[56] Yet there was considerable diversity among households: some families grew food on only an eighth of an acre, while others were working twenty acres of cropland.[57]

Agricultural life within the Blue Ridge was labor intensive.[58] Farming tools and techniques reflected the extensive use of the land, characterized by low-maintenance crops and a relatively superficial exploitation of the soil and local resources. Most farmers planted small crops of beans and other legumes that might have returned nutrients to the soil, but instead of rotating crops they left worn-out fields fallow, prolonging the time needed to replenish the soil. Some hollow farmers adapted to diminishing fertility by practicing a basic method of fallow, as one farmer reported: "When my land gits wore out after I done planted corn on hit for 3 or 4 year, I jus lets it lie faller 2 or 3 years till the weeds an' growin' things makes hit rich agin'." Most hollow farmers made no further effort to ensure agricultural conservation according to the standards of scientific agriculture. Crop rotation was limited, and although corn and beans were rotated or intermingled in small garden plots, corn was often the only crop in larger fields. Mountain farmers used no commercial fertilizers and few natural fertilizers, laying little manure on their fields even when they had livestock producing it. The tendency to combine nutrient-reducing crops with the disinclination to fertilize led to soil depletion, and farmers adapted by regularly clearing nearby forest for use as new fields. In order to clear new land, mountain farmers girdled large trees and chopped out the small trees and undergrowth, much like their eighteenth-century predecessors. Then, using grubbing hoes and mattocks or a horse, they broke the ground for the first time and planted a crop of corn and beans or potatoes. Girdled trees added nutrients to the soil as they decomposed, augmenting the humus that had accumulated under the trees while the land was in forest. Consequently, there would be productive crops for several years before the land began to lose fertility, although eventually the cycle would begin again on new land, often within a decade.[59]

In part because of these exhaustive agricultural practices, by the turn of the twentieth century many residents of the Blue Ridge hollows came to rely, at least partially, on additional sources of income. These wages and supplies remained almost completely invisible to those who sought to survey the productivity of mountain farms, but they came in the form of cash or supplies from a local mountain resort, valley farmers, and country stores on the fringes of the mountains. Frequently, families acquired cash through the sale of logs and shingles to the local sawmill, or by bartering chestnuts, dried fruit, apple butter, herbs and plants, eggs, dairy products, and liquor in exchange for commodities at nearby gap and hollow stores. The hollow farmers' main points of contact with the outside world were country stores located on the fringes of the mountains and seasonal work on valley farms and at a local resort.[60]

Of these, the most important external influence on the economy of the Madison County hollows was the mountain resort, Skyland Lodge, which served as a base of operations for most visitors to the Blue Ridge. By the turn of the twentieth century, some mountain residents had been attracted to the uppermost hollows in part because of the jobs offered by the resort. The owner, George Freeman Pollock, had discovered the mountains on a zoological collecting trip, and the landscape captivated him.[61] Pollock imagined the mountains as the site of a spectacular summer escape for wealthy Washingtonians and began to develop a resort on the Stony Man plateau in the 1880s; by 1920 it contained fifty cottages with all of the necessary comforts. Pollock owned and managed the lodge, became intimately involved with the communities that surrounded his land, and then during the mid-1920s he became one of the earliest advocates for a Blue Ridge national park.[62]

Pollock had initially been attracted to the scenic purity of the mountains, but he soon built his resort to meet the expectations of its sophisticated patrons, often at the price of significant financial distress to himself—and with ramifications that spread into the neighboring communities. Skyland Lodge exercised a considerable influence on the local economy through its demand for fresh food and its employment of seasonal laborers who served guests and managed the property. Pollock estimated that "fifty or more mountain people within a radius of ten miles . . . made at least a part of their living off of Skyland." He stressed that many mountain people "depended altogether on us for their livelihood. We gave them a market for their baskets, fruit and berries; gave them employment working in the garden and cutting wood; and all of the trails for miles around Skyland . . . were built by mountain people." By 1930 a significant minority of mountain families depended on the supplement of cash and supplies from Pollock and his guests for a critical component of their household economy.[63]

Pollock recognized the interconnectedness of the resort and local communities, and although the two depended upon each other for services and assistance, the partnership was rarely an easy one. Families in Corbin Hollow earned their living primarily from wage labor at Skyland.[64] Corbin Hollow, with its poor agricultural land, was most dependent on employment by the resort and the charity of its guests, and in part because of its proximity to the resort it received disproportionate attention from park promoters and the press. The furor over Corbin Hollow's poverty was exaggerated by the reality that the hollow was one of few locations within the mountains that was economically and agriculturally unviable for the long term.[65]

Other mountain families supplemented their income with work as caretakers for Shenandoah Valley farmers who grazed livestock in bluegrass balds. As Forest Service examiner Hall reported in 1914, "Prosperous valley farmers are also making use of this mountain region by purchasing lands which are suitable for growing blue grass and making them into summer pastures, thereby saving the products of their home farms for winter feed and largely increasing the number of stock they can raise."[66] Mountaintop pastures provided excellent forage for cattle, and 20 percent of the Madison County hollow residents supported themselves as caretakers for livestock summered in the mountains.[67]

Local stores supplied a third important source of cash and supplies for mountain families. These country markets, located either in the larger mountain communities like Weakley and Jewell Hollows or in nearby hamlets like Nethers, provided a market for crop surpluses and supplied commodities that were not produced on mountain farms.[68] Country stores provided products the mountain region could not produce, like salt, coffee, sugar, flour, canned goods, crackers, and candy. Families frequently bartered and traded, using poultry production and the sale of dairy, chestnuts, and hams to provide for their annual needs. For example, Sherman and Henry described the multiple functions of the Weakley Hollow store:

"The 'store' is but a tiny frame building selling mainly stock, feed, sugar, coffee, baking powder, lard and chewing tobacco. Here also teeth are pulled, and horses shod with home-made shoes. The store serves for the exchange of goods and as a medium for the disposal of some of the surplus products of the community."[69] Local stores offered a crucial outlet for produce as well as a supplement to the crops grown on mountain farms.[70] Farmers described trading eggs, chickens, and occasionally hams to the store for kerosene, coffee, and cloth.[71] Although some did without store-bought items, substituting homegrown corn flour for wheat flour, or honey and sorghum for sugar, virtually no one was completely separated from at least some market exchanges that brought consumer goods into the mountains.[72] Archaeologists have unearthed thousands of artifacts testifying to the range of consumer goods acquired by mountain families, some though purchase or barter, others acquired by gifts from resort visitors.[73]

These diverse strategies for self-sufficiency in the mountains reflected agricultural practices that remained prevalent in the Blue Ridge long after they had been replaced by modern technology in much of the rest of the nation. Although the economic implications of this lifestyle included lower yields and less efficient production, it also required limited capital investment and permitted farmers to adjust their market interactions at their own discretion. Many households perceived that their independence from outsiders was an advantage. However, when they came into contact with communities that lay just a few miles away, in the lowlands of the Piedmont and the Shenandoah Valley, these interactions often presaged trouble.

COMMUNITY: COMING DOWN FROM THE MOUNTAINS

Just as contemporary economists and sociologists were fascinated by the social and economic lives of the hollows, national press periodically descended upon the mountains to write feature stories focused on the region's disconnection from modern society. Sociologists, folklorists, and economists all shared the curiosity that prompted one commentator to muse: "Passing by some of these little 'farms' one wonders how people ever do make a living on them. Behind the little log house the long-eroded fields lie bare and desolate; they speak almost aloud of thankless struggle and poverty. The poorest man with the least equipment and the most meager training is on the poorest land."[74] As a consequence, some of the mountain communities in the Blue Ridge received sporadic academic and journalistic attention during the 1920s and 1930s. Whereas the poorest residents of Corbin Hollow were the subjects of countless newspaper articles, their neighbors who owned the best-located and most-developed farms and often produced a surplus for market were never interviewed by journalists in search of colorful anecdotes.[75] The majority of descriptions of the Blue Ridge mountain folk discussed the maladaptations to modern life. During the early 1930s, accounts of Corbin Hollow's economic marginality became central to the National Park Service's justifications for removing all mountain residents from the Blue Ridge in order to create the Shenandoah National Park.[76]

Competing evidence that highlighted the usual viability of Blue Ridge farms emerged in light of a devastating drought that struck the southeastern United States in the summer of 1930, and it brought the attention of Congress and state officials to conditions in the mountains. Extreme heat accompanied low precipitation, parching the soil; crops died and people suffered in both the city and the countryside.[77] Experts estimated that the Virginia corn crop would amount to only 30 percent of normal, and although this was a hardship for many commercial farmers, it posed a critical threat to subsistence producers who typically grew no surpluses. Incidentally, this regional economic crisis provides additional evidence that scarcity of food and supplies in the hollow communities was exceptional. In November, a concerned state official wrote that the mountain people were facing "not only privation but starvation."[78] Conditions only worsened as the winter progressed, and desperate cries went out for aid to southeastern farmers by the end of the year.

Predictably, most of the press attention during the drought focused on the plight of valley farmers, but local businessmen and state officials also worried about its implications for mountain families. Descriptions of drought conditions convey additional details on the economic relations of mountain families, complicating the dire descriptions of mountain scarcity of the preceding years. Accounts of hardship in the mountains describe massive shortages for all farm products, and as local realtor Ferdinand Zerkel reported: "This Fall, tomatoes were very nearly a complete failure, due to the drought. The same holds good as to Beans." Corn, the staple of both the human and domesticated animal diets, "amounted to virtually nothing for these people this year."[79] Even those cash crops that usually supplemented the income of mountain families were decimated: "Every garden truck was seriously hurt and some of the wild berry crops that often help the mountain people suffered in an unprecedented way this year."[80] These descriptions reinforce the notion that mountain families were typically able to support themselves in years of average precipitation—and further undermine the argument that the mountain economy was already in shambles.

The drought compounded the problems caused earlier in the decade by the devastation of the chestnut crop, and in 1930 the residents of the mountains faced true economic distress. Since no local, state, or federal relief funds existed to assist farmers in purchasing food or supplies to replace their losses, those who knew of the crop damage in the mountains struggled to find aid for these cash-poor communities. One local businessman reported of typical conditions: "The people in these mountains have homes with small patches, where they raise a little corn and some vegetables. With the corn they feed their hogs and chickens, and they can and put away their vegetables for the winter." Dry years disrupted these perennial agricultural patterns. In 1930, the writer reported, mountain farmers "did not raise any corn or any vegetables, so they have had to dispose of their hogs and chickens and their pantry shelves are bare."[81] These reports reinforce that these households were not normally surviving merely on salt pork and dried corn; thus, the descriptions of this natural disaster illustrate the diversity of the annual practices of self-sufficient farms. Descriptions of the plight of mountain farmers not only suggest that 1930–31 presented exceptional challenges for the survival of mountain farmers, but they also illustrate why mountain farmers traditionally used a combination of strategies to feed their families.[82]

In spite of scattered episodes of outside assistance in extraordinary circumstances like the 1930 drought, the political and economic distance of the Blue Ridge hollows from the institutions of local government meant that the people of the mountains were at a perennial disadvantage for services when compared with their lowcountry neighbors. The mountain people, although never as disengaged from regional markets as most visitors believed, were frequently far enough away from the centers of power that their interests went unacknowledged by county and state governments. They were therefore more vulnerable to political, economic, and natural forces beyond their control, particularly during hard times. A periodic inconvenience for mountain communities, this condition developed into a serious liability as plans progressed for the Shenandoah National Park in the late 1920s and 1930s. During this period the prerogative of the people of the mountains was subsumed within regional and national enthusiasm for a Blue Ridge national park.

The Blue Ridge landscape was responsible for both the distinctiveness of upcountry culture and the residents' lack of visibility within regional politics, markets, and social organizations well into the twentieth century. These remote mountain farms represented a place apart, largely overlooked by county governments. The political map of the region emphasized the hollows' distance from centers of power: mountain ridges served as natural boundaries, which meant that the eight counties containing upcountry land met along the crest of the mountains, with upcountry communities perpetually at the margins. This aspect of local geography distanced mountain residents from local decision making, and county policymakers had little incentive to conceive of the mountain region as central to their official functions. Furthermore, the mountains remained sparsely settled in comparison with the nearby Shenandoah Valley and Piedmont, with their prime agricultural soils and regional markets.

The patterns of economic and political life that characterized county and state affairs did not penetrate the mountains. Into the twentieth century, politicians were inclined to leave upcountry communities alone. There were a variety of reasons for this aloofness among neighboring communities. Although mountain families often grazed valley livestock and sent their sons and husbands into the valleys as agricultural workers, these tended to be seasonal labors. Outside the grazing and harvest seasons few contacts occurred between the two groups. Moreover, as an article in the *Richmond News Leader* reported, "the topography of these areas makes for a very finely divided and concentrated control of power. Those located at the foot of the mountains have for years been in power and despite their contacts with more progressive peoples they do not see the obligation placed upon them to provide schools for the mountain children. State-provided funds, distributed on the basis of the total number of children of school age in the whole county, are used to provide schools only for those children outside of these mountain hollows."

Under this system the mountain hollows were destined to remain at a perpetual disadvantage.[83]

Community structure and the distribution of political and economic capital not only affected political participation and schools, but also extended to agricultural improvement, an area with important implications for the livelihoods of mountain families. County organizations and local politics in the valleys were too far removed for regular interaction. Moreover, even if the hollow farmers desired to participate in the political process in Virginia during the 1930s, illiterate people who could not demonstrate ownership of taxable property valued above $250 were restricted from voting.[84] The relative disfranchisement of mountain communities led Miriam Sizer to turn from a student of the people into their advocate; in her assessment the voting laws and the lack of taxable property contributed to the unwillingness of county officials to provide schools and other services for mountain communities. Sizer believed that local elites concentrated most of their attention on managing county resources in order to maintain their own primacy. By this logic, county officials had no interest in expanding educational opportunities for mountain children or encouraging the franchise in mountain communities. In fact, mountain schools were both infrequently and irregularly staffed, and when a school did operate it was often funded by the charitable commitments of regional benefactors or religious institutions.[85] Similarly, few of the resources available through federal agricultural programs extended into the mountains, in spite of widespread concern about the backwardness of the upcountry economy.

Beginning in 1914 the nationwide county agent system established federal funding and support for state programs to bring up-to-date methods to all farmers. Yet local politics also determined the activities of the county agents. In 1930 Sizer approached E. V. Breeden, the county agent for Madison County, and suggested that he begin to work with the poor mountain farmers. Breeden replied that the county supervisors determined his obligations and that his schedule was filled with lowland activities. Having just been hired for the position, Breeden wanted to maintain county officials' good will, and he hesitated to push for the expansion of his work into the mountains.[86] Sizer observed, "The group that controls Madison County is an entrenched oligarchy . . . the machine is too powerful and entrenched for one person to cope with successfully," and she blamed the insularity of county politics for neglecting the needs of the mountain sections. Nevertheless she pressed for agricultural, educational, and economic assistance for the mountain communities.[87] The lack of political influence of the Blue Ridge mountain people compounded their invisibility to the state's agricultural bureaucracy, and the small scale of mountain farms perpetuated this omission, in spite of the intentions of federal initiatives.[88]

Sizer's interest in agricultural education reflected the broader interest in efficiency and the scientific management of farms that characterized programs for social and agricultural reform in the 1920s and 1930s. Studies in agricultural economics continually demonstrated the potential for farm improvement through scientific techniques, and Sizer's brother, a county agent elsewhere in Virginia, kept her informed about the benefits of agricultural extension. Perhaps as a result, Sizer persevered in her attempt to get Breeden into the mountains, and when she again "reminded him . . . (as gently as possible) that these Nicholson Hollow farmers as taxpayers paid part of his salary, and were hence entitled to a proportionate part of his time," he acquiesced. Breeden gave a talk in Nicholson Hollow, and a member of the audience later approached the county agent after his hogs came down with cholera. The county agent returned to inoculate the livestock, but later, after an outbreak of hog cholera in Richards Hollow, Sizer reported that no one in the community, only two miles distant from Nicholson Hollow, "had ever heard of a County Agent and did not know what one is."[89] The limited reach of agricultural extension into the mountains was not unusual, and it represents the reality that the impact of agricultural improvement did not occur evenly throughout the United States for years. Not until the New Deal, when federal officials sponsored national rehabilitation projects for poor Americans, would mountain farmers have the opportunity to receive sustained agricultural aid and advice; even then its application remained inconsistent and underfunded. Services for marginal farmers continued to remain only as good as a community's strongest politically connected advocates.

During the first two decades of the twentieth century the Blue Ridge Mountains witnessed dramatic ecological changes. The years preceding the creation of a national park in this region saw the growth and expansion of hollow settlements onto less fertile and less viable land, as well as the destruction of one of the most valuable natural resources that the mountain people had enjoyed for centuries. Yet the changes that took place in the upcountry during the 1910s and 1920s would soon come to seem minuscule in comparison to the transformation of the mountains during the 1930s.

During the late 1920s, and especially in the early 1930s, the demands of various groups on the mountains and their scenic and natural resources were increasingly in competition. The Madison County hollows remained on the margins of the national economy, but further change was afoot in the mountains as soon as the Blue Ridge became part of the National Park Service's plan to expand the national recreational landscape. During the 1920s, local advocacy for a national park in the Blue Ridge initiated the transition from subsistence farms to managed wilderness, and resort owner George Freeman Pollock's activities during the early twentieth century foreshadowed parts of the later government-sponsored conversion from farms to forest. First, however, the attention of the federal government was attracted to the mountains of northwestern Virginia due to the efforts of Pollock and his associates. These "Park Nuts" found that as mountain farms struggled during the tight years of the 1920s and early 1930s they were able to market the recreational potential of the region, in the process convincing national parks officials and Virginia politicians to embrace the creation of a new national park in the Blue Ridge region. The disrupted state of the mountains facilitated their project, as residents were less prepared than ever before to defend their land against outside interests. Once the federal and state governments committed to turning the northern Blue Ridge into a national park, an entirely new dynamic in local relations developed, and during the subsequent decade of negotiations the prerogative of the isolated farmers was subsumed within a larger national movement.

During the 1920s the accounts of conditions in the mountains presented by Sherman and Henry, Pollock, and visitors became the standard interpretation of mountain culture and viability, paving the way for developments during the 1930s that turned the region from an autonomous and little-explored corner of the world into a centerpiece of the national park system. This narrative ensured that mountain farmers would be forced to the margins as the Commonwealth of Virginia and the National Park Service committed to turning the Blue Ridge forest into a playground for the people of the East. The political and economic marginality of mountain residents was a distinct disadvantage for these people as they sought to keep their farms from being taken for a national park.

Integral to the larger project of improving land use during the early twentieth century was the imperative to coordinate the conversion of poor land from inefficient uses to purposes that served the greater good. In the minds of government planners, the displacement of small communities was an unfortunate consequence of this grand project of the emergent nation-state. The people of the Blue Ridge experienced the downside of land use planning, in part because of their history of disfranchisement within the Commonwealth of Virginia and their marginality to the planning process for the Shenandoah National Park. Meanwhile, developments during the same period in the mountains of Vermont illustrate that local expertise and communal knowledge could, by contrast, be turned to the advantage of economically disadvantaged areas, ensuring the protection of mountain farms. In their search for a sustainable local model for economic advancement, contemporary Vermonters seized the initiative in regional planning, establishing the basis for the state's more active negations with New Deal–era federal plans for land conversion and economic uplift.

CHAPTER TWO

Customs in Common

COMMUNITY AND AGRICULTURE IN THE GREEN MOUNTAINS

IN 1928, several hundred concerned citizens met in a large auditorium in Burlington, Vermont, to convene an investigation of conditions within rural communities. This group, the Vermont Commission on Country Life (VCCL), shared a sense of urgency about future prospects for the development of Vermont, uniting in an attempt to improve the state's economy and communities that was prompted by the spectre of rural decline. The commission's research covered a larger cross-section of the state than Sherman and Henry's team in the Blue Ridge, and its vision for the future was both more optimistic and more open-ended than its Virginia counterpart. Recognizing the complexity of local economic relations and believing in the importance of a measured, careful assessment of the state's future, the commission aspired to revitalize areas that had long appeared consigned to neglect and disrepair. Ultimately, the commissioners embraced a novel approach to rural uplift: one based in community values, regional cooperation, and native pride. During subsequent decades this type of approach to economic and social problems dominated conversations about local development and state planning. Vermonters' careful consideration of the state's future during the 1920s, as they contemplated the fate of their upcountry communities, helped them to prepare for the challenges and the opportunities of the 1930s.

Over the course of two years, these "Two Hundred Vermonters" ventured around the state surveying rural roads, religion, and recreation.[1] Yet unlike the authors of *Hollow Folk,* the investigators who collectively penned *Rural Vermont: A Program for the Future* were locals, members of the thinking classes. Widely read and with a finger on the pulse of national conditions, the participants in the VCCL recognized the symptoms of decline in rural communities and sought a local solution to regional problems, conceptualizing an innovative approach to land reform. Like other agricultural areas during the 1920s, Vermont struggled to maintain a viable economy in the face of rural depopulation and the booming growth of American cities. In many ways the Green Mountains share the topography of Southern Appalachia, and yet the culture of New England endowed this upcountry with a strikingly different social and political landscape, with strong political and economic connections to adjoining valley communities.

During the nineteenth century land use in Vermont was relatively continuous—both valley areas and the Green Mountains were widely cleared and covered with fields and grazing land. Early in the century the expansion of the sheep industry and the clearing of hundreds of thousands of acres for pasture had transformed the mountain landscape, and it was scattered with towns, roads, and farms. Yet steady population increases through the 1850s were followed by more than seventy years of minimal growth and the considerable redistribution of population outside of the mountains.[2] From 1850 through 1920, Vermont's population regularly lagged behind national trends, increasing only 11 percent while the United States grew by 78 percent.[3] By the early twentieth century the state's economy had been considerably altered by the persistent outmigration from mountain communities. Only a patchwork of village settlements remained in the upcountry, and much of the mountain region had returned to forest. Rural Vermonters, particularly the residents of hill towns, confronted a plethora of changes. Remaining farmers tried to maintain small, self-sustaining farms with only limited interactions with regional markets, and when markets disappeared many farmsteads faded back into forest.

By the 1920s Vermont's mountain townships increasingly struggled to remain viable. The dislocations of this era spurred both introspection and a propensity toward reform, which in turn laid the foundation for later initiatives promoting the development of Vermont's resources and infrastructure. Because they were intimately connected to the larger economy of the state, the struggle of Vermont's mountain communities took place in full view of their lowcountry neighbors. During this period, research into conditions in the Green Mountains addressed the economic decline within hill towns with the preconception that community uplift would better serve the needs of the people and the land. Consequently, Vermont land reformers sought improvement from within, restoring local values and resources to promote the economic and cultural interests of the state.

SURVEYING THE LANDSCAPE

Vermont's upcountry occupies more than a third of its landmass, exerting a powerful influence on the local culture and economy. The Green Mountains bisect the state throughout the hundred and fifty-seven miles of its length, ranging in width between twenty-one and thirty-six miles and fading into rolling hills along the Champlain Valley to the west and the Connecticut River Valley to the east. Whereas the Blue Ridge in northern Virginia is primarily one narrow tier of mountains moving northward along the state's western edge, the Green Mountains run through the center of the state, dominating the landscape.[4]

Vermont's mountain towns have historically produced fewer crops than their valley counterparts, and they have been more tangentially connected to regional markets. The mountains have an average growing season of only one hundred days, which means they are best suited for grazing and forestry. The rolling hills of the Champlain and Connecticut River Valleys are more viable for agriculture than the rocky mountain soils.[5] As in much of the rest of the Appalachian range, the mountain topography and soils make farming a challenge.[6] Vermont's mountains are primarily classified as rough stony land, many of them composed of Berkshire gneiss. These are poor soils for cultivating crops, but the less rocky parts provide excellent meadow and pasture land.[7] Vermont's deciduous hardwood forests, which dominate below 2,400 feet, are typically hemlock-northern hardwood, with a mixture of sugar maple, beech, yellow birch, basswood, red oak, white ash, and the coniferous hemlock. A boreal forest of red spruce and balsam fir blankets the higher elevations, beginning around 3,000 feet.[8]

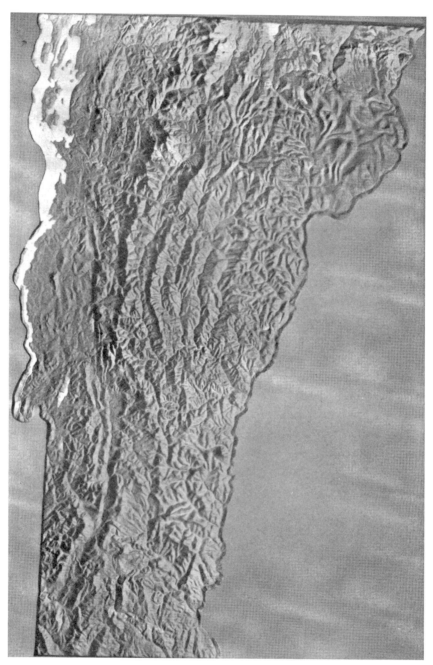

Relief map of Vermont landforms, commissioned as part of the report compiled by the
Vermont Commission on Country Life, *Rural Vermont: A Program for the Future* (1931),
frontispiece.

The importance of the Green Mountain forests was impossible to ignore, in part because of the scale of clearing during the nineteenth century; by the 1880s an estimated two-thirds of the state had been cut by loggers and farmers. Vermont's economic fortunes have long been intertwined with the forests within its borders, and the state's native forests have fueled several economic booms. Yet even during the period of peak harvest, native Vermonter George Perkins Marsh sought to raise public awareness about the effects of deforestation with his landmark *Man and Nature* in 1864. The recognition of the value of forest cover and the dangers of watershed depletion were widespread, and in 1886 Vermont's secretary of the Board of Agriculture paraphrased the consensus on the relation between forests and watersheds: "This growing tendency to floods and droughts can be directly ascribed to the clearing up of woodlands, by which the rains quickly find their way into the streams, often swelling them into destructive floods, instead of sinking into the earth to re-appear as springs."[9]

During the last decades of the nineteenth century the volume of lumber production dropped steadily, and land that had been logged in the boom years of the 1870s and 1880s increasingly returned to forest. Due in part to the ease of afforestation in the mountains, the 1883 state agricultural report predicted that Vermont's economy would come to depend increasingly on forests. One contributor, E. R. Pember, described the upcountry as an area inhospitable for agriculture, "made up as it is of almost barren rocks, soil filled to overflowing with stones and boulders, hillsides steep and inaccessible, so that reclaiming by the plow is impossible and what little vegetation there is seems hardly worth the necessary effort of the stock to obtain it." Pember recommended that Vermonters abandon their decades-old struggle with mountain farms, arguing, "There is one use that can be made of such land which promises adequate return and that is to let it grow up to forest. It was once covered with timber and time will so cover it again if given the opportunity." This sentiment was echoed with increasing regularity as agricultural production in the mountains continued to decline. As upland pastures returned to forest, the land sprouted stands of white pine; by 1900 the concentration of high-value pine ranging in age from twenty to sixty years set off a renewed logging boom in northern New England.[10]

Across the Green Mountains, farming and forests coexisted, providing the basis for a mixed economy. During the early twentieth century, the hill towns' restricted economy and changing settlement patterns drew attention to the crucial interdependence of farm and forest and the potential of forestlands to regenerate local economies. During the 1930s an estimated 3.75 million acres were covered by farm woodlots, and these forests were regularly harvested, due in part to the demands of local woodworking industries and the economic exigencies of farm maintenance.[11] Because many upland farmers depended on an income from their farm woodlots, families were often forced to give up their farms once local timber resources were depleted. J. Russell Smith observed this transformation in progress during the early twentieth century: "These people had been living on small farms which produced a part of the family support, the rest being obtained from work in the forest in winter. When the timber of the region was exhausted, the land alone could not yield a living and emigration was inevitable." The primary ecological consequence was afforestation, a process that took hold in Vermont during the late nineteenth century. By the 1920s, much of the land that had once been cleared for agriculture had returned to forest. Thereafter, Smith continued, "the forest proceeds with quiet persistence to claim the land as it awaits an agricultural reconstruction with farming that will fit the land."[12]

By the turn of the twentieth century, it had become increasingly clear that the forest would be central to Vermont's economic future.[13] In 1911, the promotional *Homeseekers' Guide* boasted: "In no section of the country are there more advantages combined for timber raising than in Vermont. Even our rougher mountain soils are covered with excellent soil; and soil makes just as much difference for the raising of lumber or pulp as for hay or potatoes. We have valuable and rapid growing trees such as the white pine, spruce, white ash, basswood and poplar, and other valuable tho slower growing species such as the cedar, maple and birch. . . . Many extensive industries in the state or nearby furnish a ready market for an unlimited supply of lumber of various grades."[14] Pulpwood and building materials created from spruce and pine provided a quick and easy product for wood industries, and between 1900 and 1930, white pine again dominated lumber production in the southern half of

Vermont. As the valuable white pine was harvested, however, its removal left behind hardwoods that had been growing in the understory, and since the 1930s the lower-elevation forests have returned to hardwood dominance, setting the stage for Vermont's famous fall foliage season.[15]

In spite of the historical dominance of the forest, Vermont's mountains were settled in the state's earliest days, having been surveyed and arranged into towns in the late eighteenth century. The six-mile-square New England township provided the framework for Vermont's civil divisions. In many cases, towns were laid out from afar, without regard to the landscape they encompassed, often with unusual results. Because of the diversity of mountain terrain, early settlers developed several villages scattered in the most opportune locations around the township, often located in the wider river valleys.[16] Hill towns with several small village centers were the dominant settlement paradigm in the Green Mountains.

During the late nineteenth century Vermont's hill towns suffered from a rural exodus. Over the decades, struggling Vermonters sold or abandoned unprofitable farms, often using cash from last-ditch timber sales to finance their departure. Rather than remain on difficult-to-farm land, the daughters and sons of Vermont left the state in search of jobs or more fertile land. Although some new farmers were attracted to the up-country by low land prices, outmigration dominated Vermont's population shifts, and mountain villages shrunk as the surrounding farms withered.[17] As a 1927 article in *National Geographic Magazine* reported: "It is . . . no indictment of the State that the number of farms in operation decreased in the 15 years preceding 1925 from 32,709 to 27,786. The young man who has learned in college the profession of farming does not battle unrelenting Nature with the savage fury of the pioneer, who had but an ax and rifle as tools. He circumvents her. He prefers to devote his energy to a local farm that can be made profitable rather than to break his heart on stony hills."[18]

With each decade fewer farmers attempted to wrest a living from upland fields, and declining numbers of residents were contributing to the maintenance of local services. These demographic changes reshaped the Vermont landscape, and as early as 1878 the consequences for mountain districts had become apparent. For example, J. H. Putnam bemoaned the implications of rural depopulation: "Scattered over these hills and up and down the valleys of all these towns, we find old houses deserted and going to decay; sometimes the house is gone and the barn left, very often all the buildings have been removed and nothing marks the spot where once they stood. . . . Where once existed populous, prosperous, and thriving neighborhoods, there is now naught but momentoes."[19] Farm abandonment in the thinnest-soiled and rockiest elevations was the result of the accumulated economic pressures facing communities distant from regional markets. Between 1900 and 1930 the total number of farms in Vermont declined by almost 25 percent, while total acreage dropped 18 percent, a decrease of over 8,000 properties and 828,000 acres in thirty years. By 1930, only 31 percent of Vermonters remained on farms.[20]

Mountain farms located in the river valleys proved the most viable within the hill towns, and they often survived the longest. By the first decades of the twentieth century, most of the farms still in operation clustered along the slender river valleys, although even there the topography restricted agriculture.[21] The expanse of arable land along the riverbeds hemmed in valley farms, and location frequently correlated with crop production and profitability. Mountain farms were far less reliant upon the dairy industry than those in more fertile areas, and they focused primarily on mixed production, including large crops of potatoes and corn. Household production continued to dominate in upcountry areas, and considerable diversity existed within the hill towns, even as the acreage in production had declined. In 1930, Vermont's farms averaged ninety-six acres of cleared land, with fewer than sixteen acres per farm devoted to other crops, and 84 percent in hay and pasture lands, but mountain farms had a mean of thirty-three acres in pasture land, one hundred and four acres in woodland, and thirty-nine acres in crops.[22]

YANKEE SELF-SUFFICIENCY

Upcountry Vermont's economic prospects were a matter of concern not only to the farmers who worked to maintain their operations, but also to state officials and researchers who sought to ensure the future viability of the state's expansive mountain landscape. Consequently, the hill towns were the subject of both study and reflection, as writers, researchers, and policymakers all endeavored to understand how the ideal of Yankee self-sufficiency might best be realized given the state's evolving economic paradigm.

View of Jamaica, Vermont, showing cattle grazing in a hillside pasture with the village of Jamaica below, early twentieth century. The surrounding landscape is a combination of forest, cleared land, and farms, a representative portrait of the Green Mountain region. Courtesy Vermont Historical Society.

Changing national markets for food and fiber affected the New England landscape from the 1910s through the 1930s as increasing numbers of farmers left marginal lands for other employments.[23] The limited productivity of the long-used soil, compounded by the difficulty of gaining access to markets for crops, provided significant disincentives against devoting substantial resources to upcountry farming. Although some hill farmers still attempted to make a living solely from agriculture, by the 1920s an upcountry household often depended on a range of employments to provide for its needs. Families who had abandoned full-time agricultural production depended on wage work to secure their livelihood, supplementing livestock and gardens with work off the farm. This was a regional pattern, and by 1940, the U.S. Census reported that 42 percent of all New England farmers integrated nonfarm employment into their annual subsistence strategies.[24] Even those farmers who owned sizeable acreages often farmed only a limited amount of land. One survey noted: "Although a man may own 150 acres of land, he will cultivate only an acre or two, and earn his living at road work, lumbering, ferning and other odd jobs at different times of the year."[25] Mountain farmers deployed a diverse array of survival strategies, which drove the region's production farther away from agriculture. Rural sociologist Elin Anderson surveyed the southern hill town of Jamaica and acknowledged: "Earning a living is something of a haphazard affair for most people in the town. Few work at steady jobs or own private businesses such as store, garage or woodturning factory. Few too persist at farming. Most of the townspeople have long since decided that to work as hard as the farmers of the town do to earn so little, isn't worth the effort. They prefer rather to raise 'just a little for ourselves' and earn their living by other means than farming." Many households discovered over time that the flexibility accompanying jobs in the lumber industry, seasonal work collecting ferns, or maintaining local roads offered an alternative to full-time farming and a cushion in times of need.[26] Among a 1929 sample of farmers from the central Green Mountains, 72 percent obtained most of their income from the farm, while another 21 percent received a majority of their income from work off the farm, and 7 percent earned most of their income from nonfarm sources. These hill farms showed considerable diversity in their crops; 94 percent grew potatoes, 18 percent cut oats for grain, and 90 percent planted gardens. By providing the basic foodstuffs for themselves, rural households were able to direct the cash earned from off-farm work toward other priorities than their subsistence.[27]

Whereas in Virginia local observers generally interpreted the self-sufficient practices of mountain farmers to be a maladjustment to contemporary conditions, many New Englanders portrayed the straitened farm economy as Yankee frugality, a laudable symbol of independence and self-reliance. Author Dorothy Canfield Fisher celebrated the practicality of Vermont farmers as an asset rather than a sign of backwardness. The Works Progress Administration's guide to Vermont, published in 1937, began with one of Fisher's essays, which echoed the writings of contemporary back-to-the-landers:

> Everybody in Vermont is still in a situation close enough to
> the primitive and natural to be not wholly conditioned by the
> amount of cash in his pockets. . . . At any rate, it is true that
> people in normal health can, *by their own efforts without cash,* to
> some extent make their environment and daily life more to

their taste. If a man wants more vegetables, he can raise them
in his garden and with his wife can or dry or put away in his
cellar what they do not use in summer. If he wants more heat
in the winter . . . swinging his own axe he can add to his fuel.
If he wants more fruit in his diet, he and his wife and the
children can pick, on Sundays and holidays, raspberries and
blueberries by the bushel, and there are always apples to be had
for the taking away, plenty good enough to make canned
applesauce out of. If he wants an extra room or a porch added
to his house, lumber is cheap, all his neighbors understand
raising a frame and are willing to help him do this, so that . . .
he can build on what he likes. He is not, that is . . . gripped
fast . . . in the rigid, impersonal framework of a society organized uniquely around money.[28]

Fisher's description focuses on the flexibility that accompanied self-
sufficiency and celebrates the advantages of independent living. Although she may have delighted in the ability of mountain farmers to
make their own way, demographic evidence suggests that many of her
neighbors either abandoned their hill farms for less rocky pastures or
turned to other occupations to supplement their incomes, thus relin-
quishing the freedom that Fisher found so endearing. Whereas in 1830
virtually every farm in northern New England had been "almost entirely
self-sufficing," by 1930, only 6 percent of Vermont farms were still classified as such.[29]

Other descriptions of rural life in Vermont from the early twentieth
century stressed the moribund standard of living, reduced soil fertility,
diminished market viability, and the flight of the most promising neighbors and children from the farm. Accounts of the fearful state of New
England towns from the late nineteenth and early twentieth centuries
were common. Articles from *Harper's*, *Scribner's*, *The New Republic*, *The
Atlantic Monthly*, and later *The Outlook* and *Ladies' Home Journal*,
stressed the failings of upcountry rural life, ironically paving the way for
the colonization of these areas with second homes by the affluent sub-
scribers of these magazines.[30] The population decline in rural Vermont
had become a cause for concern by the turn of the twentieth century, and
it was treated at length in a number of academic studies and popular ar-

ticles. For example, the *Vermont Agricultural Report for 1903* included an assessment of conditions in rural Vermont that compared figures on local population growth and decline, miles of road, and economic viability during the late nineteenth and early twentieth centuries. The survey focused on the 84 percent of Vermont townships with fewer than two thousand residents, exposing the deteriorating economic conditions in many towns. From 1890 to 1900, 101 towns (56 percent) lost more than 5 percent of their population, and two-thirds experienced a population decrease of more than 10 percent. The ramifications of steep, regular population decline were readily apparent: while the population density of Vermont towns with a growing population was 131 persons per square mile, in towns with declining population the population density averaged 24 persons per square mile.[31] Thus, the mountain communities least able to support good roads and effective schools were those faced with the greatest pressure to pay dearly for them. The disparity in what these towns could offer in terms of services, education, and employment were the source of much discussion among advocates of rural reform.

Because Vermont's political structure centralized the functions of government in the township, towns were able to exert a significant influence on state and local politics. Consequently, Vermont communities retained a noticeably democratic character, and voters shaped local policy through traditional institutions like the town meeting.[32] Property ownership determined the burden of taxes for landowners, and town governments required that residents support local services and government, including the maintenance of schools and roads. Local governments administered town schools, roads, and improvements. The towns guarded their autonomy carefully, and only in the late nineteenth century did state agencies emerge to exert some planning and oversight powers in an attempt to improve services statewide.[33]

Because of the local scale of government, land abandonment afflicted both communities and municipal services. Hill towns were particularly strapped by farm abandonment because townships were expected to support state functions and provide for local services. Small towns with few taxpayers meant that individuals had to shoulder a particularly high tax burden. In many places even a high tax rate failed to ensure that the income generated by local taxes was sufficient to fund state and local services. Figures relating to local roads bear out this inequity: in 1900,

86 of Vermont's 246 towns had thirteen or fewer people supporting each mile of road, whereas in "urban" areas, the costs of road maintenance were shared by seventy-four inhabitants to the mile. The implications of this imbalance were clear: town roads in declining rural areas were more apt to fall into disrepair–to the disadvantage of all Vermonters.[34] Because so many of the towns with reduced population were located along the Green Mountain range, the poor condition of their roads affected travel statewide, particularly since these roads were the major thoroughfares between eastern and western Vermont. Thus, when a hill town in central Vermont failed to maintain its roads adequately, residents and businesses from neighboring towns who used its roads to travel from the Champlain Valley to the Connecticut River Valley and points between were impeded in their ability to traverse the mountain passes.[35]

By the 1920s taxation and town services had become an important issue in statewide discussions of land utilization. Most hill-town landowners, whether they were subsistence farmers or the owners of marketable woodlots, were heavily taxed. This tax burden increased in the late nineteenth century as the need for a reliable statewide road network challenged the independence of Vermont townships. The first state-aid road system in the nation was created in New Jersey in 1891, followed in 1892 by Massachusetts, the leader in innovation among New England states.[36] In 1892 Vermont's General Assembly took its first step toward improving the state's roads, mandating the election of a road commissioner for each town and requiring that each township impose new taxes on the town grand list (the enumeration of real estate and taxable property): a twenty-cent tax to be dedicated to the maintenance of town roads as well as five cents in order to maintain state highways.[37] Despite these high tax assessments, most towns were unable to raise enough revenue to support the services they were required to provide for their residents, and therefore much of the cost of maintaining upcountry roads had to be subsidized by the state. Vermont's 1927–28 budget demonstrates the imbalance: whereas a representative thirteen hill towns paid an average of $700 per year into the treasury, they received an average of $3,370 for road and bridge maintenance and the construction and upkeep of town schools. In 1928 the state's eighty-seven mountain towns received approximately $293,190 in state funds, while they contributed $60,900.

This deficit was funded by property taxes paid by the more populous and prosperous towns outside the mountains.[38] As these figures illustrate, the burden placed by the hill towns on the state's finances—and on the resources of valley towns—incentivized state policymakers to evaluate the viability of upcountry communities.[39]

Population declines also had social consequences, compounding the changes in finances and settlement patterns with important cultural adjustments in mountain communities. The shift from agricultural production to wage labor in rural communities was dislocating, particularly since village businesses were oriented around the needs of an agricultural population. "Gristmills, grain and feed stores, sawmills, and creameries, all depend on the raw materials of the farm," sociologist Genieve Lamson emphasized. "The banking facilities and retail businesses have grown up in the service of an agricultural community. The local merchant feels the varied fortunes of the farmer in the volume of his trade."[40] Even the nonagricultural residents of mountain communities dreaded the continued departure of farmers, because they realized that it was improbable that other industries would emerge to replace businesses dedicated to serving farm enterprises.[41]

PRODUCTION

Vermonters had responded to the pressures of declining fertility and farm abandonment as early as the 1840s, when the state embraced a program of agricultural improvement. For decades the question of agricultural viability remained a topic of much discussion, and the Board of Agriculture, created in 1870, dedicated its early work to examining the problem of diminishing yields and rural depopulation. Some stressed the need to convert Vermont farms to livestock production. In 1878 J. H. Putnam presented a paper typical of the era, blaming mismanagement for the abandonment of Vermont farms and strongly encouraging his contemporaries to adjust their production to the capabilities of the land.[42] Instead of the soil-depleting cultivation that he attributed to the outdated practices of earlier eras, Putnam encouraged farmers to embrace forage crops and expand their production of livestock. "The farmers of these hills must realize that grass is king in Vermont, and that it is the easiest raised and most paying crop of the farm." His prescription for an improved agriculture entailed reorganizing the farm: "Upon these old hills make grass a specialty; make the farms produce all they are capable of producing, and farming will be profitable, for then those other farm products, such as butter, cheese, beef, wool and mutton will follow in abundance."[43]

Marketing livestock never attained the expected heights in Vermont, in part because regional urban markets began in the 1880s to be subsumed within the orbit of Chicago meatpackers who employed refrigerated railcars to secure a majority share of the nation's meat markets. Nevertheless, by the end of the nineteenth century, Vermont's proximity to the Boston and New York markets for dairy products offered a prime opportunity for farmers to establish regional demand for their products.[44] The dominant agricultural paradigm in lowcountry Vermont soon became the dairy farm; by 1930 the dairy industry generated roughly 70 percent of Vermont's agricultural income.[45] The place of hill farms in the state's agricultural economy was growing increasingly marginal, but into the breach stepped a revitalized forestry industry.

As upcountry Vermonters assessed the economic potential of their hills other advocates of economic growth turned increasingly to forestry. In 1882 the legislature appointed a committee to study the forest situation in Vermont, followed in 1892 by the establishment of a state forestry commission within the Department of Agriculture.[46] Beginning in 1892, the Board of Agriculture annual reports began to include papers on forestry and roads, reflecting the importance of these two topics to the state's agricultural economy.[47] These state-level initiatives were driven by the widespread fear, articulated in 1894 by Governor Urban Woodbury, that "owners of timberlands in our state are pursuing a ruinous policy in the method used in harvesting timber."[48] With so many farms being abandoned and the remaining forests under assault, Vermont policymakers devoted increasing attention to the question of how best to manage the state's woodlands.

Further organization of the forest agencies accompanied the turn of the century, and wood products manufacturer Marshall Hapgood first broached the idea of creating a Vermont national forest reserve. In 1907 Hapgood wrote in *The Vermonter* expressing his concern about unchecked logging on Vermont's remaining forests: "The State should absolutely control these forest stretches. . . . They should be absolutely reserved as public property for combined watershed, game, scenic and lumber uses. . . . Only under State or Government ownership can we have true guardianship."[49] In 1904 the Forestry Association of Vermont was founded, while the state government initiated a fire protection program in cooperation with the towns and created the office of forestry commissioner.[50] Subsequent legislation created the Vermont state forest system in 1908, and the legislature authorized the Board of Agriculture to hire a forester to oversee forest management.[51] The state forester's responsibilities included managing state forest holdings, and in 1911 the position was expanded to include advising private landowners interested in forest management on their own land. Vermont purchased its first forestland in 1909, and during the 1910s it established twelve more state forests totaling almost 30,000 acres, among them the 4,500 acre tract surrounding Camel's Hump, part of which was donated by avid conservationist Joseph Battell.[52]

These state initiatives reflected a growing awareness of the need for a comprehensive land management plan, and for some form of oversight of local conditions. Vermont's hill towns were a natural target for increased state activity. Beginning in the 1920s, Vermont agricultural economists and rural sociologists began to devote significant attention to the problems facing mountain communities, and the data they collected offer a useful window into the operation of self-sufficient farms in the Green Mountains. Researchers studied the economies of mixed-employment communities and small farms scattered through the mountains. These communities had been hit particularly hard by outmigration and the declining fortunes of hill towns.[53] The failure of increasing numbers of self-sustaining farms had led researchers to conclude that the "physical and economic handicaps to farming in the locality apparently made extensive farm abandonment inevitable."[54]

Several studies from the late 1920s focused in on economic and sociological problems in Vermont's mountain communities, and accumulating abundant data on local conditions. Two towns within the Green Mountain range offer an insight into upcountry economies. Ripton in central Vermont is exemplary of the changes that took place in towns dominated by forestry, while Jamaica in southern Vermont was representative of towns with a predominantly agricultural economy. These towns were evocative of larger patterns in the mountains, and each received careful study by economists and sociologists. The topography of these towns illustrates the diversity and economic viability of landscapes within the Green Mountain range. A brief overview of the economic and demographic evolution within these towns during the early twentieth century sets the stage for the variety of attempts to improve their rural economy that followed. Ripton's elevation ranged from 1,200 feet in the village center along the tumbling Middlebury River to 3,823 feet at the heights of Bread Loaf Mountain. By contrast, the wide and meandering West River passes through Jamaica, providing large flats in the center of town; significant portions of the town are located at low elevations, around 600 feet, even as the surrounding peaks reach heights of up to 2,051 feet.[55] State-aid gravel roads bisected both towns, and although these roads suffered decades of neglect due to the towns' small tax bases and limited resources to make improvements, by the 1920s these towns had begun to benefit from the state legislature's decision to supplement town road funds with state money.

Ripton, typical of mountain towns at higher elevations, had once depended almost completely on the forest products industry. With a restricted growing season and limited potential for commercial agriculture, its distance from rail lines further hindered market production and exports. From 1830 to 1840, however, it was the site of at least twelve sawmills, and as the 1860 *Vermont Quarterly Gazetteer* reported, "lumber bore so high a price on the market, there was a perfect furor; almost every available millseat was occupied, and the lots were stripped of their spruces; but . . . when everybody was expecting to get rich, lumber went down in price, and the mills have gone to decay."[56] By 1860, a new boom had begun, and four new sawmills were processing more lumber than ever before. Yet Ripton suffered from another decline in the logging industry beginning in the late nineteenth century, a change reflected in its population: in 1880, Ripton had a population of 617, with a manufacturing base consisting of one clapboard, shingle, and butter tub factory; four lumber mills; and two shingle mills.[57] Forty years later, Ripton's population had declined to 250, and it supported only two lumber manufacturers.[58] By 1940, after the hard years of the Depression and the first years of national forest acquisition, the town's population dropped to 212, and lumber operations had stopped completely.[59] Ripton's declining wood products industry was representative of larger trends in the Vermont mountains: the number of lumber manufacturing firms

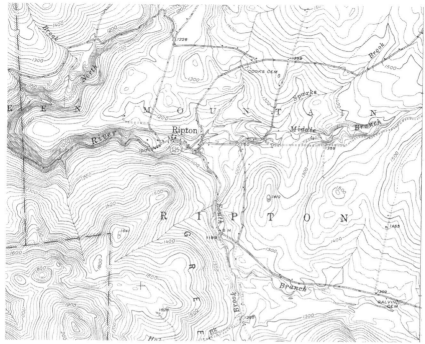

Topographic map of Ripton, Vermont. *East Middlebury, VT, Quadrangle,* 1945, surveyed 1944. U.S. Geological Survey 7.5 Minute Series. Courtesy of the University of New Hampshire Library Digital Collections Initiative.

in a sample of hill towns studied by economists C. F. Clayton and L. J. Peet in the early 1930s had dropped from seventy-three in 1880 to twenty in 1929.[60]

By contrast, Jamaica, which was representative of the more agriculturally oriented hill towns, had more residents making their living from farming than from forestry. Much like its counterparts in the Blue Ridge, Jamaica was often described as a place that "belongs to another Vermont. Its stony hill farms are slowly being reclaimed by the forest. Long stretches of rugged mountains, rushing streams and narrow valleys separate its people into isolated little communities whose only bond is the common payment of taxes to the town."[61] In comparison with dairy farms, which produced the majority of the state's crops, these farm operations were far less capitalized: whereas Vermont's commercial farmers expended an estimated $694 per year on food ($319 in actual out-of-pocket expenses),

Jamaica farmers "earn little more than five or six hundred dollars a year, and some earn less." The market penetration of Jamaica farmers was still relatively limited, and the town remained dependent on a mixed economy. In 1930, the forty-three farms operated in Jamaica were worth on average $3,081.70; these farms had a mean size of 158.35 acres, of which 27.95 acres were in cultivation.[62] Jamaica's many small farmers were typical of the majority of hill farmers in the Green Mountain region. Sociologist Elin Anderson reported, "This has been estimated as a good earning average for isolated sections of the country as a whole," but "it seems very little on which to raise a family." In spite of this straitened economy, farms and town both continued to function, as "citizens of [Jamaica] generally pay their debts, are seldom in arrears with their taxes, and usually manage to save a little nest egg for later years."[63] Notwithstanding the limited economic opportunities within mountain villages, there remained considerable independence and local pride. The interest in preserving what remained of mountain culture motivated the studies of upcountry communities and the regional economy was part of what drove the publication of *Rural Vermont*.

COMMUNITY

As in Virginia, where George Freeman Pollock was intrigued by his mountain neighbors, the communities of upcountry Vermont attracted the attention of regional elites during the first decades of the twentieth century. The concern about conditions in the hill towns derived from the inequitable tax burden, transportation difficulties, and economic and social conditions. Initially, in 1925 Henry Perkins, a zoology professor at the University of Vermont, created a statewide program to study patterns of heredity and the viability of Vermont's genetic stock.[64] This project, which Perkins named the Eugenics Survey of Vermont (ESV), supplemented other efforts to document rural Vermont society, and it eventually evolved into a more comprehensive study of rural communities.[65] ESV researchers shared with Progressive planners a concern with efficiency and social control, and the organization pursued its interest in social purity through extensive studies of Vermont's rural populations. It began with an approach that merged eugenics research and social work, but by the late 1920s it had moved closer to rural sociology, in 1928 reconstituting itself as the more comprehensive Vermont Commission on

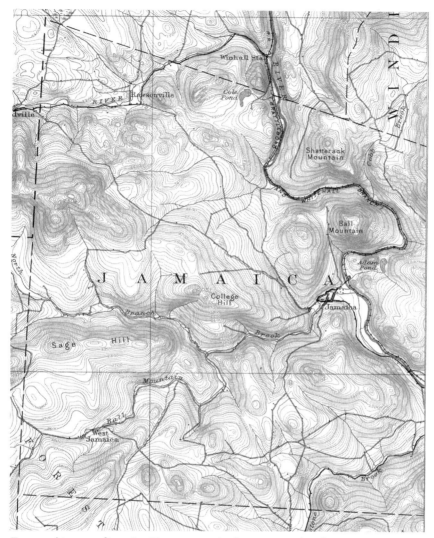

Topographic map of Jamaica, Vermont. *Londonderry, VT, Quadrangle*, 1899, surveyed 1898. U.S. Geological Survey 15 Minute Series. Courtesy of the University of New Hampshire Library Digital Collections Initiative.

Country Life.[66] As Perkins later observed, the Eugenics Survey of Vermont's studies had "brought the realization home that environmental influences, as powerful as inherited characteristics in molding a character, called for separate and thorough study and appraisal. Consequently, the Country Life Commission was organized . . . to make a study of environmental factors, which helped to mold the character of Vermonters, with the aim to plan more wisely for the future welfare of the state." Between the privately funded research of the ESV and the VCCL and the complementary state-funded research of the Vermont Agricultural Experiment Station (VAES), researchers produced several surveys of Vermont's hill towns during the late 1920s.[67]

The most comprehensive articulation of a vision for Vermont's future emerged in the Vermont Commission on Country Life's 1931 publication *Rural Vermont: A Program for the Future*. From its inception, the commission sought tacitly to investigate and improve conditions in the state's rural sections. *Rural Vermont* shared many characteristics with its famous predecessor, the 1908 United States Country Life Commission's *Report of the Commission on Country Life*, but its authors tempered their message to reflect the particular needs of the people and the land of hardscrabble Vermont.[68] The "Two Hundred Vermonters" who cowrote *Rural Vermont* represented the state's elite and Progressive element. The investigators divided themselves into study groups on agriculture, topography and climate, medical facilities, rural government, and the conservation of Vermont traditions and ideals, collectively aspiring to coordinate a realignment in the state's social and cultural landscape. As geographer John Wright described the volume, "It is unique in that it is based on close coöperation between scientific specialists and the people concerned, as represented by their community leaders." The vision and enthusiasm of the contributing authors, who were respected local figures, were critical to the success of the VCCL's project.[69]

The commission's credentials were bolstered by the collaboration of Henry C. Taylor, a professor at Northwestern University, who added scholarly legitimacy to the commission's research program. Taylor's participation was a coup for the Vermont survey. Widely regarded as a leader in the field of practical agricultural economics, he had served as the first director of the U.S. Department of Agriculture's Bureau of Agricultural Economics (BAE). [70] Taylor brought cachet and credibility to the commission, and he helped to publicize its work beyond the state. Taylor sought to publicize the commission's work beyond Vermont, and in a 1930 article for the *Journal of Farm Economics* he merged the growing literature on the national submarginal land problem and the human dimension of the commission's research in Vermont.

The VCCL's research program and its assessment of conditions within the state provided a framework for better understanding the interrelated issues that confronted rural Vermont. In his *Journal of Farm Economics* article Taylor explained that the project was driven by a query: "Are there 'pockets of degeneracy' hidden among our hills?"[71] Cognizant of the particular nature of what he called Vermont's "conservative progressivism," he clarified that the VCCL approached the problem of rural development from an angle that prioritized the "life of the people" over land use.[72] The commission's focus on social concerns demonstrated its commitment to ensuring the continued stability of Vermont communities. This was an unusual approach to studying rural life, and an editorial comment in *New England's Prospect: 1933* described the scope and scale of the project in admiring terms: "The Vermont survey was much more comprehensive in its scope than any other recent survey in New England. It was an attempt to study and plan for a region as a whole, to cut across the boundary lines between the many special fields of investigation. In this respect it was in line with a widespread movement in the social sciences and illustrates a practical application of a type of study about which there is much discussion at the present time."[73] The reaction to *Rural Vermont*'s assessment of the state's prospects was overwhelmingly positive, and in an attempt to lay the groundwork for community engagement with the rural issues it reviewed, the VCCL provided a copy of the book to every library in the state.

As part of their larger project, the ESV and VCCL also sponsored several sociological and economic studies to provide the necessary data upon which the commission could base its assessment of rural conditions. These studies included the most significant work in agricultural economics and rural sociology produced in Vermont during the early twentieth century. As the titles of the reports demonstrate, the research was focused on the people of Vermont. For example, Elin Anderson coordinated the research and writing for *Selective Migration from Three Rural Vermont Towns and Its Significance*, which looked at the causes and effects of rural depopulation; Genieve Lamson's *A Study of Agricultural Populations in Selected Vermont Towns* addressed quality of life on commercial farms in Vermont farming communities; and the Vermont Agricultural Experiment Station's complementary study, C. F. Clayton and L. J. Peet's *Land Utilization as a Basis of Rural Economic Organization,* evaluated the implications of maladjustments in land use upon hill farmers and their communities.[74]

Researchers affiliated with the VCCL reformulated long-standing concerns about rural depopulation into a research program steeped in Progressive ideas. In 1930, Perkins sent Anderson to examine the town of Jamaica as an exemplar of poor rural areas where agricultural production and limited commerce did not appear adequate to support the diffuse population. Anderson's study of local conditions confirmed that although Jamaica was surviving according to time-honored practices, little chance existed for agricultural improvement, as local farmers realized almost no profit from their land.[75] Anderson's report presented a social-scientific analysis of Jamaica and other Vermont communities and offered a range of recommendations for improving local and regional land utilization. Anderson and her collaborators investigated town grand lists, mortgage information, migration statistics, town clerks' records, and residents' recollections in an attempt to examine the viability of Vermont's hill towns. The conclusions published in *Selective Migration* speak to the researchers' conversance with the fields of rural sociology and agricultural economics, as well as their familiarity with studies of land utilization that had been conducted elsewhere in the United States.

Although the language of Anderson's report addresses the improvement of rural communities primarily in eugenic terms, at its core it boils down to a recommendation for improved land management and government intervention in land utilization.[76] The descriptions of the marginal town of Jamaica (called Sylvania in the report) echoes the language of *Hollow Folk* and other accounts of rural poverty during the 1920s and 1930s: "Sylvania is another world. One of the first outposts as one coasts eastward down the mountain ridge silently speaks for it. It is a home— bleak and weather-beaten. In the dooryard are strewn parts of implements and sticks of wood. Near the road a few chickens roam and a cow grazes. In the rear is a small garden, the only bit of cultivated land. At one side is an old Ford car, the one hint of farm machinery. Beyond this home are miles of wilderness, then another solitary human habitation, and then more wilderness before the first little community . . . is reached."

This passage evokes what Anderson perceived as the desolation of life in a declining hill town.[77]

Anderson framed the need for land use reform in social terms, rather than in conservationists' terms; nevertheless, the impact of reorganizing the landscape would be the same. Sharing the perspective of planners elsewhere, Anderson recommended: "To maintain people of fine stock in the rural communities two conditions are most essential. One is that in the rural sections which are fertile and well suited to cultivation conditions be so improved that people who really love the land are encouraged to remain. The other is that in the rural sections where the land is poor and little suited to cultivation the people be encouraged to leave for more progressive communities, lest deterioration in the quality of the stock of future citizens occur."[78] The overarching question that remained was how to ensure that the hill towns would survive, and even begin to thrive again.

STUDYING THE MOUNTAINS

By the late 1920s, agricultural economists and rural sociologists around the country had come to believe that reorganizing rural settlement was critical for the nation's further economic growth. Land use planning advocates in the Northeast were simultaneously suggesting that "the State encourage people who live on marginal land to move to the more progressive communities . . . by taking over all marginal land." Many of the contributors to *Rural Vermont* endorsed a statewide program for land use planning, which "would demand first a careful study of each township to determine reorganization on the basis of the uses for which the land is best suited." *Selective Migration* observed that "it may appear at first a costly program, but in the long run it will repay a hundredfold in human values even more than in land values. Deterioration can take place only in poor isolated communities where the potential capacities of the people are not challenged into use."[79] This report thereby integrated the ESV's agenda for uplift into the larger program of rural renewal, merging an analysis of rural economics and agricultural change into a proposal for securing the future viability of Vermont communities and their Yankee stock. Anderson concluded, along with most other observers of rural society, that significant adaptations needed to be made in order for the American village to continue to thrive into the second half of the twentieth century. This was a practical approach to land use planning, and by the 1920s

similar calls for broader readjustments in the uses of the Vermont uplands abounded.

The question of how to ensure efficient land use was central to the
rural research of the 1920s, and Taylor described the predicament faced
by land use planners: "In Vermont there are considerable areas where
the use to which land should be put is uncertain. Land which was
once used for farming but which is now being abandoned for that purpose because people can do better for themselves elsewhere. . . . Should
these lands return to forests? Should they at the same time be used for
summer residence, or can there be found some new form of agriculture
well suited to this land?"[80] In this vein, in 1929 the Vermont Commission on Country Life encouraged surveying hill towns "with a view to
gathering facts which will form the basis of developing the principles of
land utilization, applicable to the various parts of the state of Vermont
where, owing to soil, topography and climatic factors, uncertainty exists
as to the probable use to which this land should be put."[81] The product
of this research, a four-year survey of land utilization in Vermont's hill
towns, appeared in 1933 as the Vermont Agricultural Experiment Station
Bulletin 357, *Land Utilization as a Basis of Rural Economic Organization,
Based on a Study of Land Utilization and Related Problems in 13 Hill Towns
of Vermont*, compiled by BAE agricultural economist C. F. Clayton and
VAES economist L. J. Peet.[82] Bulletin 357 represented the most comprehensive analysis of the hill farm problem to date, either in Vermont or
elsewhere, and it laid the groundwork for further research into the status of what these researchers defined as marginal communities.

Land Utilization as a Basis of Rural Economic Organization examined
conditions in thirteen hill towns arrayed along the crest of the Green
Mountain range. These towns were "essentially similar" in topography
and soils to another seventy-four towns in the state, all of which had suffered from depopulation and economic stagnation during the decades
prior to the Depression. The impact of these demographic changes was
hard to overlook: while the eighty-seven towns encompassed 35 percent
of the land area of the state, by 1930 they contained only 15 percent of the
population, and their uncertain future concerned land economists and
Vermont boosters alike. By 1930, these thirteen towns had an average
population density of nine persons to the square mile, compared with
thirty-nine throughout the rest of Vermont.[83]

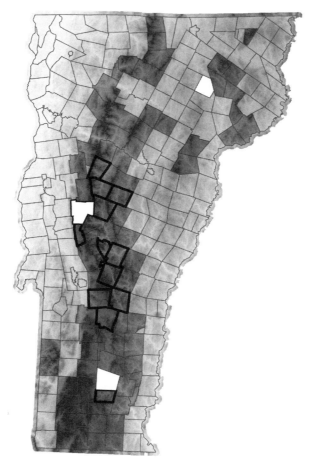

Township map of Vermont with submarginal towns marked in dark gray. The towns outlined in black are the thirteen communities studied in depth by Clayton and Peet: from north to south, Fayston, Warren, Roxbury, Granville, Ripton (highlighted in white), Goshen, Pittsfield, Stockbridge, Sherburne, Shrewsbury, Plymouth, Mount Holly, and Wardsboro. Jamaica, also highlighted in white, is located directly above Wardsboro. The town of Sheffield, in the northeastern corner of the state, is highlighted in white and is discussed in chapter 5. Map designed by author from data provided by the Vermont Center for Geographic Information, Inc.

Clayton and Peet treaded familiar ground with their research, echoing decades of observations about the challenges of mountain agriculture. These communities, as others had noted, exemplified the consequences of depopulation on rural governance and the local economy: "The combination of a sparse and declining population and the physical

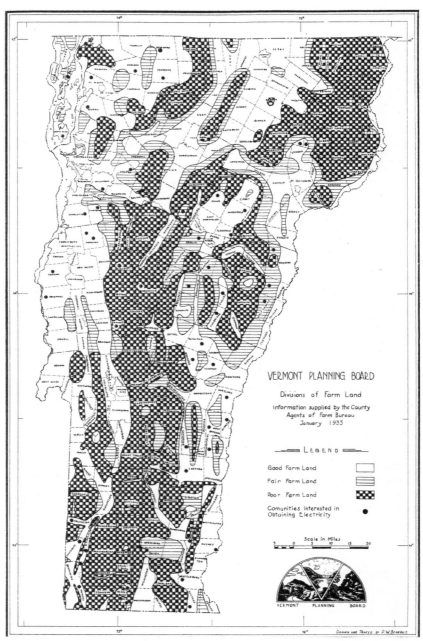

Divisions of Farm Land, showing the agricultural lands in Vermont. Areas of submarginal land for agriculture are clustered in the Green Mountains and the Northeastern Highlands. From the 1935 "Graphic Survey: A First Step in State Planning for Vermont," p. 14. University of Vermont, Special Collections, Bailey Howe Library.

limitations of the land has left many of these towns with a very slender economic basis for the maintenance of public facilities and services." In particular, Clayton and Peet's research showed how significantly land use practices had changed during the 1920s. The depopulation of the hill towns from 1919 to 1929 was marked: the total number of farms in these thirteen towns dropped from 962 to 721, a 25 percent decrease, and the proportion of cultivated land on fully operated farms shrunk from 70.6 percent to 54.7 percent. Similarly, the number of unoccupied farms in these towns rose from 431 in 1919 to 640 in 1929, an increase of 48.5 percent, which had significant consequences for the town tax base and local schools.[84]

Continued farm abandonment meant that the acreage in forest and woodland in mountainous parts of the state was steadily growing as the hill towns became less economically desirable for development. The amount of open, cultivated land in the thirteen towns compared with the total amount classed as woodland (a ratio land economists often used to ascertain degrees of land abandonment) demonstrated the shifting patterns of land use: in 1929, 31,358 acres were planted in field crops, 35,457 were in pasture, and another 264,995 acres were covered by farm forest. These acreages represented a dramatic decline in cultivated lands since the mid-nineteenth century, when only an estimated 38 percent of the state was covered by forest. These adjustments in land cover presented a challenge for farmers, yet simultaneously an opportunity for these towns, because abandoned land naturally transitioned into second-growth timber, which eventually matured into a potentially valuable resource. As a consequence, one of policymakers' primary concerns was ensuring the conservation of the timber resources, since hill towns were more than three-quarters forest by 1929.[85]

NEW AVENUES TOWARD RURAL ADVANCEMENT:
TOURISM AND TREES

As the VCCL initiated extensive discussions on how best to improve the fortunes of upcountry Vermont, people embraced several initiatives they hoped might secure increased prosperity for mountain communities and the state as a whole. Vermonters agreed that the state's future was tied to its ability to commit to the conservation of natural and scenic resources, and they increasingly turned their attention to making the most of the abandoned homes and regenerating forests of upcountry Vermont. Foremost among the strategies for bolstering the economy of upcountry Vermont were cultivating an enhanced forest products industry and developing a program to promote summer tourism.

The proposal for expanding the vacation industry in Vermont first emerged in the late nineteenth century. The cool climate of the Green Mountains had begun to attract summer visitors, and by the 1890s an estimated sixty thousand vacationers traveled to Vermont. One unanticipated consequence of emigration from agricultural areas, and from hill towns in particular, was that visitors could be lured to Vermont not only for the scenery but also because hundreds of abandoned farms were available for purchase at affordable prices. Beginning in the early 1890s the state encouraged people to take up abandoned farms, either as business opportunities or vacation homes, thereby selling its depopulated farms to nostalgic summer visitors, in what some might call a classic example of Yankee ingenuity.[86] The Vermont Board of Agriculture collaborated with the nascent State Division of Publicity, established in 1891, to publish brochures advertising land, farms, and summer homes for sale, under various titles and in various formats, beginning with the 1891 *Vermont, Its Resources and Attractions, With a List of Desirable Homes for Sale,* and extending through the 1940s with publications like *Vermont Farms and Summer Homes for Sale.*[87] In 1916, Vermont writer Walter Crockett (who would later serve on the VCCL Committee on Land Utilization) celebrated the affordability and accessibility of the state: "Vermont stands as ready to furnish an enjoyable vacation to the person who has only a few dollars to spend, as to the tourist possessed of great wealth."[88]

The Bureau of Publicity distributed its publications throughout the surrounding region and succeeded in luring people to the Vermont mountains, both to farm and to vacation. The enthusiasm for outside investment was conveyed through a 1916 textbook intended for Vermont schoolchildren, *Vermont, Its Resources and Opportunities,* which encouraged tourism, claiming: "A great opportunity awaits Vermont as a summer tourist state. The beauty and variety of its scenery, the ease with which it may be reached, and the good quality of its roads, combine to make it the ideal vacation region of the country." This classroom text echoed the language directed toward prospective home buyers, suggesting that "attention should be called to the superior advantages which

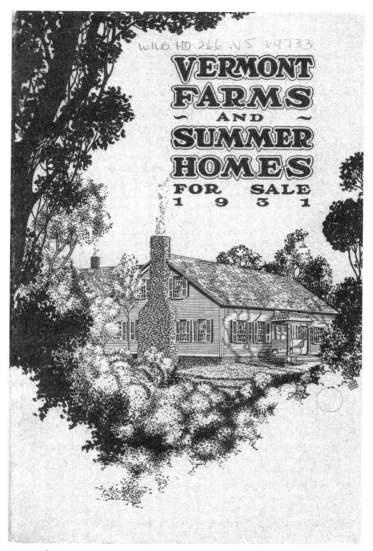

Cover of "Vermont Farms and Summer Homes for Sale, 1931," published by the Vermont Bureau of Publicity. This publication was part of a multi-pronged annual campaign to encourage outside investment in Vermont farms and summer homes. Courtesy of the University of Vermont, Special Collections, Bailey Howe Library.

Vermont offers in the matter of sites for summer homes with the great number of lakes and ponds, hills and mountains within its borders, there is no limit to the desirable sites that can be sold at very reasonable prices. There should be thousands of such summer homes distributed throughout every town and city in the state."[89] Encouraging investment from out-of-state buyers was an increasingly frequent topic of discussion in state newspapers and magazines, and attracting visitors who could take advantage of the state's scenery and bucolic countryside appealed to many Vermont boosters.

During the late 1920s the Vermont Commission on Country Life sought to promote both recreational use and rural reform, while guarding Vermont's agricultural productivity. For example, the VCCL's Committee on Summer Residents and Tourists recommended that areas where the "scenery is beautiful and the soil is not very productive" should be set aside for recreational use. It cautioned, however, against replacing the state's "productive farms with a non-agricultural class of residents." The pastoral aesthetic, no less than the importance of agriculture to the state's economy, encouraged the protection of those viable farms that contributed so much to the state's identity.[90]

Increasingly, the notion that the purchase of vacation homes by seasonal visitors might begin to compensate for rural depopulation began to gain credibility. Already by the 1920s some communities had discovered that the problems of depopulation and farm abandonment were moderated by the purchase of summer home properties, and boosters encouraged this type of "adjustment" of the local economy.[91] With the publication of Rural Vermont this idea spread even more quickly, and the push to develop a summer home industry rose to an even higher level. The VCCL commissioned two studies of summer residents, H. D. Pearl's A Study of the Effects of Summer Developments in Vermont on the Native Population and Pearl R. Brown's A Survey of the Effects of the Recreational Industry in the Rural and Village Homes of Vermont and a Survey of the Value of Vermont Properties Used by Summer Residents and Tourists. These reports observed that in a notable contrast to the rest of the small mountain towns of Vermont, a few hill communities "within the past few years have prospered to a limited extent through summer guests, tourists and summer residents. The prosperity of these towns is so marked that it seems the only way in which the state can bring back to

Vermont some of the capital that has been leaving the state for fifty years." The push to promote Vermont as a vacationland, filled with well-maintained summer homes, was under way.[92] Boosters stressed the benefits of Vermont's low land prices, and in a 1931 radio address Governor Stanley Wilson promoted the conversion of abandoned farms to summer homes, encouraging prospective landowners to consider that "the price of a cheap automobile will buy an abandoned farm with considerable land, and unlimited opportunities for development."[93]

Vermont's mountain scenery and low land prices presented a number of opportunities for summer home development, and there was ample evidence of the potential for further growth. For example, the town of Jamaica offered inducements to homebuyers, in 1912 voting to waive property taxes for five years on abandoned farms that were purchased and improved by either local residents or summer visitors.[94] There was still plenty of room in the town for new residents: in 1930, only 155 of the 232 habitable houses in town were occupied year-round, with another 20 in use as summer homes.[95] The number of summer residences rose steadily, however, and by 1940, "Camps and Homes Recently Bought in Jamaica" listed 53 summer residences.[96] The 1931 report describing conditions in Jamaica enumerated the attractions of this community for visitors: "The town is an ideal place for a rest cure, but not so ideal a place in which to spend a lifetime."[97] Elin Anderson's notes described the town as "wild and picturesque, beautiful and not developed as a summer place," sited in a prime location for recreational development.[98] In the year following the publication of *Selective Migration*, back-to-the-landers Helen and Scott Nearing bought the Jamaica farm on which they established the self-sufficient lifestyle chronicled in *Living the Good Life*, later a canonical guide for back-to-the-landers.[99] From the beginning of their experiment with country living, the Nearings encouraged other like-minded people to buy into Vermont, although ironically the massive development of a ski area on once-depopulated Stratton Mountain during the 1950s drove the Nearings away.

As the Nearings and other ambitious new arrivals in Vermont hill towns observed, abandoned farms offered an abundance of opportunities for summer visitors and new year-round residents. Publicity advertising Vermont property mushroomed during the early 1930s, when ever-greater numbers of Americans sought refuge from the ravages of modern life. As one poet described, hill farms promised a welcome escape for a reasonable price:

> Little homes of old Vermont
> Rock-walled farms with hill and stream,
> What quaint tendernesses haunt,
> Where lilacs flaunt and roses dream!
> "Hill-farms selling for a song."[100]

These "hill-farms selling for a song" were close enough to urban centers to provide a country retreat, but far enough from the cities to allow residents some insulation from unwanted market pressures. Nevertheless, the economic correction provided by out-of-state real estate purchases remained somewhat limited: whereas from 1919 through 1929 over two hundred farm homes were vacated in thirteen towns along the spine of the Green Mountains, only forty-seven of them returned to use as summer homes during that period. *Rural Vermont* reported that many opportunities for investment remained: "If there are comparable numbers of such houses in other hill towns of Vermont, some 1,000 idle and unoccupied farmhouses are available for sale for recreational purposes."[101] In the meantime, abandoned farms continued to return to forest, providing another economic possibility for Vermont's mountain region.

Since the turn of the twentieth century, developing the forests that were reclaiming abandoned farms during the previous decades offered another option for revitalizing the Vermont economy. Boosters recognized that a renewed forestry program had the potential to stimulate economic growth. In 1903 the State Board of Agriculture acknowledged that an agricultural revival seemed unlikely in the hill towns, concluding: "The mountain side, isolated sections of rural Vermont are declining, and ought . . . in the light of the industrial spirit of to-day, for the economic and social good of the people, to be turned into carefully managed timber orchards."[102] The mountain forests, however, a mix of hardwoods and softwoods, had the potential to invigorate the state's diminishing wood products industry, once an important force in the regional economy. The mountains provided an ideal environment for growing high-quality timber, and since vast swaths of the Green Mountains had returned to forest since the late nineteenth century, these woodlands required a program of management and protection, as well as sensible use. As the Bureau of Publicity's *Industrial Vermont* observed in 1914, the state's forests contained great potential: "The timber resources of Vermont are great. Over considerable areas of the Green mountain section of the state, timber is the only crop that can be raised. If common prudence is used, if the forest resources of the state are conserved, if the people of Vermont learn that it is better to cut only merchantable timber rather than strip the hillsides of every green thing, then it is possible to add largely to the industrial wealth of the state. Vermont is becoming aroused to the possibilities of its development along many lines."[103] A decade later, the Vermont Commission on Country Life echoed this sentiment, proposing resuscitating the wood products industry in the hill towns as a strategy for ensuring their long-term survival. The economic future of the hill towns was thus linked to the viability of the forests, and many Vermonters looked to the forest products industry to fuel economic regeneration and the stability of the mountain region.

The economic future of Vermont's hill towns had been imperiled long before the onset of the nationwide depression, and the main contribution of social-scientific research in the late 1920s was the investigation of options for strengthening local economies and ameliorating conditions in the towns. The question of how best to manage Vermont's resources concerned more than merely figures relating to land valuation and board feet of lumber. Vermont's program for improving hill towns suggested that it was both inevitable and desirable that some people would continue to choose to live in the mountains. Consequently, economists and local leaders envisioned a reorganization of local communities with a modified pattern of settlement, including clusters of farms and village homes in better areas and the abandonment of roads and farms in the less accessible and less fertile parts of the towns. As J. Russell Smith observed about the broader Northeastern Highlands region of New England, "The future of this region seems plain. If we ever come to regard ourselves as custodians of our continent rather than its destroyers, this upland will have careful forestry, systematic resort-development, and agriculture in selected spots in the lower levels."[104] By the late 1920s, Smith had been joined by many others in a chorus calling for better land use and more careful management of the nation's resources.

During the 1920s and 1930s Vermonters developed many of the same ideas about rural renewal as those academics from other parts of the country working in agricultural economics and rural sociology. Vermont's rural program had analogues in other regions also suffering from farm abandonment and poor resource management. What was distinctive about Vermont was how a powerful local movement sought to regenerate Vermont's rural economy based upon the resources at hand. Vermonters concerned with the social and economic health of the upcountry proactively endorsed planning for local management of forest and recreational resources, the concentration of population on better land, and the removal of underused schools and roads that inefficient population distribution had created. Upon the implementation of these changes, many expected that the hill towns would once again be able to sustain themselves through limited farming combined with seasonal employment in woodworking and tourist industries.

Most significant within the program for revitalizing the hill towns was the growing realization that there would eventually be a need for greater town and state participation in the conversion of abandoned farms to managed forests. For the first time, state leaders realized substantive improvements in the economies of the hill towns would come about only through broad changes in land use policy. Acknowledging the regional importance of the hill town problem, and reflecting the collaboration between state and federal agencies, Clayton and Peet's *Land Utilization as a Basis for Rural Economic Organization* foreshadowed developments that were to come in the 1930s by encouraging all levels of government to coordinate research and direct planning toward modifying land use and population distribution in these towns.[105] By highlighting the major challenges facing Vermont hill towns, this publication offered a model for local and regional action.

Many of the concerns shared by Vermonters were even more universal than they imagined, and research on the rural depopulation and agricultural inefficiency in the hill towns fit into other work simultaneously taking place nationwide. The academics who analyzed Vermont both benefited from and contributed to this larger national discourse about the future of rural America. Yet among the differences between the approach of Vermonters and the other researchers to land use planning was Vermonters' hesitation to use state power to promote land use change. In large part, these concerns about the role of government in implementing reform would have an important influence on Vermont's negotiations with the federal government during the 1930s, particularly over federal coordination of statewide conservation and resettlement programs.

CHAPTER THREE

Academics and Partisans

FEDERAL LAND USE PLANNING, 1900–1933

BEGINNING AROUND THE TURN of the twentieth century, as rural communities increasingly struggled to discern their economic future, federal intervention in the management of parks, forests, and agriculture expanded, signaling a new phase in the evolution of the nation-state. This was famously the age of reclamation in the arid West, of experiments in dryland farming, and of the quest to rationalize agricultural production. Yet alongside federal efforts in the West to turn "wastelands" to productive purposes emerged a parallel turn toward improving land utilization in the East—one that entailed removing uneconomic farms and forests from production and returning them to the public domain. Land use planning was premised upon the idea that the use of submarginal land for agriculture and forestry undermined the economic viability of local communities and the nation. Academic researchers initially recognized the opportunity for reshaping the eastern landscape through land reform, and they laid out an agenda for reform that reached state governments during the late 1920s. These projects would not reach fruition, however, until the massive increase in federal spending during the New Deal reallocated vast sums of money for conservation and recreation.

During the first decades of the century, conservation reemerged as a concept that promised to reinvigorate the rural economy. Land grant universities took the initiative in encouraging agricultural and natural resource conservation, educating a cohort of scholars who would drive the expansion of federal programs from the 1910s through the 1940s. States also demonstrated a newfound willingness to stake a claim to federal funding for developing local industries and infrastructure, including roads, tourism, and recreation, in order to create new business opportunities and combat economic distress. Collectively, these initiatives changed the face of the American landscape, helping to drive the dramatic reorganization of the national economy during the 1920s and 1930s. The combined influence of these programs reshaped the American economy and environment.[1]

The conditions facing rural communities in the Blue Ridge and Green Mountains were not unusual in the industrializing economy of early twentieth-century America. Local and state officials in declining agricultural areas frequently faced resource depletion, an inadequate tax base, and communities ill prepared for the rapidly modernizing society. This was the age of what some have termed the Second Great Transformation of American society, characterized by economic centralization, the expansion of state power and professional expertise, and the rise of an urban-dominated consumer culture.[2] These developments frequently passed over older agricultural communities, however, leaving many rural Americans detached from the exuberance and ambition of the era. The sense that rural communities were being left behind increasingly spurred academics and, eventually, federal officials, to develop new research programs and policy initiatives that sought to improve conditions within the hinterland.

The 1920s, although often portrayed as the age of normalcy, were a period of innovation and experimentation in land utilization and regional planning. During these years the agricultural economy was upended by depression, and shaken by the culmination of decades of unsustainable practices. This combination led to an opening for reformers seeking to promote more efficient agriculture and forestry. Ultimately, the economic dislocations of the first decades of the century drove planners to propose a previously unimaginable range of programs for reforming rural land use. New ideas included converting private land to national parks and forests, removing unviable farms from production, and employing the powers of government to improve rural services. This movement originated in the state universities of the Northeast and

Midwest, where academics began to confront problems in agriculture and forestry early in the twentieth century. By the 1930s, federal policy-makers had joined this movement and begun to conceptualize an integrated nationwide approach to land management. The Hoover administration embraced the idea of comprehensive land use planning, yet not until the middle years of the decade, under Roosevelt's New Deal, did federal agencies have both the funding and the manpower to begin to implement a program for rationalizing the national economy. Then, through attempts to reorganize ownership, both private and public, the federal government sought to establish the rural economy on a more solid foundation.

Whereas farming, forestry, and recreation are generally portrayed as separate issues, and historians have often examined them accordingly, these three aspects of land management were frequently intertwined within the policy arena during the early twentieth century. Progressive policymakers viewed these aspects of rural America as interdependent and sought to implement reforms that would make each of them as efficient and profitable as possible. Conservationists, economists, and sociologists surveyed the rural landscape in search of a solution to the economic and social problems that faced the nation, and by the 1930s many of them had come to endorse a new vision for reforming land use. In 1931, Secretary of Agriculture Arthur Hyde suggested, "Public provision should be made for the utilization of this land for purposes other than farming. There seems to be an opportunity here for Federal cooperation with State and local governments to promote the economic stability of distressed areas. A study should be made to determine what classes of land are ill-adapted to private cultivation, grazing, or timber growing, and to indicate what benefits might be derived from the public acquisition of such areas."[3]

The study of land utilization, also known as land use planning, emerged in the early twentieth century as a solution to the problems of conservation, integrating resource management, recreation, and agriculture into a comprehensive vision for conserving the nation's resources. The academic literature of the 1920s was full of research on land utilization, and scholars embraced the prospect of reforming national land use according to the principles of best use. Much like the related and simultaneously emerging field of ecology, this approach sought to balance and maximize the dynamic aspects of the land, an idea that was central to plans for improving the nation's future.[4]

Conservation planners proposed to reorganize the American landscape, uplifting rural people and bolstering the struggling national economy. Land use planning took an inclusive approach to resource management, eliminating the misleading dialectics that have too often pitted conservation against preservation, progressive against conservative approaches to land management, and social against economic reform. By more effectively managing natural resources, land use planners believed that they could help struggling farmers refocus their efforts on profitable enterprises, while benefiting the nation by opening scenic areas to recreation, wildlife management, and public use.

The merger of conservation and agricultural planning predated the environmental crises of the 1930s by more than a decade.[5] Its product, land use planning, evolved as a discipline designed to confront problems in resource management. The ecological damage associated with unsustainable agriculture and forestry had long concerned both policymakers and economists, and during the 1920s researchers in institutions including the Bureau of Agricultural Economics and state extension services began to design alternatives to the destructive practices they associated with struggling marginal farms. Between 1920 and 1933, these planners laid the groundwork for New Deal conservation and land utilization programs in Appalachia and elsewhere. Advocates of land use planning established a research program within the U.S. Department of Agriculture (USDA) that foreshadowed New Deal land policy, and during those years expansions of the national parks and forests emerged alongside a comprehensive program for reforming agricultural land use. These ideas established a basis for the preservation and forest management projects that were implemented in the Blue Ridge and Green Mountains during the mid- to late 1920s, and for an even more visionary approach to land use that emerged in the federal government during the early 1930s.

During these decades many policymakers began to view land use planning as a solution to rural economic and social problems. Proposals for improving land utilization enjoyed widespread support among policymakers and academics in a remarkably nonpartisan collaboration between groups from different parts of the political spectrum. Ameliorating

conditions in rural America and conserving worn-out land drove a push
for agricultural reform, generating momentum for land use planning
during the second half of the Hoover presidency. It was only during the
most contentious days of the New Deal that conservative Democrats and
Republicans revolted against the idea of land use reform: some critics
were concerned about the growth in government that the land utilization research signaled, while others believed that the rights of individuals and property owners were trampled by programs to reform land use
in the United States. With the rapid pace of change during the mid-
1930s, once-universal ideas about improving land use ultimately fueled
some of the most bitter conflicts in Washington over federal programs
and the role of government.

CONSERVING APPALACHIA

The reformist energy typically associated with the New Deal had been
gradually building for decades. During the last quarter of the nineteenth
century, conservationists had started to push for the protection of lands
remaining in the public domain, while at the turn of the century, reformers began to turn their attention to improving the quality of rural
life.[6] In these years a new series of public land policies sought the protection and efficient use of natural resources alongside the expansion of
the system of national, state, and local parks and forests. Then, during
the 1910s and 1920s, practitioners of the emerging disciplines of agricultural economics and rural sociology joined conservationists in evaluating the management of the rural landscape, and researchers, advocates,
and policymakers began to conceive of new programs for land use
directed at specific problem areas, like the Appalachian Mountains.
The emerging alliances between early twentieth-century agricultural
economists and conservationists demonstrate how the concept of proper
land utilization laid the groundwork for the idea of resettling at-risk
agricultural populations and converting their submarginal farms to
government-managed forests. Simultaneously, the federal government
began to extend its reach into the eastern mountains, orchestrating the
transformation of significant portions of the mountains from private
smallholdings to public lands. The creation of new eastern national
parks and national forests during the 1910s and 1920s illustrates that
the New Deal was not the first occasion during which proponents of

agricultural improvement joined with resource managers to protect the nation's natural advantages.

As many scholars have acknowledged, the conservation movement marked a new phase in the emergence of the nation-state, and particularly in the influence of the state and federal governments on regulating land policy. The formal practice of planned management of the public lands can be traced to President Theodore Roosevelt's 1903 Public Lands Commission and the 1908 National Conservation Commission's inventory of natural resources.[7] As Roosevelt noted in the Conservation Commission's first report, "All we are asking . . . is that the National Government shall proceed as a private business man would. . . . The same measure of prudence . . . of foresight demanded from him as an individual, are demanded from us as a nation."[8] The idea of a planned approach to managing the public lands represented a new perspective on American resources, and conservationists' focus on efficiency, sustainable use, and the value of expertise offered a new paradigm for resource management.[9]

During the 1910s, the momentum conservationists had generated in their efforts to protect American forests, watersheds, and natural resources began to be extended onto the farm.[10] Economists and sociologists who focused on agriculture shared an interest in rural culture, and President Theodore Roosevelt tapped several of them to study the state of "country life" in America.[11] In the early decades of the century, the Commission on Country Life, led by Cornell horticulturalist Liberty Hyde Bailey, had undertaken a program of research and initiated a series of national conversations about the quality of rural life.[12] Agricultural economists were increasingly aware of the destruction created by shortsighted farming and logging, as well as of the economic costs of these practices for rural communities. The flourishing field of research in agricultural efficiency further encouraged planning for the improved economic and ecological uses of the land. In economics, sociology, and resource management, researchers engaged with contemporary questions about efficient use. The agricultural economists and rural sociologists who entered the federal government or advised federal policymakers during the 1910s and 1920s deployed the resources of their disciplines to develop new public policies.

The accumulated effects of economic dislocation and reduced productivity inspired a new movement to protect fragile areas from unbounded exploitation. Resource managers and conservationists came to believe that returning large areas of abused land to public management was the most effective means of protecting the remaining trees and soils. During the 1910s Congress established the rationale for creating eastern national forests and parks, thereby reframing federal land policy to serve the public interest over the individual.[13] Glenn Frank, the president of the University of Wisconsin, analogized this momentous reversal: "[It] is . . . the guidance of American civilization in the transition from its pioneer youth of shortsighted exploitation to the productive maturity of statesmanlike development." The new challenge for modern Americans was that "we must learn to dress the land we have deflowered. We have been little more than high-pressure salesmen of our resources. We must become high-minded statesmen of our resources." In the end, Frank predicted, "conservation may well prove the acid test of the ability of American democracy to pull itself together in a vast cooperative venture."[14] This new conservation vision had the potential to dramatically reorder the nation's most vulnerable landscapes, and it would have an undeniable impact on the Appalachian Mountains.

Three principal avenues of federal conservation planning laid the groundwork for federal land management during the twentieth century. The first had its origins in the federal government's recognition that the public domain contained areas that had inherent value to the American people and should be preserved for the benefit of all citizens: the national park system. The second brought a utilitarian angle to the notion that resources should be conserved, and it established a protocol for reserving forest lands for management by the federal government in the interest of all the people: the national forest system. The third, state-sponsored research in agricultural economics, was based upon the idea that planned agricultural production would serve the interests not only of farmers, but also of the communities of which they were a part and, by extension, of the nation as a whole. From these threads emerged the vision of a form of regional planning that could integrate these interrelated strands of the national interest into a coherent program.

NATIONAL PARKS

The National Park Service originated in a dramatic display of federal prerogative: Congress' decision to set aside a commercially attractive parcel of the public domain in order to protect it through federal management. In this 1872 act Yellowstone National Park was formed through an unprecedented allocation of more than two million acres intended for the use and enjoyment of the people. This first national park was created so that the region's unusual and scenic features would be preserved and held forever in trust, instead of being allowed to fall into private hands and turned to personal profit. Thereafter, Congress established other national parks and reservations on some of the West's most majestic landscapes. These disparate parcels were located in ecologically and culturally unique places. "The fundamental purpose of the said parks, monuments, and reservations," read the National Park Service Organic Act in 1916, "is to conserve the scenery and the natural and historic objects and the wildlife therein and to provide for the enjoyment of the same in such manner and by such means as will leave them unimpaired for the enjoyment of future generations." This was a tall order, particularly as protecting scenery and wildlife and opening these areas to public access were not necessarily compatible. The inherent competition between preservation and recreation would have a lasting impact on the agency.[15]

The national parks contained the most memorable natural features the continent had to offer, and they benefited from hearty public support. During the National Park Service's initial period of consolidation and institution building, from 1916 until roughly 1919, it added new parks from the nation's vast expanse of public lands west of the Mississippi River but could not expand into the more populous private lands of the East.[16] The western parks served primarily a limited segment of the population: those with the time and the money to take extended vacations by train or automobile. Yet beyond the ranks of middle-class and cross-country tourists, during the first decades of the century a broader constituency of Americans was beginning to vacation, and parks advocates argued that their access to public recreation areas was impaired by the distance of the national parks from population centers. The popularity of Coney Island and Atlantic City, and of resorts in the Catskills and the Poconos, testified to the growing importance of recreational outlets for those living in American cities.

When the National Park Service turned its attention to institution building, parks advocates recognized that federal funds depended upon the goodwill of Congress and its constituencies; therefore, the expansion of the park system after 1919 was born of political expediency. Political calculations, as well as public-spiritedness, drove the expansion of the national park system into the East.[17] The western states and territories received all the benefit of federal parks appropriations, even as eastern taxpayers funded most of the development and maintenance of the national park system. By the mid-1920s, parks advocates insisted that the rest of the nation was entitled to "a definite policy for the creation of additional national parks in the eastern section for the public use and general welfare of its millions of inhabitants."[18] New parks in the East, in areas with scenic appeal and recreational potential, were designed not only to preserve a part of the region for public use, but also to introduce the majority of Americans to the pleasures of outdoor adventuring. In 1918, 350,000 Americans visited the national parks, whereas after a series of expansions into the East during the 1920s, that number jumped to 2.8 million by 1928, and 4 million in 1935.[19]

The movement to create new national parks arose from the desire to preserve natural areas while simultaneously offering recreational opportunities to the American people. In February 1924 President Calvin Coolidge endorsed the development of a park in the Southern Appalachian Mountains, and he encouraged the examination of suitable areas for expansion.[20] Park advocates stressed the value of accessible national parks to residents of the congested cities, and the potential value of a museum of nature showcasing the region's natural features. Secretary of the Interior Hubert Work emphasized the regenerative power of outdoor recreation: "We feel restricted in the artificial atmosphere of the city and annually long to reestablish contact with the soil to refresh our tired minds and bodies. The great open spaces call us and we want our children and our children's children to know some parts of their native America as it appeared to our fathers."[21] As the creation of new national parks guarded the scenic resources of the nation's most compelling landscapes, Work suggested, it also protected the most noble and energetic characteristics of the American people, thus fulfilling the nation's best interests.

NATIONAL FORESTS

The national forest system also had its origins in the expansive public lands of the West, in forests designated to combat the appropriation of public resources by private interests and the desire to protect remaining forests from unbridled exploitation. The 1891 Forest Reserve Act laid the groundwork for conserving western forests, and shortly thereafter the federal government began implementing a management plan on these lands. In 1905 the forest reserves were placed within the USDA's Forestry Bureau, which was later that year renamed the Forest Service.[22] Like the national parks, the national forests could only be created out of the remaining public domain, which confined them to the western United States.

Not until the second decade of the twentieth century did the national forests expand to include formerly private lands in the East. Beginning in the late nineteenth century, conservationists had begun to push for a system of national forests in the eastern mountains, and groups like the Appalachian National Park Association lobbied for a system of eastern national forests.[23] Using the rationale that forest protection should be a national undertaking, and that all regions should be assisted in protecting their forestland, conservationists launched an expansive lobbying campaign. Arguing that the eastern forests were critically endangered by logging, fire, and improper maintenance, conservationists pushed for federal protection of the mountain forests of Appalachia. The editors of *Harper's Weekly* highlighted the regional imbalance of federal spending, including the investment in reclamation and recreation in the West, suggesting: "As the East contributes willingly to the development of the water-powers and even to the establishment of national parks in the West . . . so the West may be counted upon to support generously this far less costly plan for affording national relief to the East."[24]

During the early twentieth century, concerns stemming from the growing awareness of the ecological consequences of over-logging spawned new initiatives to preserve the eastern forest. A chorus of influential voices in conservation organizations and the federal government emerged in support of a system of eastern national forests. The consequences of continued exploitation of eastern mountain forests threatened to undermine the eastern landscape, argued H. B. Ayres and W. W. Ashe's 1905 *The Southern Appalachian Forests*, a report urging the expansion of federal oversight over forest resources. Ayers and Ashe suggested that one of the principal shortcomings of private ownership was the limited ability of private owners to effectively protect their forest holdings. "Individual owners are to a great extent helpless in preventing . . . unwise cuttings, clearings, and forest fires. Some of them can care for their own lands, but they can not, owing to their small holdings and small incomes, regulate the policy which controls adjacent areas. Only cooperation on a large scale, such as government ownership could provide, can . . . preserve these resources to the best advantage."[25] Added to this logic, the Southern Appalachian forest was being aggressively harvested, and 1909 was the culmination of decades of regional timber production; in that year 36 percent of the hardwoods harvested nationwide came from the Appalachian Mountains, mostly from the rich and scenic forests of western North Carolina and eastern Tennessee.[26] Finally, in 1911, responding in part to concerns about overharvesting of the nation's remaining forest resources, Congress approved the Weeks Act, legislation authorizing the government's purchase of private land in the eastern states to expand the national forest system.[27]

The Weeks Act reversed the centuries-old practice of federal land distribution and initiated a program for repurchasing private land for national forests, thereby returning private land to the public domain. This legislation also established a precedent for expanding the system of public lands into the eastern United States, offering federal aid to states engaged in protecting timberlands at the headwaters of navigable streams.[28] Initially, the eastern forest acquisition program was limited to protecting the navigable waterways, a power reserved for Congress through the interstate commerce clause. Through this innovation federal land managers were able to extend their expertise into conservation planning in the East.[29] In the following years, as Forest Service examiners conducted acquisition surveys, they discovered that many of the most endangered mountain forests were not linked directly to navigable waterways. Thereafter, the 1924 Clarke-McNary Act expanded the Weeks Act's provisions for fire control and extended the forest service's mandate beyond navigable waterways to include the purchase of land to promote reforestation, making possible the creation of new national forests nationwide.[30] The impact of these laws was dramatic: whereas in 1922 the U.S. government owned 2,148,648 acres east of the Mississippi River, by 1930 more than four million acres in the Southern Appalachian Mountains had been added to the national forests. In 1935 the U.S. Forest Service was the largest landowner in the Appalachian region.[31] As a consequence, visitation to the national forests increased more than ten-fold, from three million to thirty-two million visitors annually between 1917 and 1931.[32]

As the Clarke-McNary Act established the basis for further national forest expansion, it laid a challenge at the feet of the National Park Service, an agency that had begun to compete with the Forest Service for both land and resources nationwide.[33] During the 1920s, the Forest Service began a coherent program of developing recreational facilities in the national forests, thus pairing its conservation mandate with recreation. During the mid-1930s, Secretary of Agriculture Henry A. Wallace acknowledged the Forest Service's increasingly broad agenda: "The whole idea has been to devote the land and all its resources to its highest possible use; to fit national forest lands for such uses as their character, that of their resources and the needs of the public will permit. That means selective logging, which will maintain the present lumber industry and prevent ghost towns, and developing camp grounds or renting land . . . for summer homes, perhaps where attractive trout streams are handy to good roads."[34] The Forest Service was able to capitalize on its full potential, creating a range of new attractions within its boundaries. It was partially in response to the challenge posed by this new initiative that in 1924 the Park Service began its push to expand the national park system into the East.[35] The two agencies became rivals as both committed to expanding their territory in the eastern states. The directors of the national park and forest services both increasingly sought to dominate the recreational facilities of the nation. The benefits of this competition accrued to the American public, as they were able to enjoy the new public lands of the densely populated East.

AGRICULTURE IN THE ACADEMY

The ambition to protect scenery and manage forest resources that spawned the National Park Service and the U.S. Forest Service were evocative of a new era in planning for a modern national economy. As Congress acted to develop the park and forest systems, researchers began to evaluate the challenges facing rural landowners and communities in a quest to promote efficient land use. Two graduate programs in particular, at the University of Wisconsin and Cornell University, helped to launch the careers of leading land use planners. From Wisconsin emerged an influential cohort of institutional economists, while Cornell's faculty developed an applied research agenda that matched the expertise of agricultural extension to the needs of county and state land use planning.

Institutional economists envisioned that the solution to the farm problem might be achieved through the application of conservation planning in agriculture.[36] During the first decades of the century academic research in economics and sociology increasingly focused on applying scientific knowledge to problems of production.[37] Similarly, the expansion of research on land utilization reflected the emergence of new areas of inquiry within the academy. Economist John D. Black summarized the consensus among people who studied the land: "The land-utilization problem, as it confronts us today, is a principal phase of our great national problem of conservation of our natural resources."[38] By 1929, land use planners in the state and federal governments had begun to dedicate significant resources, both human and financial, to planning for more efficient land use. As L. Dudley Stamp wrote in a 1934 article in *Science*, "Planning the land for the future is essentially the work of securing the optimum use for the benefit of all. . . . It is essential to balance the often conflicting claims of the farmer, forester, miner, industrialist, home-owner, traveler, pleasure-seeker; to secure a balance between town and country development, between the economic and esthetic needs of the nation."[39]

As the field of land use planning matured, researchers often focused on specific "problem areas" as the topic of their surveys, and during the first decades of the twentieth century, these areas were frequently in the eastern mountains. Ultimately, Virginia and Vermont's Appalachian landscapes provided an ideal setting for these rural sociologists' and agricultural economists' studies. Land utilization researchers tended to focus on areas that were geographically close to the centers of population but that remained incompletely integrated into the agricultural trends, politics, or finances of modern life. Rural sociologists, intrigued by the apparent economic and cultural independence of mountain communities, studied them as relics of frontier society, examining the culture in search of a primitive and pure American past.[40] As scholars' interest in the condition of agriculture began to spread beyond profitable farming communities, agricultural economists analyzed the operations of the poorest mountain farms and sought to improve land use. Inefficient agricultural land uses, the diminishing forests, rural poverty, and social unrest were both individually and severally the subject of research and policy in Appalachia and beyond, and policymakers increasingly identified the interconnections between these national problems.

The movement to reform land use grew out of planners' firsthand experience with the problems of agriculture. Many of these academics came from the farm and had watched their communities struggle with the economic changes that faced rural areas. Most of the influential rural social scientists were the product of upper-middle-class Midwestern farms, and they dedicated their careers to critically evaluating the larger social and economic forces at play in the agricultural economy.[41] These scholars shared what Jim Scott has characterized as a *métis* vision, merging personal experience in rural communities with the "practical knowledge" of the functioning of agricultural systems.[42] Farm-raised institutional economists like Henry A. Wallace, Henry C. Taylor, and M. L. Wilson often exhibited both sympathy with and concern for the future of agricultural communities, and they spent their careers exploring ways to ensure rural prosperity and efficient land use. This research was a form of social engineering that promoted a new method of establishing order in the agricultural economy.[43]

Economics was the discipline most attuned to the social issues that convulsed the United States in the 1880s and 1890s, and its practical applications drove research during the early twentieth century.[44] The economics program at the University of Wisconsin produced an influential cohort of policy-oriented academics who helped to frame the national conversation about agricultural production and land use planning. Institutional economists Richard Ely and John R. Commons had established a program in political economy where reformist intellectuals examined the intersections between agriculture and efficient management. Many Wisconsin students had experienced firsthand the insecurity of modern agriculture, and they believed that individual farmers needed access to scientific and economic guidance in the business of agriculture. Institutional economists, working as both "partisans and political activists," offered critical interventions in the framing of national farm policy during the first half of the twentieth century.[45] These scholars believed that government should exercise a positive influence on social change and that members of the academy should act as proponents of reform. John Dewey best expressed the idea of holistic social planning, suggesting that " 'reforms' that deal now with this abuse and now with that without having a social goal based upon an inclusive plan, differ entirely from effort at re-forming, in its literal sense, the institutional scheme of things."[46]

The community of institutional economists shared common roots: while Rexford Tugwell studied under Scott Nearing and Simon Patten at the University of Pennsylvania, and Iowa-trained Henry A. Wallace followed the economic thought of Thorstein Veblen, most of the rest of the influential forces in agricultural economics had ties to the University of Wisconsin. M. L. Wilson studied with Commons, while John D. Black, L. C. Gray, and Henry C. Taylor studied under Ely, whose proposed land policy provided for scientific planning and the regulation of natural resources. Ely argued that social control over the means of production would permit the "coordination and balance of economic forces," thus insuring "prosperity for all economic groups" and making agriculture serve the needs of the people.[47]

Ely, Commons, and Taylor encouraged their students to probe the connections between theory and practice in order to apply their research to contemporary problems, both local and national, merging ideas about "a positive state, reformist institution-building, [and] applied technical expertise," with a demonstrable influence on public policy.[48] These economists sought a model for improving production that would help farmers "rationalize the output and marketing of their individual farms," as well as improve the economic condition of communities and the nation. Their practical approach to education produced a cohort of intellectuals who were prepared to work not only in the academy, but also within government, where they found expanded opportunities for implementing their ideas. For example, Taylor left Wisconsin in 1919 for a position in the USDA, and in 1922 Secretary of Agriculture Henry C. Wallace appointed him to direct the new Bureau of Agricultural Economics, which quickly grew into one of the most influential research divisions in the federal government and was central to the land utilization programs of the 1920s through the 1940s. Although Taylor returned to academia in the mid-1920s, he later influenced the public sector again through his work with the Vermont Commission on Country Life and the Farm Foundation.[49]

Beginning in the early 1920s a cohort of researchers within the USDA promoted a program for improving research on land use within the federal government.[50] The agricultural economists who had been trained at Cornell, Wisconsin, and other universities had spread around the country, working in Washington, DC, and numerous state capitals, as well as throughout rural America. As these social scientists applied the methods of their disciplines to the most pressing economic and social problems facing the nation, federal policy began to follow this momentum. In 1921 Secretary Wallace appointed a Committee on Land Utilization, with L. C. Gray of the Division of Land Economics as chairman and a membership from various divisions of the department. This committee prognosticated about probable future land use nationwide, and although it called for an "economic classification of land," it did not possess the resources or the data to analyze the local and regional variations in land use and productivity. Instead, it proposed developing an expansive research program to assess land utilization, claiming, "What is needed is a classification on broad general lines which will give us a reasonably accurate inventory of the potential agricultural and forest resources of the nation, mapped out in broad outlines, and localized according to the commonly recognized geographical units." Thereafter, researchers in the USDA and state governments began to gather these data and to apply them to local economic conditions.[51] The Bureau of Agricultural Economics supported this mode of government research, and in 1923 BAE chief Taylor observed that "experiences in gathering facts regarding land settlement have confirmed the belief that turning the light into dark places is an effective method of bringing about reforms."[52] Hidden within these dark corners of the nation, according to Taylor and his colleagues, were the submarginal farms of the Appalachian Mountains, and it was there that these scholars discovered an application for their ambitious project of land use reform.

The groundwork that scholars laid during the 1920s established the eastern mountains as a central laboratory for regional planning and improved land utilization. During the early 1930s, the federal government embraced the intellectual project of land use planning, and reformers quickly moved to implement far-reaching plans to assist poor communities nationwide. With the advent of the New Deal, as the federal government expanded the funding of conservation and social programs, reforming land use moved into the realm of federal policy. As the analysis of agricultural problems matured, New Dealers came to believe that the problem of chronic rural poverty was a consequence, both ecological and sociological, of the unwise use of agricultural resources.

THE PROBLEM OF SUBMARGINAL LANDS

Policymakers reacted to declining economic conditions in the rural United States by calling for a program for categorizing and modifying land use. Central to this project was counteracting the impact of poor land on individuals and communities.[53] These marginal lands, often described in agricultural economics as "submarginal lands," had been among the first to suffer from the soil depletion that accompanied decades of farming. As Americans idealized efficiency and improvement, particularly during the Progressive Era, the existence of submarginal conditions in both rural and urban areas increasingly became the source of public concern and policy decisions. L. C. Gray described the concept of unsuitable agricultural lands succinctly: "Submarginal land is land that, under proper conditions of utilization, it will not pay to cultivate according to the normal standards of return to labor and capital that tend to prevail throughout the competitive field." The terminology was significant because, as Gray continued, "the term, 'submarginal,' formerly the exclusive possession of the economist, within the last few years has entered the vocabulary of the man on the street. . . . It has become his generic term for characterizing a wide group of problems that have come to the forefront in our national consciousness."[54] From the outset, the economic and ecological consequences of the continued use of poor farmland for agriculture was a significant force in attracting the attention of local, state, and federal governments to the condition of struggling mountain farmers.

Farmers working unviable land presented a public policy challenge, as Ely observed: "The shifts in agriculture and the over-expansion and settlement on submarginal lands have left thousands of stranded farmers, many of whom fail to make a decent living and most of whom create excessive costs."[55] Economists judged that farmland had become unviable primarily because of the impact of market forces and competing regions, and they identified three types of submarginal lands in the country: those characterized by a declining competitive advantage because of a declining margin of profitability, as in Northern Appalachia; lands distant from markets, where production was traditionally low per capita and the land was overpopulated for its carrying capacity, as in Southern Appalachia; and the deforested, resource-depleted cut-over around the Great Lakes, in the South, and in the Pacific Northwest.[56]

Resolving the problem of submarginal lands was one of the grand intellectual and planning projects of the early twentieth century. In New York State, an influential contingent of land use planners took an applied approach to the problems of land utilization as Cornell University's agricultural extension program searched for a solution to wasted resources and overproduction. A practical approach to local problem areas began in 1923 when the Chenango County Farm Bureau asked Cornell to conduct a study of the consequences of farm abandonment in rural parts of the county. That investigation inspired a program of surveys and extension projects that anchored New York's innovative land use research in the latter years of the decade.[57] While other university and state extension programs were simultaneously confronting similar challenges of reorganizing agriculture and the rural landscape, Cornell, with its vibrant program in rural sociology and esteemed agricultural school, consistently led the nation in applied solutions and planning innovations.

New York's county-level planning soon metamorphosed into a larger program that combined conservation initiatives and relief programs throughout the state. The clear economic advantages of land use planning had become a central inspiration for this policy initiative, and it was bolstered by the election of an ardent conservationist to the governorship. Following the election of 1928, governor-elect Franklin D. Roosevelt called agricultural leaders from throughout New York to confer on farm relief, and the consensus emerged among this group that abandoned farms should be converted to timber cultivation. In early January 1929 Roosevelt appointed an Agricultural Advisory Commission to evaluate plans for agricultural relief and promote conversion of marginal land to its best use, arguing, "We must begin to work out a plan for using every acre for the purpose to which that particular acre is best suited."[58]

Roosevelt's professors at Harvard and Columbia had been advocates of economic reform who embraced government regulation and intervention in cases where the market was not serving the needs of the individual.[59] He was predisposed to support the ideas behind regional planning, alongside the suggestion that government might intervene to manage both public and private lands, legitimizing a movement that had been building in urgency during the previous few years. This vision was informed by the work of members of the Regional Planning Association of America (RPAA), planners and social reformers who allied in 1923, stressing the importance of planning at a regional scale, with due attention to conservation, resource use, and metropolitan growth.[60] Early in his tenure as governor, Roosevelt began to articulate his vision for an expanded land use planning program in New York. He disclosed, "I have long been interested in the general subject of city and of regional planning. The present proposed survey of the whole State is merely an intelligent broadening of the planning which heretofore has been localized. It is a study for a state-wide plan which will include the use of every acre in the whole State. So far as I know this is the first time in the United States that the city or regional plan idea has been extended to take in a whole state."[61] Roosevelt contended that the land use planner could account for the complicated functioning of the local economy and resource base, and that it was possible to apply this same approach to the state as a whole.

During Roosevelt's tenure as governor, the momentum behind land use planning continued to build. As Cornell's county surveys progressed, the governor observed that each successive report "proved again what is a matter of common knowledge among agricultural experts, to wit—that a large percentage of the land now in cultivation as farms has no right to remain as farm land." Roosevelt used this growing base of evidence to promote a state-wide examination of the soils, climate, land uses, and people of the state, suggesting that an informed land policy had the potential to help New Yorkers "attain the highest maximum efficiency in planning farm to market roads, rural electrification and telephones, and scientific allocation of school facilities," as well as determine where poor farm land should be converted to forests and wilderness areas. The New York legislature extended the program of land use planning statewide.

As governor, Roosevelt linked reforestation to agricultural policy, encouraging collaboration among farm economists, conservationists, and land use planners, as he would continue to do as president.[62] The governor also promoted a reforestation program "on a scale that has never before been attempted by any state," arguing that tens of thousands of abandoned acres should be reclaimed and "put to their proper use—the growing of trees and the furnishing of recreational opportunities."[63] In 1931, the state legislature introduced an amendment to the state constitution, the Hewitt Reforestation Amendment, which was designed to ensure regular appropriations to support reforestation on the state's most vulnerable land, and to extend the program eventually to all idle land.[64] In a statewide referendum voters approved this avenue toward long-range planning and allocated twenty million dollars for the purchase and reforestation of poor and abandoned farmland on an estimated one million acres.[65] New York voters thereby demonstrated an awareness that their state had both an opportunity and an obligation to take responsibility for improving land use, and with this act they helped to launch a conservation program that would serve as a model for the rest of the nation. The state took responsibility for reversing the cycle of rural decline after a over a century during which this land had "broken the hearts and pocketbooks of thousands of families who have attempted to farm it." This program allocated resources to improve conditions in viable agricultural areas, while converting submarginal farms and abandoned land to other uses.[66]

In 1931 Governor Roosevelt argued that rural poverty threatened the prosperity of the entire nation. "The continued maintenance of farms on land which [is] not adapted to farming will be a drag on the social development of rural life. Such farms cannot support an American standard of living; as Americans we cannot encourage a lower standard of living to continue on them."[67] Roosevelt was central in promoting the scientific readjustment of rural land to the most efficient use possible, thus joining a chorus calling for significant changes in government's approach to the economic and social crisis that confronted rural America. Governor Roosevelt's advocacy of state-level land use reform emerged as a model that was widely cited within agricultural circles during the first years of the 1930s. Agricultural economists and rural sociologists nationwide took note of New York's expansive ambitions and planning successes, which eventually took on nationwide significance with Roosevelt's election as president.[68]

TO THE FEDERAL LEVEL

After the boom years of World War I, the economic dislocations associated with postwar overproduction and the consequent decline in crop prices shook American agriculture to its foundations. Policymakers increasingly recognized the social and economic challenges posed by agricultural inefficiency. Consequently, the unsettled rural economy concerned politicians as well as planners, and both Democrats and Republicans spent the 1920s debating the future of American agriculture. Agricultural economists and politicians sought a remedy for deflated commodity prices, and some seized upon the idea of price controls and government intervention in the marketing of agricultural surpluses.[69] In this milieu, a variety of proposals for bolstering the rural economy gained a foothold, including a plan introduced in Congress by Senator Charles McNary (R-OR) and Representative Gilbert Haugen (R-IA) designed to provide a guaranteed price for agricultural commodities through federal purchase of all surplus crops.[70]

The agrarian economists did not endorse this form of market manipulation as a long-term solution to the economic crisis, however, and they continued to support land use planning instead, arguing that it was the most sustainable route to an improved rural and national economy. In fact, progressive-minded politicians and planners began to envision a new role for the state in resolving economic and social problems. By the late 1920s the academic ideas that had hitherto been presented primarily in conference papers and government bulletins began to be considered as a basis for a national land use policy.[71] Withdrawing submarginal land from production emerged as a viable and comprehensive approach to promoting efficient land use, conserving fertility, reducing crop surpluses, and raising the social and economic standards of historically depressed agricultural areas.

In this vein, the National Democratic Committee commissioned a study of plans for farm relief during the 1928 presidential campaign, and concluded that submarginal farming "constitutes a drain on our national well-being to the degree that the acquisition of such lands by the public is warranted." This report foreshadowed much of the agenda of the New Deal planning agencies, describing the longstanding economic and social problems in submarginal areas and proposing "the extensive purchase of such submarginal lands as are suitable for forestation." The author, Edwin Seligman, a Columbia University professor of political economy, argued that the moment had finally arrived for reforming rural land use. Depressed agricultural land prices provided a major incentive for acquiring submarginal lands "available for purchase at comparatively low figures," and, Seligman proposed, "The funds obtained by the owners would enable them to buy farms in the better regions."[72] With increasing enthusiasm, politicians considered the prospect of reorganizing rural settlement and the agricultural landscape. Farmland-repurchasing programs had the additional advantage of bolstering the national conservation agenda. Seligman's report predicted that these projects would "appeal to everyone interested in the policy of conservation," because they would "preserve the soils of many hillsides that are now washing down into the rivers and which frequently cover the more fertile valley lands with worthless and destructive gravel," while offering new opportunities to farmers, protecting the mountain forests, and revitalizing rural communities.[73]

After the financial crash in 1929 and the onset of the nationwide depression, and especially by 1931, federal policymakers joined the nation's planners and agricultural economists in acknowledging that land utilization and overproduction were the most pressing concerns facing American agriculture. The leading thinkers within agricultural economics, including M. L. Wilson, Henry A. Wallace, and L. C. Gray, entered the upper ranks of the agricultural establishment in Washington during the Hoover administration, and they remained pivotal in determining federal conservation policy during the Depression decade. As a result, the principal accomplishments of the agricultural and natural resource conservation movements during the 1930s took place primarily within the federal government.

Rationalizing land use and eliminating farms promised to provide a reliable path to economic stability. As economist A. G. Black observed in 1929: "A carefully guarded policy of purchasing wornout farm lands in areas where agriculture is dying out at present, and thus assisting the owners to move out, has much to recommend it. No way could be devised for spending $25,000,000 of money a year that would relieve agriculture more and save more individual suffering than to spend it upon the purchase of such land."[74] Even before the onset of the Depression the movement was afoot to develop an expansive federal initiative to reform land use. Although ultimately this was not the primary avenue the federal government pursued for moderating economic dislocation during the 1930s, it did eventually gain currency during the Second New Deal.

In the early 1930s, an estimated one hundred million submarginal acres nationwide remained in agricultural production, and the deteriorating condition of these lands led to several initiatives spearheaded by President Hoover. Secretary of Agriculture Henry Hyde described the administration's policy in 1930: "In the United States there are millions of acres of lands which, because of location, soil exhaustion or natural infertility, cannot be made to produce a living equal to the American standard. These are known as submarginal lands. From the standpoint of national agricultural efficiency, as well as individual efficiency, they ought not to be farmed. . . . They should be taken out of production, reforested and held until some coming generation needs them."[75] In 1931 the Hoover administration began a more active phase, implementing changes in fiscal policy and federal spending, as well as signaling new momentum for land use reform. That October, an influential group of scholars and policymakers came together at the National Conference on Land Utilization to discuss land use in the face of economic depression, and three days of meetings spurred a new intensity in plans for national land use policy.[76]

The energy generated by the Conference on Land Utilization spurred the Hoover administration to form a National Land-Use Planning Committee, a group that followed the lead of those states that had begun to formulate a proactive approach to land classification and land utilization.[77] Although the committee held only advisory powers, its participants were dedicated to pursuing the interagency coordination of federal land use policy. Members of the committee, among them M. L. Wilson, Mordecai Ezekiel, and L. C. Gray, were products of the midwestern agricultural colleges, and there they had been imbued in the principles of agricultural efficiency and conservation of resources. They had each, often independently, dedicated their careers to studying the farm problem, and the economic crisis of the Depression provided a new forum for their ideas. President Hoover was impressed by the committee's work and promised support for their recommendations; he pushed for the inclusion of a submarginal land program in the 1932 Republican platform. In a campaign speech in Des Moines, Iowa, in June 1932, the president appropriated the planners' language, proposing the creation of a program to "divert lands from unprofitable to profitable use, and to avoid the cultivation of lands the chief return of which is the poverty and misery of those who live on them."[78] By the fall of 1932, the National Land-Use Planning Committee was collaborating with the state governments of Georgia and Minnesota, both of which had requested assistance in developing "a sound land use program." Interest in land use planning was spreading into new regions of the country.[79]

In the meantime, Hoover's presidential opponent was able to recruit several of the proponents of land use planning who served on Hoover's committee to help draft the Democratic Party's plans for economic recovery, in the process converting life-long Republicans M. L. Wilson and Henry A. Wallace to the Roosevelt camp.[80] Yet the Hoover administration's groundwork was an important backdrop for Roosevelt's program. Columbia professor Rexford Tugwell, another member of Hoover's committee, joined Wilson and Howard Tolley in formulating Roosevelt's agricultural policy from early 1932.[81] As Tugwell later reflected, "The ideas embodied in the New Deal legislation were a compilation of those which had come to maturity under Hoover's aegis. . . . We all of us owed much to Hoover, [especially] for his enlargements of knowledge, for his encouragement to scholars, for his organization of research. . . . The brains trust got much of its material from the Hoover committees or from the work done under their auspices."[82] Thus, the stage was set by 1932 for the federal government to begin implementing agricultural reform and land use planning.[83] *Brains Trust*

The Democratic campaign platform during the 1932 election embraced a number of interrelated issues dear to the hearts of progressive economists, including federal planning for agriculture, land use, regional development, and transportation policy. As one of Roosevelt's chief advisors, Raymond Moley, described the centrality of conservation to the candidate's philosophy of government in 1932: "Roosevelt had advocated reforestation, land utilization, the relief of the farmers from an inequitable tax burden, and the curative possibilities of diversifying our industrial life by sending a proportion of it into the rural districts. The central problem of agriculture—the paradox of scarcity in the midst of plenty—he saw as a problem of conservation."[84] Roosevelt himself spoke a few times during the campaign directly to the agricultural situation: in Atlanta, Georgia, he assured his audience: "During these weeks I have made it abundantly clear that I propose a national agricultural policy which will direct itself not only to the better use of our hundreds of millions of acres of every type of land in the United States, but also to the rehabilitation of that half of our population which is living on or directly concerned with the products of the soil. Our object must be the rebuilding of the rural civilization of America."[85]

In mid-September 1932 Roosevelt unveiled the centerpiece of his program for agriculture in Topeka, Kansas.[86] Roosevelt used this speech to speak directly to rural America, emphasizing his familiarity with agricultural problems, his record on farm policy in New York State, and Hoover's failure to assist the American farmer. Roosevelt outlined a few "quick-acting remedies" for agriculture and proposed three permanent measures for reforming American agriculture that spoke to the interests of planners and farmers alike. Therein lay the culmination of the land use planners' vision for reforming the nation's agriculture. First, Roosevelt suggested, was the reorganization of the USDA with the intention of developing a national program of land use planning. Second, he promoted creating a "definite policy looking toward the planned use of land," calling for a national soil survey and the future distribution of population and production according to the best possible practices. Third, he proposed the reduction and redistribution of taxes, particularly through the reorganization of local governments in rural areas. Roosevelt concluded: "These three objectives, my friends, are of the sort that will require slow moving development.... They constitute a necessary building for the future."[87] Although the New Deal's primary agricultural program, the Agricultural Adjustment Administration, ultimately took a very different tack than that proposed in Roosevelt's speech, the candidate had formally embraced a program for system-wide agricultural reform.

The conservation movement was revitalized by the push for national land use planning during the Great Depression, and the New Deal's land reform projects were deeply rooted in Progressive ideas about efficient use. With the creation of the New Deal the greatest ambitions of land use planners appeared en route to fulfillment. As one Department of Agriculture staffer observed in 1934, "The events of the past year ... have demonstrated that in periods of emergency it is from the body of research workers that administrators and advisers are recruited. They alone often times possess the detailed, accurate and timely knowledge necessary to grapple successfully with important problems." The planners had the opportunity of a lifetime to attempt to ensure that years of research dedicated to land use reform were on the verge of being converted to action.[88]

From the first days of the Brains Trust, academics and intellectuals were central to federal agricultural policy and integral to the design of a wide range of farm programs.[89]   *Not enough*   *Brains Trust*

By the end of the 1930s, millions of acres of land had come under federal management and in various stages of improvement through enhanced conservation initiatives and the labor of relief workers. In the intervening years, the subsidies and supervision provided to agriculture and the public lands through federal agencies had combined to transform the nation's landscapes of production and leisure. In the process, conservation and recreation had become an even more fundamental aspect of federal land policy. This adaptation of economic and social programs to rural areas represented the culmination of the New Deal's mission to reform land use. It signaled a moment of confluence in the broader history of agricultural policies, American public lands, and the conservation and preservation movements.

PART TWO PROJECTS

CHAPTER FOUR

Designing the Shenandoah National Park

THE 1920S AND 1930S were a period of government expansion that brought the state and federal governments into realms of unprecedented influence. Many of the land use planners' ideas about conserving the nation's natural resources were implemented in Appalachia as the federal government consolidated vast new acreages of parks and forests. In large part, the surge of interest in new national parks during the early 1920s revealed the changing priorities of government and society as they related to nature and private property during the early twentieth century.

This era in the evolution of the federal government provided an unprecedented opportunity for transforming the American landscape. In Virginia's Blue Ridge Mountains, policymakers reinterpreted the forest as a primeval landscape—an ideal site for the Park Service's dual mission of preservation and recreational development. The advocates of a new national park described the mountains as a landscape worthy of federal protection—one that boasted magnificent scenery, ample habitat for wildlife, and unmatched accessibility to the American people. Conservationists stressed the value of multi-use public lands and a truly national system of parks and forests, and they pushed actively to add as much land as possible to federal management. Residents of the Shenandoah Valley, local politicians, and business interests enthusiastically anticipated the economic benefits and the prestige of having the first eastern national park placed in their region. As a consequence, from 1924 to 1936, state and federal officials attempted to revise the history of the landscape populated by the subjects of *Hollow Folk*—by removing the people from the narrative. The Blue Ridge consequently became the site of an emerging conflict between local attempts to reassert their prerogative and the nationalizing project of the burgeoning nation-state.

Creating a rationale for developing a park in the Blue Ridge premised upon its natural features required promoters to rhetorically erase the human imprint upon the landscape, replacing it with an unpeopled and pristine nature, "a sanctuary, where man might come eons later to rediscover himself among nature's birds and trees and among her eternal hills."[1] The small farmers and grazers who had used the mountains for centuries were thus written out of the history of the park, even though their presence was indisputable. Furthermore, many of the people living in the Blue Ridge were not willing to sacrifice their homes and farms for a national park, and so the transition from farms to forest did not occur without a struggle.

The history of the Shenandoah National Park supplements the growing history of the national parks by demonstrating the complexity of multiple-purpose, top-down park development.[2] The enthusiasm of National Park Service officials, urban visitors, local boosters, and conservationists drove the Shenandoah project, with each group seeking a different version of the park. They were pitted against mountain residents, many of whom resisted the momentum to create a new national park. This chapter contextualizes the impediments to designating a new national park on private land, illustrating how the trajectory of conservation planning was contingent on political and economic forces that far exceeded the control of any one constituency.

In the end, partisan politics, economic depression, and the growing popularity of the automobile all affected the creation of the Shenandoah during the 1920s and early 1930s. The conversion of this region into a national recreation area and museum of nature was threatened by Virginia's difficulty acquiring money to pay for mountain farmers' lands; the challenges raised by mountain landowners themselves; and the inherent conflict between preservation and recreation that surrounded the park road, Skyline Drive. The Shenandoah National Park project encountered numerous obstacles during the 1920s and 1930s, but it also demonstrates how the expanding federal government developed a variety of resources to resolve the trickiest problems of land use planning.

VISION

The designation of the Shenandoah National Park came at an important moment in the evolution of the National Park Service's mission, as the agency sought to reframe its approach to conservation and the public lands. In 1924, responding to political considerations as well as competition from the rapidly expanding national forest system, the Department of the Interior turned its attention toward the Southern Appalachian Mountains in search of suitable areas for new national parks, proposing to develop a multipurpose landscape of conservation and recreation areas. The Shenandoah National Park was one of the first areas to be converted to public use under the auspices of the federal government, and it thus represents an important phase in the evolution of the National Park Service's mandate. The acquisition of private land for parks signaled a significant policy shift, as the Park Service had previously had acted only as a steward for those dramatic landscapes that remained within the public domain.[3]

Park advocates offered several reasons for expanding the system into the Southern Appalachians: preserving remaining forests, reclaiming the natural beauty of the mountains for public enjoyment, and creating a recreational outlet for the residents of the urban East. Increased mobility among middle-class Americans, and their access to automobiles and leisure time, helped spur the Park Service to advocate for additional parks. Using the argument that although significant scenic and natural areas existed in the East, these areas remained inaccessible to the majority of the population, the Park Service committed itself to ensuring that these areas were preserved for posterity. When Park Service Director Stephen Mather perceived an opportunity to expand the system, he targeted Appalachia as the optimal site for a new park, proposing that it should serve as a museum of nature: "There should be a typical section of the Appalachian Range established as a national park with its native flora and fauna conserved and made accessible for public use." Mather highlighted the history, natural features, and aesthetic value of the Southern Appalachian region, arguing that areas of scenic and scientific value could be readily acquired "for the benefit and use of all the people."[4]

The National Park Service developed an improvised image of pure, primeval nature in the Eastern mountains. The resulting narrative inspired Secretary of the Interior Hubert Work to observe during a visit in 1925: "Here in the Blue Ridge of Virginia, in the very heart of civilized America, lies preserved for our use a bit of nature that is identical with the virgin territory found by Captain John Smith and his heroic followers. Its very inaccessibility has kept it intact, and in the hurried distractions of modern life your forefathers have not had the time to conquer this wilderness, which is one of the few remaining in the East." The idea of an overlooked and pristine mountaintop forest within easy traveling range of the majority of eastern cities, available for the enjoyment of all Americans, became a powerful image in the push for new parks in the East.[5]

In February 1924, Secretary Work appointed a committee to explore the eastern mountains in search of the most suitable location for a new national park. The committee consisted of five leading citizens, described as "outstanding experts on parks and students of out-door life": Representative Henry W. Temple, Republican congressman from southwestern Pennsylvania and an avid advocate for outdoor recreation; Major William A. Welch, the general manager of the Palisades Interstate Park; Colonel Glenn S. Smith, a respected topographer with the U.S. Geological Survey; Harlan P. Kelsey, horticulturalist and former president of the Appalachian Mountain Club; and William C. Gregg, an industrialist and organizing member of the National Parks Committee. The committee was directed to find a location for a new park that could serve the "two-thirds of our population living east of the Mississippi." The motivation was clear: forty million Americans lived within hours of the nation's capital, and the Park Service sought to serve their recreational needs.[6]

The members of the Southern Appalachian National Park Committee (SANPC) traveled the region in search of an ideal and accessible representation of sublime nature. In the process, the National Park Service's directive to conserve and restore parts of the mountain landscape led the committee to acknowledge the contemporary assaults upon the region's ecological balance. Park advocates from throughout Appalachia had been warning of the threats posed by development, particularly from lumber companies moving into the last remaining old-growth forests, sheltered on "steep mountain side or hidden away in deep lonely cove." Therefore, the plans for a new park were intended not only to preserve scenery, but also to reserve a piece of the eastern forest for posterity.[7]

The idea of a national park in Appalachia resonated with politicians and boosters regionwide, and committees formed throughout the Southeast to promote the attractions of their local landscapes. Competition was brisk, and the stakes were high. Consequently, the SANPC was kept moving along the Appalachian range, drawn from ridge to hollow by the exultant claims of local and state officials. The SANPC prepared a questionnaire to be completed by proponents of potential park areas, inquiring about human occupancy, forest cover, the history of industrial development, and unusual landscape features, which permitted the committee to vet the submissions before agreeing to visit over two dozen proposed sites.[8]

The Commonwealth of Virginia was particularly well situated to promote its mountains. Not only was the state located adjacent to the Nation's Capital, but state political leaders also embodied a mixture of optimism, confidence, and fiscal conservatism as they sought a new economic foundation for the region. Virginia's New South business progressives focused on the extension of public services, including roads and parks, as a cornerstone of the state's economic expansion.[9] Moreover, Virginians had already demonstrated an interest in developing the scenic and cultural features of their state. In particular, the Shenandoah Valley, an area famous for its Civil War history and bountiful agriculture, had inspired the efforts of local boosters. In January 1924, a month before Secretary Work announced his plan for new eastern parks, representatives of local business and political interests came together as Shenandoah Valley, Inc. This group proposed to "tell the world of the developed and undeveloped resources, and the scenic and historic attractions of the beautiful Valley," including the region's potential national parks and forests. In the summer of 1924 Shenandoah Valley, Inc., recommended creating a park along the western border of the Shenandoah Valley, even as another contingent that summered at George Freeman Pollock's Skyland Lodge along the Valley's eastern edge had already submitted their own document. The Skyland advocates envisioned a park encompassing between 50,000 and 100,000 acres, stretching ten miles along the crest of the Blue Ridge, and they assured the committee that there would be around 25,000 acres of prime mountain forest available.[10]

The Skyland partisans' response to the SANPC questionnaire downplayed the presence of year-round inhabitants of the region, while acknowledging that there were a few small farms in the mountains, "of no great value." The questionnaire's query regarding improvements within the proposed area, including "towns, factories, mines, farms, quarries, hydroelectric power plants, or other developments," received the reply that the region was "absolutely free" of development. Yet the improvements at Skyland alone, which in 1920 was composed of more than fifty cottages, a sophisticated spring-water system, a dining hall, an amusement hall, lawn-tennis courts, a rifle range, a livery stable, several bath houses, and a swimming pool, suggest that the resort was hardly an undeveloped wilderness. However, Skyland's recreational potential evidently removed it from the category of undesirable developments in the eyes of the SANPC, a testament to the conflicting criteria and visions among park planners about the requirements for a national park.[11] The questionnaire also claimed that the proposed area contained a "virgin forest area," including "large quantities of very fine hemlock, spruce, oak, ash, poplar, and chestnut; all kinds of hardwood, which in large portions of this area have never been touched with the axe," an assertion belied by foresters' reports as well as contemporary photographs of the area. The Skyland contingent cited growing pressure on local timber resources, suggesting that not only were there large quantities of merchantable timber within the mountains, but also that "negotiations are active for its exploitation in the immediate future."[12] Pollock perceived that only federal purchase could save the thousands of forested acres near Skyland that were beyond his control. So, while its beauty and recreational potential were a selling point for the Blue Ridge, so too was its vulnerability to development—and the larger threat posed by the timber industry.

Resort owner and chief booster Pollock had competing instincts regarding the fate of his beloved mountain resort. Without an heir and in his fifties, Pollock foresaw an uncertain future for Skyland, and he sought to prevent it from falling into the hands of timber companies. He had embraced the preservation of the forest as one of his motivating purposes since his early days in the mountains, styling himself as an important protector of the forests. However, Pollock's preservationist instincts conflicted with his desire as a host to put on a good show for his patrons at Skyland. An extensive consumer of the mountain forest

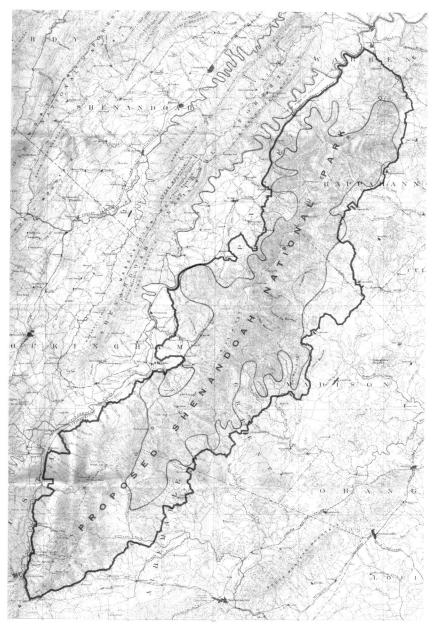

Map featuring the maximum boundaries of the Shenandoah National Park in 1927. The inner line depicts the area surveyed by Forest Examiner Hall in 1914. The narrow Shenandoah Valley is bracketed by the Blue Ridge on the east and Massanutten Mountain on the west (where Shenandoah Valley, Inc., proposed creating a national park). From the National Archives and Records Administration, College Park, MD, 79/10A/440/10.

Skyland Campers at Old Rag Mountain, shown cooking the midday meal. Note the bonfire prepared to the right of the picture, in preparation for the evening's festivities. Courtesy National Archives and Records Administration, College Park, MD.

himself, Pollock was driven to harvest vast quantities of wood for the comfort and entertainment of his guests. For example, the 1912 Skyland Catalogue recounted that one recent Fourth of July was enlivened by a 300-cord bonfire consisting of a pile of wood forty feet in diameter and fifty feet tall, saturated with gasoline so that its flames rose one hundred feet in the air.[13] The scale of Skyland's wood use suggests that the timber resources of the mountains were under threat from more than commercial logging operations.[14]

Pollock's questionnaire offered an appealing pitch for a new national park, and its lively description inspired the like-minded members of the Southern Appalachian National Park Committee to visit the area. A born marketer, Pollock envisioned a great future for the Blue Ridge, and he highlighted the region's proximity to eastern cities where "a population of over *twenty-million*" resides "*within a few hours' and few dollars' journey.*" Washington, DC, was located only eighty miles to the east, and thus: "The cheapness, quickness and comfort of accessibility make this an ideal *all-year-round* playground." Like the other areas jockeying for a national park, the Blue Ridge boasted a vocal constituency that demonstrated its enthusiasm for the park idea. Local and regional businessmen, chambers of commerce, and outdoor enthusiasts quickly enlisted to contribute money and time to the campaign to secure the park. New regional organizations emerged to coordinate these efforts, and numerous advocates worked tirelessly to convince the SANPC to endorse a national park in northwestern Virginia.[15]

In September 1924, two members of the SANPC spent three days exploring the Blue Ridge Mountains around Skyland. There they found "several areas . . . that contained topographic features of great scenic value, where waterfalls, cascades, cliffs, and mountain peaks, with beautiful valleys lying in their midst, gave ample assurance that any or all of these areas were possible for development into a national park which would compare favorably with any of the existing national parks in the West." Reporting favorably on the site, the visitors recommended that the remainder of the committee take a week-long inspection tour on horseback that fall to investigate the area further. The committee also met with local leaders, including Virginia governor E. Lee Trinkle, Congressman T. W. Harrison, and *National Geographic* associate editor William J. Showalter, all of whom supported a Blue Ridge park. Presaging the later omission of mountain people from park plans, these tours did not include a visit to the hollow communities just a few miles from Skyland.[16]

The Virginia Blue Ridge attracted the committee "because of beauty and grandeur of scenery, presence of a wonderful variety of trees and plant life, and possibilities of harboring and developing the animal life common in the precolonial days but now nearly extinct." The SANPC embraced the idea of setting the region aside as a natural preserve, to be bolstered by reintroductions of flora and fauna, and envisioned cultivating the region's recreational potential for tourists.[17] When in December 1924, the SANPC reported on its investigations, it recommended the creation of two national parks: in the Blue Ridge surrounding Skyland and the Great Smoky Mountains of North Carolina and Tennessee. The central location of the Blue Ridge proved a crucial advantage in its competition for park status. In fact, the committee judged the Blue Ridge as "the outstanding and logical place for the creation of the first national park in the southern Appalachians," because of its prime accessibility and scenic appeal. Shortly thereafter, Director Mather declared that both sites "possess scenery of a high order and of national importance, and are readily susceptible of development for recreational purposes." In Washington, enthusiasm was building behind the idea of a new national park in the eastern United States.[18]

MOMENTUM

At the federal level, the momentum behind the new park continued to build. In December 1924 Congressman Temple of the SANPC and Senator Claude Swanson (D-VA) introduced legislation to initiate the process of securing land in the Southern Appalachians.[19] This act authorized the secretary of the interior to determine park boundaries and reappointed the SANPC, charging it with defining park boundaries and overseeing the selection, donation, and acquisition of lands for the new eastern parks. Shortly thereafter, and building on the precedent from land donated to create Lafayette National Park (now Acadia) in Maine, the Department of the Interior stipulated that further approval of the parks was contingent upon the donation of the land to the federal government. Because the National Park Service had no authority to buy land itself, Congress laid the responsibility for acquiring the Blue Ridge park on the citizens of Virginia, who were expected to raise funds, purchase the land, and present it to the federal government. Park advocates shared Secretary Work's confidence that "donations of land within this area by the State and private individuals will leave only fragmentary parcels to be otherwise acquired."[20]

The enthusiasm for land acquisition and fundraising made the creation of the park seem assured in its early years, and contributed to the sense of inevitability that drove the initial phase of the Shenandoah National Park development. The Blue Ridge site's combination of accessibility and scenery suited the National Park Service's mission, and park partisans nationwide quickly endorsed the Shenandoah project. The Shenandoah's location played a vital role as a feature of the regional fundraising campaign, and Promoters noted the ease with which Americans of all classes could travel to the park. Two centuries of internal improvements had opened up the areas around the mountains for easy travel, facilitating access to the region. One of the many advertising brochures endorsing the park stressed: "With rail and motor roads already flanking its boundaries, it would be visited, not annually, but monthly and weekly throughout the year by thousands of lovers of the outdoors, who have never gone to Arizona or Maine and probably never will." However, even as the proximity of the Blue Ridge to centers of population made it an attractive location, this new paradigm of park creation created an administrative challenge for the National Park Service.[21]

In spite of the decade-long history of acquisition of private property for national forests, first established under the 1911 Weeks Act, there was no precedent for creating a national park from privately held lands. In April 1925 the Shenandoah National Park Association (SNPA) incorporated to oversee the acquisition of land for the nascent park. Embracing its new mandate, the SNPA kicked off its campaign for pledges in the late summer of 1925. People throughout Virginia rallied behind the Shenandoah project, and the park benefited further from the election of Shenandoah Valley resident Harry Flood Byrd to the governorship in November 1925. A newspaper publisher (the *Winchester Star* and the *Harrisonburg News-Record*), Byrd had strong ties with Skyland: he had inherited his father's cottage at Skyland, "Byrd's Nest," and shared a social connection with the Skyland park advocates. An enthusiastic proponent of tourism and infrastructure, Byrd embraced the Shenandoah National Park as one of the cornerstones of the state's economic program. Like many Virginians, he took tourism seriously, and as he observed in 1927: "A satisfied visitor is our best investment."[22]

Byrd had established his reputation as a state legislator by advocating a well-designed and well-maintained network of state and county roads; as governor he promoted automobility as a centerpiece of the state's planning program.[23] His pay-as-you-go philosophy represented an attempt to apply common-sense business practices to the practice of governing, and it quickly turned Virginia's state deficit into a surplus.[24] Byrd also looked to improve the fortunes of the state through tourism and economic development. Viewing automobile tourism as a cost-effective boost to the state's economy, he argued that "America is on wheels and Virginia is now awake to the dollar value of the tourist traffic."[25] Upon his election as governor in the fall of 1925, Byrd assumed control over the park fundraising campaign and encouraged the development of the state's "latent resources" by creating a new State Conservation and Development Commission (SCDC). He appointed his former campaign manager, Front Royal businessman William Carson, to head the new state commission,

Governor Harry Flood Byrd and the State Conservation and Development Commission at Skyland, November 1927. From left to right, front: Rufus S. Roberts, Thomas L. Farrar, Col. Glenn S. Smith, George Freeman Pollock; on step: William E. Carson, Governor Harry Flood Byrd; on porch: L. Ferdinand Zerkel, Sam Irwin, Charles T. O'Neill, Arno B. Cammerer, Elmer O. Fippen, and Lee Long. From *Shenandoah National Park, Official Pictorial Book* (n.p.: National Survey Institute, 1929), 4.

which was composed of the "ablest and most outstanding businessmen in Virginia." Byrd charged the commission with emphasizing Virginia's unique past to promote its natural and historical resources, with the ambition of attracting tourists and their money to the state.[26]

Once the administrative structure was in place, Virginians turned to the task of acquiring land for the park. Virginia's initial fundraising campaign, "Buy an Acre at $6," generated enthusiasm for the park by aiming at the largest possible donor base. According to fundraising lore, SNPA member Dan Wine pitched the slogan under the premise that "if thousands of people would just buy one acre," the park could be purchased both quickly and efficiently. Not only did wealthy contributors seize on this slogan, but small donors and even groups of schoolchildren also joined together to contribute to the Shenandoah fund. An editorial in the *Washington Star* observed, "This Shenandoah National Park 'sale' is a veritable real estate boom. There are big profits in sight. These profits will take the form of pleasurable excursions in the future. Everybody can participate, can 'get in on the ground floor,' as the phrase runs. There are no choice sites. One acre is just as attractive as another and just as certain to yield a rich return." Even cash-poor George Freeman Pollock pledged 1,000 acres of his own land. Support among federal officials was no less enthusiastic, and Secretary Work's donation, one of the first, received a great deal of publicity. This enthusiasm invigorated the campaign: fundraising began in late February 1926, and by April Virginians had promised over $1.2 million toward the park. As the park project began to appear more secure, Congress authorized the creation of the Shenandoah National Park once Virginia presented a minimum of 250,000 acres to the United States government. The legislation clarified the federal government's position regarding land acquisition, emphasizing "that the United States shall not purchase by appropriation of public moneys any land within the aforesaid areas, but that such lands shall be secured by the United States only by public or private donation."[27]

The Virginian parks officials, daunted by the scale and the expense of land acquisition, had increasingly begun to dread the complex task before them. The Commonwealth's responsibilities encompassed not only fundraising and a financial outlay in order to purchase the land, but also designating the territory needed to meet the congressional mandate. The scale of the purchase was considerable: Congress established boundaries stipulating a length of sixty-six miles and a width of between eight and eighteen miles—making for a maximum area of 521,000 acres, or a minimum of 250,000 acres.[28] In August 1927, Virginia completed its official survey of the Shenandoah area, reporting that the estimated cost of acquisition would be nearly six million dollars. This survey also registered an unexpected challenge in land acquisition, since more than two thousand homes had been identified within the designated purchase area. As voluntary sales and land donations continued to trickle in, the SCDC suddenly recognized the full extent of its logistical and financial challenges. Compounding the higher-than-anticipated costs of acquiring the park land, fundraising for the Shenandoah National Park had also faltered. The momentum for raising funds had crested by mid-1927, and fundraisers faced the task of collecting pledges from Virginians who were experiencing the increasing financial pressures of the agricultural depression and the first stages of industrial decline.[29]

Beginning in early 1928, as the fate of the park project began to seem uncertain, the government of the Commonwealth of Virginia stepped in to assist in the park development. Virginia park boosters lobbied the legislature for support, and the Richmond Chamber of Commerce hosted a buffet supper for the members of the General Assembly in January 1928. Characteristically pro-business and pro-development, local chambers of commerce commanded the political and economic influence to lead the publicity campaign within their communities, and they had been principal supporters of the park project since its inception. The boosters recognized the political and economic necessity of legislative interest in the park; the dinner was meant to build upon Tennessee's appropriation of $1.5 million for the Great Smoky Mountains National Park. Virginians were urged to match their neighbors' support at this supper, at which officials from Washington were the guests of honor: Secretary of the Interior Work and Assistant Director of the National Park Service Arno Cammerer joined SANPC members Congressman Temple, William Gregg, Glenn Smith, and other national figures.[30]

The park lobbyists' activism succeeded. In March 1928, the Virginia General Assembly voted an unprecedented million-dollar appropriation to support land purchases for the park. Made in compliance with a request from Governor Byrd, the state's contribution was contingent on the collection of a majority of individual pledges as well as the availability of funds for acquiring the minimum acreage requirement. That same month, Virginia also acted to streamline the process of land acquisition for the park, providing for a blanket condemnation of all lands within the park boundaries. The Public Park Condemnation Act outlined a process through which the state would sue for possession of land by county within the purchase area, and the county circuit court, serving as an impartial arbiter, was charged with assessing a fair price for individual parcels. In a friendly test case, *Rudacille vs. State Commission on Conservation and Development,* the state supreme court ruled in October 1929 the procedure to be constitutional. By late 1929, therefore, after the Commonwealth's pledge of money for the park and the legislature's action to create a process for land acquisition, Virginia was in a prime position to deliver the Blue Ridge park to the U.S. government.[31]

IMPLEMENTATION

Planning for the park entailed not only logistical oversight but also cultivating potential audiences, and the Virginians involved in coordinating outreach for the project were savvy marketers. The Shenandoah park promoters, wanting to entice new visitors to the region, integrated roads into the project, capitalizing on the accessibility of the proposed park. The SANPC first presented the idea for a "skyline drive" in the Blue Ridge Mountains in its December 1924 report, suggesting: "The greatest single feature" of the proposed park "is a possible sky-line drive along the mountain top, following a continuous ridge and looking down westerly on the Shenandoah Valley, from 2,500 to 3,500 feet below, and also commanding a view of the Piedmont Plain stretching easterly to the Washington Monument. . . . Few scenic drives in the world could surpass it." The park road was conceived as a way to appeal to a wide range of constituencies, and the Virginia political organization, already enamored of road building, quickly embraced the idea. A December 1927 speech by Governor Byrd stressed the parkway's benefits to the State of Virginia, promising: "The first act of the Federal government will be to construct a skyline highway on the top of the Blue Ridge Mountains. This will be one of the great wonder roads of America." Skyline Drive became one of Byrd's pet projects and was one of few New Deal relief programs that he endorsed.[32]

The park road proved an important selling point for Virginia park advocates, and it captured the attention of many supporters. A 1929 article in *National Geographic* on Virginia featured the road as the centerpiece of plans for the proposed Shenandoah National Park: "As one motors along this skyline highway, to the east a thousand vistas of the splendid Piedmont plain will unroll before delighted eyes, and to the west the meanderings of the Shenandoah, the crazy quilt of fertile field and fine woodland, the contrasts of hill and dale, town, and country, present an ever-changing panorama."[33] The mixture of pastoral and sylvan landscapes along the road was designed to inspire visitors to the region. Between the long-range vistas and the modern boulevard, the Shenandoah road was expected to embody the best features of the increasingly popular parkway movement.

Other promotion of the park took place by word of mouth, as influential Virginians reached out to sympathetic policymakers. Governor Byrd's lieutenant in the park campaign, SCDC Chair William Carson, found his way to the ear of political forces with an interest in the park; in 1928 and 1929 he lobbied incoming president Herbert Hoover to establish a weekend retreat in the mountains. Hoover was charmed by the area and subsequently established a weekend camp on the Rapidan River. The president's presence attracted additional media coverage to the Shenandoah and northwestern Virginia, and the Rapidan Camp figured largely in the political culture of the Hoover administration; in gratitude the SCDC stocked the river for the pleasure of the fisherman-president. Carson ensured that Hoover's retreat was integrated into the Virginia tourism campaign, and in 1929 the *Norfolk Ledger-Dispatch* suggested, "If the President of the United States finds this area satisfactory for a few days outing now and then, why not thousands of other folks . . . ?" Avid explorers of the mountain landscape, the president and his wife, Lou Henry Hoover, took an active interest in the development of the park beyond the confines of their property.[34]

Hoover's enthusiastic endorsement of the region as worthy of national park protection helped to facilitate the establishment of the Shenandoah National Park. Moreover, he revived plans for the ridgeline road, and Park Service Director Horace Albright (1929–33) credited the engineer-president with initiating the construction of the roadway. Albright told of a May 1930 horseback ride from Rapidan Camp into the mountains when "the President called for me to bring my horse up alongside his. We looked at the view for a moment. Then, pointing out the flat, even contours of the ridge, he said, 'you know, Albright, this mountain top is just made . . . for a highway. There's nothing like it in the country, really, where you can see such vistas.' He paused for a few moments, gazing at the beautiful scene. Then he added, 'I think we should get a survey made for a highway here, and I think it can be built at a reasonable cost.'" With Hoover's encouragement and the cooperation of the SCDC, the ridgeline road became a viable project. Beyond reigniting the enthusiasm for the road, Hoover introduced an additional innovation that shaped the road: using unemployed Shenandoah Valley farmers as the principal

Aerial photograph from 1936 showing the grassy bald at Big Meadows and the extensive clearing that had long characterized this region of the Blue Ridge. *Aerial photograph ca. 1936, CCC Camp at Big Meadows.* Library of Congress, Prints and Photograph Division, Historic American Engineering Record, "Built in America" collection. VA-119-113

workforce. Congress had appropriated relief funds to alleviate the worst effects of the 1930–31 southeastern drought, and Hoover encouraged the use of money designated for Shenandoah Valley farmers to pay valley farmers for road construction. Construction began in July 1931 on the first segment of the nation's first skyline road.[35]

The parkway helped to revitalize the Shenandoah park advocates' public relations campaign. In October 1932, the Bureau of Public Roads opened the first stretch of Skyline Drive for a public preview. Automobiles could enter the roadway from Lee Highway and follow it along twelve winding miles to the facilities at Skyland before retracing their steps. The road opening, timed to coincide with the appearance of fall foliage (and perhaps with the final weeks of the 1932 presidential race), both promoted the Shenandoah National Park fundraising campaign and introduced the American people to the future national park. During

Jewell Hollow overlook, Skyline Drive, displaying the range of cleared and forested land in the Blue Ridge. Harry L. Staley, View from Skyline Drive in *Over the Skyline Drive in the Shenandoah National Park, From Lee Highway to Spotswood Trail* (Harrisonburg, VA: Staley and Staley, 1936), plate 2.

the six weeks the Skyline Drive remained open an estimated 30,000 visitors traveled along the unpaved road, with an unwaveringly favorable public response.[36]

SETBACKS

In spite of the enthusiasm generated by the Skyline Drive, other complications threatened the future of the Shenandoah National Park. Two challenges dogged the park planners during the early 1930s, endangering the entire project: the expense of land acquisition and the disposition of families who were unwilling or unable to move from their mountain farms. In October 1931 Cammerer and Albright met with SCDC Chairman Carson to discuss the SCDC's finances. The mandated minimum acreage continued to exceed the SCDC's budget, in spite of Cammerer's 1928 re-survey of the site, which excluded almost two hundred thousand acres from the park boundaries.[37] Acknowledging that

Parcel map showing the 1927 boundaries of the proposed Shenandoah National Park and the individual tracts contained within it. GIS data provided by Dan Hurlbert; map created by author.

the fundraising campaign had not generated sufficient funds, and reflecting concern about higher-than-expected land prices, the conferees discussed how to adjust to the new situation. During this meeting Carson, "confidentially, advised that contrary to . . . original expectations . . . we would have to face the fact that there either would be no Shenandoah Park, or have to figure whether a park of sufficient acreage could be acquired for about $2,000,000," which would buy between 150,000 and

180,000 acres. Carson also explained how each of the eight counties that had donated money to the park would likely insist on having the park include land within its boundaries, thus necessitating that the park consist of a narrow strip along the length of the mountain ridge. Believing "it was better to have a reduced park, where that appeared practicable, than no park at all," and Secretary of the Interior Ray Lyman Wilbur insisted that the park must "be an administrative, workable and scenic unit," Albright proposed reducing the size and "leaving the acquisition of the remainder for the future." Congress subsequently trimmed the boundaries of the minimum purchase area once again, to 150,000 acres, eliminating higher-priced lowland areas from the park.[38]

These negotiations over park boundaries highlighted additional tensions in land acquisition. From the outset, Virginia boosters had stressed that the area was virtually uninhabited in their solicitations for a national park. Yet there were hundreds of families living in the northern Blue Ridge, and because the National Park Service prohibited occupancy on park lands, the Shenandoah project remained contingent on these residents vacating the mountains. Beginning in the early 1930s, the incompatibility of mountain farms and the park became increasingly evident. Consequently, acquiring land and handling the needs of the mountain people would prove to be the most challenging element in the creation of the Shenandoah National Park.[39] The vagaries of jurisdiction and responsibility during the decade of land acquisition meant that nothing definitive altered the status of mountain residents for years after the designation of the park in 1924. Land condemnation began in late 1929, and in spite of the streamlined process designed by the Virginia legislature, it proved beset by complications. The Public Park Condemnation Act had been designed to assure fair purchase prices and a clear legal procedure for sales, but the reality of the court proceedings diverged from the planners' vision. The legislation had stipulated that condemnation notices be advertised first in local newspapers, yet their limited circulation undermined the effectiveness of this process. Thus, many landowners received at most only one indication that a suit was pending—what was intended to be a final notice of imminent condemnation—a letter mailed to landowners ten days before court proceedings were scheduled to end. For people living far from a post office, who rarely checked their mail, even this direct communication proved inadequate.[40]

Compounding these issues, the Virginia government steadfastly ignored the looming problem of how to manage the disposition of the hundreds of families living within the boundaries of the proposed park. Many residents were unable to afford land outside the mountains due to the courts' low valuation of their land and buildings, while squatters and tenants did not have recourse to a government settlement. Moreover, by 1932 the state had made virtually no effort to find an alternative home for the people who needed to leave the park area. The Virginia SCDC was expected to make arrangements to provide for the resettlement of the propertyless residents, but it was already overwhelmed by the task of acquiring land, and balked at coordinating social services by avoiding the discussion of removal for as long as possible. This denial set up a clash with federal officials. For the National Park Service, the case was simple: the 1925 enabling legislation for the Southern Appalachian parks required that states manage, fund, and implement the purchase of land for new national parks. Legally, Virginia was obligated to deliver unencumbered title to the land and a depopulated parcel.[41]

National park staffers understood that mishandling the removals could generate a political backlash capable of jeopardizing both the Shenandoah and future national park projects. Therefore, the agency maintained a limited view of federal responsibility for land acquisition and local welfare, and refused to intervene in local affairs, especially the extremely sensitive negotiations over land purchase and removals. In August 1931, Cammerer acknowledged the dilemma presented by mountain residents. "In the Shenandoah we will be confronted by . . . the question of innumerable squatters . . . who have little or no property rights and will have to be evicted by us if the State has not done so." He grimly foreshadowed the issues to come: "I don't think the State will plan to do this. . . . I think the State will plan to turn blanket court title for the entire park area over to the Secretary and expect him to take the park over right away, irrespective of local mountain residents. This we should not tolerate, for then we will be compelled to evict what is really the State's business to do and be subjected to all kinds of trouble. Let's keep out of it." Cammerer aptly identified the danger facing the fledgling agency: it could be hampered by the implication that it preyed on some of the nation's most vulnerable people in the desire to develop a new national park.[42]

Once the complexity of the removal question became clear, the National Park Service deployed its own sociological researcher in an attempt to assess the problem presented by mountain residents. The agency hired Miriam Sizer, Sherman and Henry's chief fieldworker, to resurvey conditions in the Madison County hollows.[43] Sizer's advocacy for the mountain communities had spurred federal officials to analyze the situation. In March 1932, Cammerer wrote to Albright, "Miss Sizer's paper on the sociological problem involved in the mountaineers of the Shenandoah section is a corker. I had hoped for the past two years that you and I, with the Secretary, Dr. Sexton, and Pollock could spend two days at Skyland just to look into this problem." Cammerer then clarified the dimensions of the problem: "The Secretary ought to see it by going into Corbin Hollow himself. . . . It's got to be done soon, otherwise, unless we get his personal reaction, we'll get orders from still higher to keep these 'poor mountaineers.' " A lifelong bureaucrat who was thoroughly averse to project complications, Cammerer repeatedly displayed a deep antipathy toward the poorest people in the mountains, whom he described as "literally the scum of the mountain people." He apparently believed that the Hoovers' sympathy for their mountain neighbors, a product of their benevolent efforts in the area around Rapidan Camp, might compromise the quick resolution of park removals.[44] In August 1933, Cammerer assumed the directorship of the National Park Service, and thereafter his frustration with the Commonwealth of Virginia and complications caused by mountain residents only grew.[45]

Cammerer's repeated insistence that the Park Service would not participate in the provision of services for displaced mountain residents created tension with Virginia officials who were already overwhelmed by the strain and the expense of land purchase.[46] Whereas a seamless process of land designation, acquisition, and transfer would have required intensive internal collaboration, Virginia's state agencies did not cooperate effectively. The lack of coordination within the state government, alongside its feeble social welfare network, left Virginia poorly equipped to manage programs for people left without resources by the park creation. Ultimately, Virginia officials were saved from failure when New Deal relief agencies stepped into the void to develop a series of programs for the resettlement and rehabilitation of the people displaced by the park.

A NEW DEAL

In spite of the obstacles presented by the disposition of mountain residents, the park project was reinvigorated in 1933 by the transition between presidential administrations. Franklin D. Roosevelt shared Hoover's enthusiastic support of conservation, and he contributed his own ideas to the Shenandoah project. Within weeks of his inauguration, President Roosevelt, Secretary of the Interior Harold Ickes, and National Park Service Director Albright joined Carson for an inspection tour of the Blue Ridge and Hoover's Rapidan Camp, which the former president had donated to the Park Service for the use of his successors. A local newspaper, the *Madison Eagle,* reported: "Roosevelt enjoyed his first full holiday since becoming President, driving Sunday in an open touring car through the rolling Virginia country to the Rapidan. . . . At Harrisonburg, Roosevelt spoke enthusiastically to reporters about the park and showed keen interest in plans for its development." Roosevelt was impressed by Hoover's vision for Skyline Drive, and admired that work on the project had been begun using the labor of the unemployed. The alignment of the road along the ridgeline, the beauty of the scenery, and the protective stone walls that lined the route, which allowed views of the surrounding valleys, caught the president's eye. Roosevelt's support for the recreational and aesthetic vision behind the Skyline Drive helped to ensure the continued funding for this public works initiative.[47]

Roosevelt recognized that the Shenandoah offered an ideal location for federal conservation projects as it was accessible to both the press and the public, and so he chose the Blue Ridge as the site of several early Civilian Conservation Corps (CCC) camps. Legislation authorizing this new relief and conservation agency passed Congress in April 1933, and the first camps in the national parks were located in the proposed Shenandoah National Park.[48] Within weeks of the camps' establishment, enrollees set to work returning a "natural" appearance to the mountains. The CCC's initial mission was to restore plant cover and clear accumulated deadwood in order to jump-start the rehabilitation of the Blue Ridge forest. As horticulturalist and former SANPC member Harlan Kelsey observed: "Primeval plant growth in this park area has been manhandled to such an extent that a large part of the area is covered with . . . an

The President Lunching in a Virginia Conservation Camp, Big Meadows, *New York Times,* August 13, 1933. Courtesy of the Forest History Society archives.

entirely different nature from what it was originally."[49] Initially, the massive infusion of laborers accelerated the restoration of a healthy forested landscape, as the corps cleared brush and dead trees (including the tens of thousands of American chestnuts killed by the chestnut blight) and fought erosion and forest fires. Later, as the recreational program of the CCC moved into full operation, workers devoted themselves to developing the water, power, and communications infrastructure for park facilities, as well as the construction of Skyline Drive and the development of hiking and riding trails.[50]

Roosevelt's enthusiasm for the CCC program motivated his second visit to the Blue Ridge; in mid-August he visited the one thousand enrollees already at work on conservation projects in the proposed park. The *New York Times* pictured Roosevelt lunching at Camp Fechner in Big Meadows with an accompanying article describing Roosevelt's whole-hearted endorsement of camp life, as well as the meal, a "regular Saturday dinner." Journalists portrayed this meal as evocative of the health and good fortune of those in the camps, who had gained an average of twelve pounds in their first several months of service, thus reinforcing the point that the physical restoration of the people, as well as the land, was a primary ambition of the corps program.[51]

The massive influx of manpower into landscapes like the Blue Ridge simultaneously generated concerns among conservationists who were invested in ensuring an ecological balance in forested landscapes.[52] Although the speed and thoroughness of the park cleanup were impressive to most observers, as early as January 1934 the local CCC naturalist began to express concern that the overgrooming of the park created an unnatural space that was not conducive to long-term wildlife repopulation, which was one of the National Park Service's objectives. Thereafter, CCC project managers had to revisit their assumptions about what was natural and healthy for the forest, and wildlife biologists stepped in to moderate overzealous CCC work projects. This type of conflict between nature protection, outdoor recreation, and aesthetics emerged repeatedly in CCC camps across the country, even as the corps' methodical approach to work relief and reforestation played an important part in the conversion of the mountains from an inhabited landscape to an appearance of primeval nature.[53]

BACKLASH

With all of the favorable attention to the Shenandoah National Park plans in the popular press, it took a long time for burgeoning critiques of the project to attract the attention of government officials. Yet beginning in the late 1920s, criticism of park development suggested several ways in which the Shenandoah project undermined traditional land use values, and they illustrate some of the issues that were in play for stakeholders in this emergent public landscape. In spite of the Shenandoah National Park's popularity with the American public, opposition emerged from across a number of groups, including conservation organizations, outdoor enthusiasts, and local landowners. For example, not all conservationists shared Hoover and Roosevelt's enthusiasm for the Skyline Drive, and the park roadway in particular developed into a source of controversy. Plans for the road set off debates over the purpose of national parks and the place of the automobile in outdoor recreation. At its heart, the road question concerned whom the parks were meant to serve— tourists, wildlife, hikers, aesthetes—and what compromises were made to serve these many constituencies.

Although a park road had been proposed in 1924, park advocates did not anticipate how significant the roadway would become to plans for the Shenandoah National Park. After years of boundary adjustments, the park evolved into a compact, "shoestring" park, in which any internal road would be more prominent and invasive than in the expansive western parks. This physical limitation was compounded by the reality that the Skyline Drive was a ridgeline road, bisecting the narrow park along its entire length and hugging the mountain ridges in order to embrace the best views. The road had the potential to open parts of the park to auto tourists, creating a parkway in the clouds, but it simultaneously fragmented protected areas designated for wildlife and outdoor recreation.

Hikers and the outdoor organizations that had designed trails and built shelters in the mountains found their recreational landscape—which they had expected to be protected forever by the new park—subsumed within the plans for the Skyline Drive.[54] The Appalachian Mountain Club (AMC) and the Potomac Appalachian Trail Club (PATC) had begun to visit the Blue Ridge during the early 1920s, taking advantage of the region's proximity to Washington to develop a trail network. Through labor-intensive, cooperative efforts and with the blessing of landowners, these hiking clubs formed a community that cherished the solitude and rigor of the mountain trails. The PATC, in particular, had enthusiastically supported the creation of the Shenandoah park, and its members worked tirelessly to promote the project. The club balked, however, when plans for the Skyline Drive were superimposed upon the Appalachian Trail. Although these groups rallied against the parkway, they did so belatedly and ineffectively, and their failure to influence the Skyline Drive's route led them to oppose the development of ridgeline roads in other areas.[55]

The debate over the proper siting of park roads eventually reached the highest levels of government. Even Secretary of the Interior Ickes cautioned against overbuilding in the parks, remarking that "the scarring of a wonderful mountain side" should be undertaken with circumspection. Outdoor organizations attempted to influence the route's location, and in 1936, PATC President Myron Avery submitted a proposal to alter the path of the parkway in order to preserve the southern section of the park as a "wilderness area." Avery's plan recommended that the road extension skirt the mountains, leaving the ridgeline in its original state and protecting the natural character for both hikers and wildlife. In spite of his efforts, construction crews continued to build the roadway along the ridgeline. Leading conservation groups thereafter rallied against road development in the newly created Appalachian parks and forests. The Wilderness Society, for example, was organized in 1935 to fight against the movement for park roads, inspired by the waste and misuse that its members saw emerging from the construction of the Skyline Drive and others like it. Ultimately, the debates over park roads brought to the forefront discussions over the best use of public lands, and paved the way for protests elsewhere, including the one that led to the rejection of the proposed Green Mountain Parkway in Vermont.[56]

Conservationists' and outdoor recreationists' critiques of land use in the Blue Ridge were only a minor distraction in the planning for the Shenandoah National Park. By contrast, other opponents of the park sought to abort the project altogether, and brought their battle to court. The transfer of lands from the state to the federal government was complicated by a federal lawsuit filed against the Commonwealth of Virginia. A Blue Ridge landowner and orchardist, Robert Via, sought to terminate the park project and have all land returned to its previous owners. Via's legal challenge contested the Virginia condemnation law under federal law, circumventing the Virginia Circuit Court ruling in the October 1929 *Rudacille* case because Via was a resident of Pennsylvania.[57] Via's lawyers argued against Virginia's donation of the park to the federal government from two angles: asserting first that a state government cannot use its power of eminent domain to seize private property for a purely federal use; and, second, that Via was denied due process because he was not personally served with papers declaring that his land was being taken. In January 1935, the U.S. District Court for Western Virginia rejected Via's claims. To the first charge, the Court responded that the Shenandoah National Park benefited the people of Virginia as well as the residents of the United States and that therefore it could not be classified as an unconstitutional transfer of power. To the second, the judges ruled that since the condemnation proceedings went through state courts and Via had been paid for his land, the "taking" was paid, and thus Via had no legal right to sue for financial damages.[58] Via's legal team appealed this decision to the U.S. Supreme Court, which as part of its critique of the expanding scope of federal power agreed to review this case in the summer of 1935. After hearing Via's lawyer's opening arguments, however, the Supreme Court released the case, issuing a memorandum decision on November 25, 1935, that sustained the lower court's ruling.[59]

With the legality of the Shenandoah National Park no longer in question, the U.S. Attorney General gave his approval to the acceptance of the park. Finally, after over a decade of planning and land purchases, on December 26, 1935, Virginia formally conveyed the title to the United States. The deed conveyed an 181,578-acre park, encompassing 1,088 individual parcels of land, which had been purchased for a total of $2,258,908.72.[60] With this transfer of jurisdiction, the federal government assumed all responsibility for further development of the park, and the National Park Service began to plan for the park's official dedication. Virginia thereby ceded further responsibility to the federal government, even though an estimated three hundred families still resided within the boundaries of the new park. The apparent incongruity of the Department of the Interior's acceptance of park lands—even though they were still encumbered by resident families—was to be resolved by New Deal relief and rehabilitation agencies. Because of this new federal initiative, Virginia was finally able to pass along most of the responsibility for the needs of the poorest park residents, and, yet as Cammerer had long feared, much of the controversy regarding the disposition of these people remained to come.[61]

By the mid-1930s, the creation of the Shenandoah National Park, a process that had been presented as a simple process of land conversion in the mid-1920s, had turned into a land use planner's worst nightmare. Although some Blue Ridge landowners were proud to have their region celebrated for scenery equal to the grandeur of Yosemite or the Grand Canyon, most, even those who supported the idea of the park, recognized that the project was a threat to their way of life. Mountain residents repeatedly voiced concern about the future of their property, and they expressed their anxiety through protests ranging from letter writing campaigns to arson. Complaints against the park were many, including opposition to claiming of private land for a public park, impatience that owners were not receiving adequate compensation for their property, and frustration with the mechanisms of removal. These protests repeated a number of themes, demonstrating the spectrum of reactions against the development of the park. Ultimately, few residents were keen to sacrifice their homes for the greater good of the American people.[62]

Blue Ridge residents corresponded with the state and federal governments as plans for the park became defined: inquiring about protocols, requesting services, or explaining why their land was unsuitable for park purposes. Some attempted to organize their neighbors to combat what they saw as an unjust use of governmental prerogative, while others engaged in covert actions against the state and federal governments. The reactions were as diverse as the people living within the park. For example, in the late 1920s Lewis Willis sought to rally his neighbors against the park, hoping to derail its development, claiming, "The national park project was conceived in ambition, brought forth by an appeal to greed, and fed on exaggerations and misstatements." Willis, who was instrumental in organizing the Land Owners' Shenandoah National Park Association, asserted the unconstitutionality of the Condemnation Act in a hearing before the Page County Circuit Court. Later, he sought to reverse the park plan, disputing the contention that the park was in the public interest. In a 1932 letter to Hoover he asserted: "We are unwilling to part with our homes to advertise a few politicians and to help a small part of our population to get their hands into tourists' pockets." Willis repeatedly suggested that greed and the desire for personal advancement had motivated prominent Virginians to support the creation of the Shenandoah National Park.[63]

Like many of his neighbors, Willis argued that the Blue Ridge Mountains were neither unique nor unspoiled: "Part of it has been cleared, plowed, and pastured; and well nigh all of it has been logged at some time or another." He contended that the economics of land seizure required correction and that county courts' appraisal of the value of mountain farms was disproportionately low. "If public necessity were proved, we would still be entitled to just compensation. . . . This is a case where sale value of the property does not represent its value to the individual owner. Many of us who are now self-supporting cannot support ourselves by investing the sale value of our lands somewhere else." Willis repeatedly alluded to the value of self-sufficiency to a mountain farmer and the fact that mountain people were at a significant disadvantage when dealing with the lowcountry economy and politics. Yet in spite of his sustained and vocal campaign against the park, Willis had no more effect on modifying the park plans than Via or the PATC.[64]

Another park opponent, and one of the most persistent correspondents with state and federal officials, Melancthon Cliser, began his campaign against the park with a letter to the new State Conservation and Development Commission in 1926. Cliser shared Willis's suspicions about the motivations of park advocates and voiced his own theory about the park idea: "This Park business has been gotten up by Mr. Pollock Proprietor of Skyland summer resort and a few large land owners who have cut the timber and left the land entirely worthless and they are glad to get something out of it." Cliser argued that his own carefully tended property, which included a small store and filling station, was included in the park in order to compensate for the abused land owned by pro-park landowners, because "it takes some good land with it to make it attractive." Cliser's home sat on a state road through the mountains, Lee Highway, which connected Washington with the Shenandoah Valley, a route through areas that the SANPC feared would be "exploited and made pest holes [with] hot dog stands, etc., automobile pest holes." In October 1935, Virginia forcibly removed Cliser and his wife from their home after he refused to close his store and filling station, "enterprises which 'interfered with the development of the park by the Government.'" While Virginia had offered Cliser a temporary lease to remain on the land until the park was dedicated, he had repeatedly warned them off his land and refused to sign the papers. Partially because of Cliser's history of vocal dissent, and partially because his home was located on a major route through the proposed park, the story of his eviction attracted newspapers from across the nation. The image of an older couple being physically removed from their home fueled the suspicion of those who questioned the motives of the state and federal governments.[65]

After his removal, Cliser's letters to the federal government became increasingly demanding. His last letter in the park files, written in the late 1940s, requested money for the purchase of an acceptable home in which he and his wife could end their days. The tone of this letter bespeaks defeat. "I had a modern home, bath, hot and cold water, electric lights, phone, store[,] service station, lunch room, 46 acres of land, plenty of wood for fuel, besides and produced plenty of vegetables and some to sell, especially potatoes and apples, the best variety. I usually kept several

Photograph of Melancthon Cliser eviction, October 1935, National Archives and Records Administration, College Park, MD, 79,/10B/1653/16.

cows and sold a considerable quantity of milk and butter." In comparison with this once-self-sufficient existence, Cliser described his current condition: "After my eviction [I] was compelled to live in an old dilapidated house and a few acres of land, but now instead of my wife baking pies and cakes, she takes in washing for a living." Cliser, then aged seventy-two, reflected, "When we started in life we started with nothing and we worked hard and made ourselves a nice home." His dignity still burned from having been deprived of what he saw as rightfully his, particularly after seeing it "taken away from us for a playground." The passions that dispossession ignited in mountain residents were the source of a great deal of trouble for the Commonwealth of Virginia and the National Park Service, and as Cliser's correspondence and the letters of many others indicate, the recriminations did not end when people left their mountain homes.[66]

Other protests against the park continued long after the project's completion. For example, the Shenandoah National Park had an unusually high rate of arson in the years following the park's dedication. Arson was one of displaced residents' most common responses to their sense of impotence after they lost their land, and "firing the woods" was a notable Southern protest strategy. Anonymous perpetrators rarely acknowledged their role in forest arsons, and yet the National Park Service's fire statistics demonstrate the extent of residents' frustration with the Shenandoah park creation. During the 1934 calendar year, fires in the designated park burned a total of 1,010 acres. Of twenty-two fires, fifteen were incendiary, burning roughly one-half of the area damaged by fire in that year. This pattern extended to the other two southern parks dedicated during the 1930s, Great Smoky Mountains National Park and Mammoth Cave National Park. All three parks had dramatically higher arson rates than the rest of the park system in 1934 (seven, fifteen, and twenty-one fires due to arson, respectively, as opposed to a maximum of two in any other national park).[67] While some have suggested that the decline in fires in the Shenandoah during the late 1930s was attributable to the work of the CCC in clearing combustible underbrush and staffing fire towers, other evidence indicates that this brush clearing was less of a deterrent than the removal of residents from the mountains.[68] A 1944 Park Service report observed: "The great decrease in the number of incendiary fires, which has followed the relocation of many of the settlers, the park's effective law enforcement program, and the special efforts on the part of the park personnel to make friends with the local residents and obtain their cooperation, is both striking and gratifying."[69] By the mid-1940s this equilibrium helped to set the stage for a period of relative cooperation between the Shenandoah staff and their neighbors.

A PARK FOR THE PEOPLE

Despite the delays caused by local opposition to the Shenandoah National Park and the difficulty of securing title to the mountains, park advocates continued to imagine a greater purpose for this newest national park. The Blue Ridge park had been designed for the use and entertainment of the American people, and during its development the Commonwealth of Virginia and the National Park Service prioritized the recreational and cultural needs of an increasingly urban nation as of paramount importance. Park promoters stressed the value of an outdoor experience close to the city, and they envisioned that the Virginia park could serve the recreational desires of all Americans. The turmoil of modern society increasingly seemed to justify the public expenditure of funds for parks, and recreation was seen as part of the answer to the industrial crisis. As Carson observed in 1929, "The Park not only means great things to Virginia, but also to those densely populated eastern states north of us, with their myriads of workers." The park represented more than simply the recreational opportunities in its hills and valleys; rather, "its attractions . . . will mean to the people . . . a development of their aesthetic sensibilities without their realizing it." The Shenandoah National Park, located within close proximity of the major eastern centers of population, thus served a wide range of the interests of the American people.[70]

The vision of a multi-purpose landscape was fulfilled on July 3, 1936, when President Roosevelt, Secretary of the Interior Ickes, Virginia governor George Peery, and Senators Harry Flood Byrd and Carter Glass, as well as other dignitaries, traveled to the Blue Ridge to dedicate the Shenandoah National Park. In his speech commemorating the occasion, President Roosevelt took a long view of the park's significance. The president used the nationally broadcast dedication ceremony to repeat several of the messages of his campaign for reelection that fall. His speech linked the goals of conservation and relief, arguing that the national parks were "in the largest sense a work of conservation. Through all of them we are preserving the beauty and wealth of the hills and the mountains and the plains and the trees and the streams." Roosevelt stressed that conservation was not solely directed at natural resources, but that it also served the people: "We are maintaining useful work for our young men. Through all of them we are enriching the character and happiness of our people." Roosevelt also used the park dedication to honor the labor of the CCC workers who were transforming the American landscape. He celebrated those who turned the land to public purposes: "Think of it—the thousands of young men, their involuntary idleness three years ago—that ended when they came here to the camps on the Blue Ridge; and since they have not been idle. Today they have ended more than their own idleness, they have ended the idleness of the Shenandoah National Park." Moreover, the president highlighted the importance of outdoor recreation for the American public, emphasizing the "need for recreational areas, for parkways, which will give to men and women of moderate means the opportunity, the invigoration and the luxury of touring and camping amid scenes of great natural beauty." Roosevelt thus demonstrated how land use planning served the needs of the people and the nation, and in the process he reinforced the messages being disseminated through the New Deal.[71] Roosevelt concluded by

dedicating the Shenandoah National Park "to this and succeeding generations of Americans for the recreation and for the re-creation which
they shall find here."[72] The utility of conservation and federal planning
were the president's principal themes during this speech, as well as
throughout his campaign for reelection.

Even before the Shenandoah National Park's dedication, the Blue
Ridge had attracted more tourists than any other park in the system. In
1935 the park boasted 611,000 visitors, 100,000 more than the next
most-visited park, and in the years that followed these figures continued
to rise.[73] In August 1939, when the last section of Skyline Drive opened
to the public, visitors could drive along the mountain ridge, enjoying the
scenery from the comfort of their cars. For one dollar, American drivers
could purchase a year's worth of access to the ninety-six-mile, $4.5 mil-
lion roadway running along the crest of the mountains, and the pleasures of visiting the surrounding park lands. In 1940 the Shenandoah
National Park led all national parks in annual visitors for the fourth con-
secutive year, with a total of 950,807 people entering the park and enjoying its forests and scenery.[74]

As anticipated, the park had not only added to Virginia's prestige
among vacation destinations and protected a section of the eastern
mountains from lumbering and haphazard development, but it had also
offered a source of jobs to people afflicted by the economic turmoil of
the Great Depression. The balance sheet, when compiled by park proponents, illustrated astounding successes. But below the surface, and
visible only occasionally to the larger public (yet of constant concern to
federal officials), was almost a decade of uncertainty over the fate of the
poorest mountain residents. Although originally a sidebar in the design
of the Shenandoah National Park, the fate of the mountain people became a major consideration in the mid-1930s as the vast majority of these
residents were forced to cede their land for the use of other Americans.
Many of the families who remained in the park through the late 1930s
were eventually integrated into the relief programs of the New Deal. Ultimately, the resettlement of the Blue Ridge farmers ultimately depended
on the social and economic programs integral to the New Deal's planning
and conservation agencies.

In the interim, however, other federal agencies were also commit-
ting resources to the Appalachian region in partnership with the states,

and the evolution of federal conservation planning in Vermont offers a suggestive counterpoint to the development of the Shenandoah. The conservation projects of the 1920s and 1930s in the Green Mountains provide striking points of contrast to the creation of the Shenandoah National Park. In Vermont, state officials selected conservation projects that were adapted to serve their approximation of the state's needs, and both policymakers and voters engaged in an active conversation about how to apply federal funds and expertise to local needs. In the process, Vermonters appropriated federal money to serve both the state's utilitarian political philosophy and a strong conservation-mindedness, which ensured greater local support and less controversy for many federal projects in the Green Mountains.

CHAPTER FIVE

Cultivating the Vermont Forest

IN THE EARLY TWENTIETH CENTURY, the state of Vermont drew on local traditions of stewardship and a history of land management as it experimented with different means of protecting mountain farms and forests. In particular, during the 1910s and 1920s it benefited from partnerships with towns and the federal government. During these decades Vermonters developed a proactive approach to managing the upcountry forest, approaching land management as part of the state's intensive evaluation of its cultural and economic resources. Due to the starkly evident consequences of land abandonment, and later the work of the Vermont Commission on Country Life and rural researchers, town and state officials readily acknowledged the centrality of natural resources to the viability of local economies. The implementation of local and state-level conservation initiatives reflected a deep concern with the economic future of the hill towns, and as the state recognized the insufficiency of local resources to support necessary programs it invited the partnership of the federal government in conservation planning. Moreover, the burgeoning economic association of the Green Mountain region with recreation spurred a practical evaluation of its "natural advantages," which spurred Vermonters to integrate tourism and forestry into plans for the state's economic future.

In spite of the steady regrowth of the forest in large parts of the state, wasteful practices endured in many locales. Early in the new century, reflecting a growing concern about the future of the state's resources, the legislature created a Committee on the Conservation of Natural Resources, and Governor John Mead appointed a commission to study the state's natural resources.[1] The commission surveyed conditions in declining communities, which were reeling from farm abandonment and the lack of centralized resource management. Forestry was a key concern, as commission member John M. Thomas explained: "The awakening of the people to the need of conservation came about principally through the rapid decrease of our forests. There is something about a denuded hillside which stirs resentment in almost every one, and those who are dead to sentiment respond to the stern fact of the rapid increase in the price of lumber."[2] During the first decades of the century the state government repeatedly addressed issues relating to the conservation of natural resources, seeking a balance between profit and management.[3]

Local and state-level planning in Vermont aspired to stabilize resource management, but eventually the state's limited finances restricted these programs, and Vermont found it advantageous to partner with the federal government on infrastructural and conservation initiatives. Consequently, during the 1920s and early 1930s several federal-state land use projects combined to transform the mountain landscape. As was the case throughout Appalachia, conservation was the realm most affected by federal policies, and during the New Deal Vermonters negotiated the implications of several varied private and federal solutions to the upcountry economic crisis. Vermont, with its proud traditions of local independence, preferred to maintain control over the scope of its collaborations, and the state was able to shape the course of local development through the 1930s.

This chapter considers the several ways in which land use planning exercised a significant influence on the expansion of the Vermont state government during the early twentieth century. In part, this expansion was due to the economic consequences of depopulation and farm abandonment that had forced the state to support the maintenance of local governments in an attempt to mediate the effects of straitened hill-town economies. The precedent of state aid for local services established a framework that later drove the design of conservation programs. Furthermore, because Vermont's mountain communities were tightly integrated into the state's political and economic landscape, regional plans accommodated their economic interests.

VISION

Vermont's nascent attempts at land use planning emerged from both local communities and the state government, and these discrete actions prepared a framework for the establishment of a larger conservation vision statewide. The declining number of farms in Vermont during the late nineteenth and early twentieth centuries was a glaring testament to the changing landscape, particularly in the state's less productive upland areas. The consequences of this population shift were dramatic: the amount of improved land in Vermont declined 34 percent between 1900 and 1930 as one-quarter of all Vermont farms were abandoned.[4] According to one Vermont Forest Service report, the exodus of people from the mountains "practically means the obliteration of declining towns and the transferring of their burdens onto the balance of the State—whether or not it is willing to accept."[5] Consequently, the state government spent the first decades of the century seeking a stable solution to demographic change. State and town forests, the inception of the Long Trail, and the encouragement of summer home development all promoted a conservation agenda within the state. The question of how best to manage the state's natural resources increasingly consumed the attention of state policymakers, because as the VCCL observed in *Rural Vermont: A Program for the Future*, "to allow such land to remain idle is not only a shameful neglect, but also as unbusiness-like as to permit money to lie idle."[6] The equal representation of hill towns in the Vermont General Assembly, along with the centrality of upcountry roads to the state's transportation network, meant that the economic interests of these mountain communities remained integral to the state's vision for its future.

During the first decades of the twentieth century, the Vermont state legislature cultivated forestry and recreation in the Green Mountains, dedicating an increasing share of limited state funds for conservation programs. Simultaneously, the imperative to conserve expenditures by increasing efficiencies in government drew the state into a new paradigm of government relations. Because the outmigration from mountain towns continued to put pressure on local economies, the state began to assume some of the burden of financing improvements in areas historically under the purview of town governments. Among these, forest management, local roads, and disaster relief generated the most visible, and the highest-impact, forms of state aid.

Proper forest management promised to strengthen local economies, and the 1915 state law permitting towns to acquire town forests was designed to improve and reclaim lands, generate a new source of revenue for the townspeople, stimulate wood-products industries, protect water supplies, and provide recreation. The legislature introduced the program for creating town forests with the intention of providing a model for local forest management. Town forests emerged as a potential solution to the financial straits of upland towns, reflecting the economic advantages of converting struggling farms to forests. The logic was clear: as one local tax assessor observed, "Our town could well afford to buy those 10 farms to close up the roads and school there. The expense of roads, bridges, and school is a lot more than the taxes they pay plus the interest on what the farms would cost us." This form of land use planning meant that marginal farms could be reforested and managed for timber production. "Under intelligent forestry these farms would in years to come return a handsome profit to the town on its investment." Towns that embraced this opportunity in subsequent years discovered firsthand the benefits that could be accrued from the conversion of hill farms to town forests, adding to their income by cultivating forest crops. However, while prescriptions abounded for the efficient management of town and state forests, these forests expanded only incrementally. By 1924 sixteen town forests contained a total of 5,000 acres. By 1930 forty-two town forests encompassed almost 9,000 acres, but these still represented only a tiny fraction of the lands best suited to forest in many of Vermont's towns.[7]

The impetus for creating town forests varied. Some forests were located to protect municipal water supplies, whereas others were simply sited on former poor farms or abandoned land. In spite of the potential loss of income from abandoned farms, the return of the forest offered quantitative advantages. The momentum behind re-ordering the mountain landscape began to win new converts, and by 1926 Vermont's secretary of agriculture E. H. Jones expressed doubt about the viability of mountain farms. In an article for the *State Forest News*, Jones confessed: "Under the changed conditions most of our abandoned farms are rightly abandoned. They may well be turned over to the Forest Service to begin again that forest growth for which they were by Nature intended."[8] By the mid-1920s the sentiment that poor farm lands would be better managed as state and town forests had permeated public opinion.

Significantly, these new community forests also opened up an opportunity for cultivating outdoor recreation within the state. As a speaker before the Vermont Maple Sugar Makers' Association observed in 1924: "If a few rough farms do revert to their natural wilderness; there will always be a demand for wood, timber, and lumber, and a farmer can harvest trees as well as any other crop. Our wooded hills break the winds and clouds; they give us good air and water; they are beautiful to the eye."[9] Moreover, town forests could offer residents an opportunity to enjoy the benefits of well-managed public lands: "The municipal forest should be a veritable wild park, a noble playground in which men, women, and children could really 'commune with nature.' "[10]

As town governments examined their internal finances they recognized that roadwork and school transportation reimbursements represented a major drain on local governments. Road work was an economic boon to individual households, but the perennial expense of road maintenance strapped town finances, while the recognition that many miles of town roads were underused drove local experimentation in reorganizing settlement patterns.[11] Vermont's town forest legislation helped to facilitate the reordering of the local landscape. For example, the northeastern town of Sheffield (see map on p. 65), which contained considerable submarginal land, embraced the town forest as an opportunity to reduce annual expenditures and reorganize settlement patterns.[12] Sheffield's town officers sought to rationalize land use and municipal services by encouraging struggling families on outlying farms to move to available land that was both closer to town and more agriculturally viable. In 1921, the town paid $400 for a 140-acre farm located several miles from the school at the end of a little-used mountain road, with the ambition of converting the land to a town forest. The economic advantages of this purchase were simple. Each year the town's annual expenses for serving this family had included roughly $200 in charges for transporting the family's children to school, on top of the cost of maintaining the road. Based upon these expenses, the selectboard calculated that within two years its investment in the farm would pay itself off. Other land purchases followed, and in 1925 Sheffield purchased a second farm for $400, saving the town an additional $225 per year on tuition and transportation, not to mention the expense of maintaining the roads. The town officers estimated that purchasing these "sparsely occupied areas where costs of local services are greater than the value of occupied tracts" permitted the town to cease maintenance on mountain roads, thus reducing expenses and improving services for all of its residents. During the five years following the town's purchase of the land it yielded an annual hay crop and the pastures began to reforest in fir and spruce.[13]

State officials endorsed the town of Sheffield's approach to modifying land use, citing it as an example of the initiative small communities could take to simplify local services. In 1925 the Vermont Forest Service encouraged other towns to undertake similar land conversion projects:

> There are in many towns of the state rocky hill farms, several miles from the railroads and markets, which are unsuited for farming. The towns are at a great expense to maintain roads to these scattered farms and usually the town must pay for transporting the children to and from the school. Such farms are of little value and at best yield a bare living to the occupants. It would be better for the occupants of such farms and also for the town, if these lands were purchased by the towns and made into town forests. By doing this the annual outlay on roads and the cost of transporting school children would be eliminated. Instead of being a liability to the town, these lands when properly forested would be an asset. Does your town have a condition as outlined above. If it does the subject should be brought up at the next town meeting. THE INDIVIDUAL AND TOWN BOTH LOSE WHEN *NON-AGRICULTURAL LAND* IS FARMED.[14]

The state Forest Service's enthusiasm for land purchases and consolidation, however, could not sufficiently support land use change in fund struggling hill towns, or reorient the priorities of the thrifty state government, so only limited parts of the mountains were preserved in this manner through the mid-1930s.

As part of a larger move to assume the neglected burdens of the towns, the state legislature expanded the state forest system in 1923 and created the Vermont Forest Service to facilitate the work of reforestation

and forest conservation.[15] By December 1929 the state had acquired by gift
and purchase 34,627 acres in nineteen state forests. During this period the
expectations of what value the forests held for Vermont's citizens expanded, and the state began to explore opportunities to develop forest
recreation, watershed management, and scenery.[16] Beautiful mountain
forests offered new opportunities for summer home development, recreation, and increased tourism, and *Vermont Beautiful* author Wallace Nutting was merely one of the first to celebrate the economic and aesthetic
opportunities presented by afforestation.[17] A 1924 Vermont Forest Service
report welcomed the expansion: "Many thousands of people use the state
forests annually for recreation, camping, hunting and fishing. As time
goes on, these forests should prove to be a big asset to the State of Vermont
as the timber cut from these forests will far more than pay for the running
expenses. In addition the tracts will help protect the headwaters of our
streams, our scenic attractions and furnish public recreational areas."[18]
The system continued to expand into the early 1930s, when funds for new
land acquisition shriveled with the onset of the Great Depression.[19]

In spite of the limited personnel and the meager resources of the
Forest Service, by 1932 Vermont foresters had created a series of plans
for forest development, and district foresters mapped the management
plans and timber-stand analyses of many municipal and state forests.[20]
Acting on its own initiative, in response to the economic contraction of
the early 1930s, the state put "several hundred Vermonters" to work in
December 1932, making use of unemployed labor to help improve forest
stands.[21] Commissioner of Forestry Perry Merrill's approach to relief
proved prescient, and when in 1933 the federal government solicited
ideas for how to use Civilian Conservation Corps workers and other relief labor, the plans the Forest Service had already generated laid the
groundwork for much of the reforestation and timber management
work that characterized New Deal forestry in Vermont.[22]

During this period other organizations also began to explore a new
vision of the value of Vermont's forests for other recreational purposes.
In 1910, twenty-three Vermonters created the Green Mountain Club
(GMC) with the ambition of building trails and shelters that would open
the Green Mountains to hikers so that the region might "play a larger
part in the life of the people."[23] The idea behind the organization, which
originated with schoolteacher James P. Taylor, entailed creating a 265-mile

hiking trail along the crest of the Green Mountains, an unprecedented recreational project for the era. Progress on the trail system proceeded rapidly, and by 1913 the club had created plans for a "Long Trail" along logging roads and footpaths stretching for 150 miles through the mountains. The Green Mountain Club thereafter developed a network of hiking trails along Vermont's ridgeline, gradually acquiring usage rights to mountain land and building bonds of cooperation with landowners and the towns whose boundaries they crossed. This first long-distance hiking trail was the inspiration for the Appalachian Trail. These hikers and volunteer trailblazers had a vested interest in preserving the state's natural and scenic areas, and their work culminated in September 1931 when the Long Trail was formally dedicated.[24]

MOMENTUM

The foundation established by state-level planning initiatives helped to lay the groundwork for the further expansion of government influence on Vermont's landscape. Around the turn of the twentieth century the state government acknowledged the need to expand its operations into local matters. As the state's responsibilities grew, other contingencies led to the further expansion of the state's prerogative. Vermonters not only cooperated on state-level planning but occasionally reached out to partner with the federal government on projects of major importance. The histories of federal road aid, flood relief, and the Green Mountain National Forest date the collaboration between the state and federal government to the 1910s and 1920s. These partnerships prefigured the projects of the New Deal and beyond.

Vermont's road program began in 1892 when the first Highway Act reallocated money for road maintenance from wealthy to poor towns, redistributing it on the basis of greatest need. This state supplement to the town road network was further expanded with the passage of the Federal-Aid Road Act of 1916, in which the federal government offered matching funds to states for the construction of rural post roads.[25] Vermont welcomed this assistance in establishing a modern road system. Yet in spite of this steady accumulation of funding sources, the state struggled to achieve more than simple maintenance on its roads, largely because of the vast mileage of roads located in hill towns, where the ravages of winter weather and spring thaw were the most harsh.

The maintenance of highways and byways repeatedly emerged as a point of conflict at all levels of government. The state's roads were critical to all of Vermont's industries—forestry, agriculture, manufacturing, and tourism—and thus formed a foundation for the state's economic development, yet they were not reliable. By any measure, improvements statewide remained relatively limited, and in 1924 Vermont had only twenty miles of hard-surface roads, far fewer than most neighboring states.[26] Road building thus emerged as the most pressing issue of the 1926 gubernatorial race, when both candidates embraced a program of roadway improvements. The victor, Republican John Weeks, proposed a statewide highway program that would build forty miles of hard-surface highway a year on a pay-as-you-go basis, funded primarily by the state gasoline tax.[27]

The roads program received an unexpected, and most unwanted, boost in 1927 when a disastrous flood swept through Vermont's mountains and valleys in early November, devastating much of the state's system of roads and bridges. Saturated soils and heavy rains combined to swell streams flowing out of the mountains, overwhelming rivers and flooding vast sections of Vermont. As Arthur Stone described the scene in his 1929 history of Vermont, "October had been a wet month, the rainfall being double the normal. The ground was saturated and there had been overflows in some localities which had caused damage. . . . On the evening of November 2, it began to rain, and continued with heavy precipitation for nearly forty-eight hours. Over the most of the State eight inches and more fell during this period. The ground could absorb none of this, and the water hurried into the already over-full streams plunging out of the mountains seeking a sufficient channel or receiving reservoir. Brooks became rivers, the rivers became torrents appalling in height and volume."[28] The Flood of 1927 caused unprecedented damage to the state's infrastructure, and in some places rivers crested twenty feet higher than their previously recorded highs. The Winooski River in north-central Vermont was the hardest hit, at forty-five feet above its normal level; it devastated the state capital at Montpelier and the industrial center at Barre.[29]

For a state already struggling to maintain a rudimentary system of public roads the flood forced a massive reconceptualization of the role of government. Suddenly, emergency investment in infrastructure was both urgent and essential. In early 1928, the Vermont Public Service Commission reported a conservative estimate of $2.48 million in damage to highways, $7.06 million in damage to bridges, and $3.9 million in damage to twelve railroads; the expected losses from the flood totaled more than $24.74 million.[30] The greatest destruction hit lowland areas, sparing many of the cash-strapped hill towns, but communities statewide suffered paralyzing damage. Communications and commerce were disrupted not only by the disaster itself, but also by the lasting consequences of an estimated 1,400 bridges destroyed by the flood.[31]

Serendipitously, Vermont's deluged communities had recourse to outside help, benefiting from the precedent set by the first major federal relief effort, the cleanup after the devastating Mississippi River flood of the summer of 1927. Daunted by the scale of destruction, Vermont welcomed assistance from the U.S. government, and Secretary of Commerce Herbert Hoover, who had coordinated the Mississippi relief effort, made a much-publicized tour to inspect damage and relief operations.[32] From the perspective of state development, the flood's greatest impact stemmed from the massive expansion in funding for roads and bridges after the floodwaters receded. During the 1927 special session of the Vermont legislature in late November, Weeks assessed the need for $8.5 million to repair state roadways and bridges. The governor announced: "Bridges and highways are no longer built and maintained principally for the good and convenience of the people of the town where they are located, but for the good and convenience of the people of the entire State."[33] In a move with significant implications for the future of state infrastructure, Weeks proposed that the state highway department manage the reconstruction effort, rather than town or county governments. The legislature approved repairs and the issuance of a bond to cover their cost, in marked contrast to Vermont's traditional pay-as-you-go approach to road maintenance and construction.[34] Responsibility for the provision of services once considered exclusively local shifted to the state level, and the structure of Vermont politics began to change as a result of this evolution.

Contemporary accounts of the post-flood reconstruction suggest that the rebuilding should be considered in the context of policymakers' advocacy for a modernized road system, given how champions of hard roads like Governor Weeks embraced flood repair as a means of further enhancing the state highway network.[35] The state and federal governments

spent almost twelve million dollars on road construction and repairs in
the two years after the flood. During the winter of 1927–28, construction
proceeded across the state at an unprecedented pace, with almost a hundred replacement bridges built during the last weeks of 1927.[36] The following year, another 1,329 bridges were erected, most of them replacing
spans washed away by the floods, and in 1929 the state erected an additional 201 bridges. Permanent funding increases document this change,
and in 1932 the legislature allocated $2.94 million for roads, an increase
of 186 percent from 1924.[37] A few years later, the Hoover administration's Reconstruction Finance Corporation supplemented these funds,
and this federal funding arrived in Vermont in August 1932, paying primarily for the work of unemployed laborers on the state's road system.[38]
By 1935, when the State Planning Commission took stock of Vermont's
transportation infrastructure, it reported that the state contained 14,386
miles of highways, of which 69 percent (9,994 miles) were maintained
by the towns; another 23 percent (3,363 miles) were state aid highways;
and 7 percent (1,029 miles) were maintained through the Federal Aid
System.[39] The improvements to the transportation network over the preceding decade transformed the state's physical and cultural landscape. A
1937 retrospective in the *Burlington Free Press*, evaluating Vermont's progress in the decade since the flood, concluded that the explosion in road
construction after the flood had permitted the state to design a modern
road system, with benefits that abounded for all residents and visitors.[40]

Disaster relief had pushed the state to a new level of activism and in
the process helped to secure its economic stability. In fact, in early 1928,
as the state was fully immersed in flood recovery and repairs, Eugenics
Survey of Vermont director Henry Perkins used the statewide emergency to help muster support for the Vermont Commission on Country
Life. Capitalizing on the disaster, Perkins solicited participation from
state leaders with a letter arguing that "the flood has made a difference to
the whole population . . . and has opened up some new possibilities. You
are anxious to see Vermont made—and to help make Vermont—a better
place in which to live."[41] The devastation of the flood, the sense of common purpose that followed, and the expanded state initiative of the late
1920s all complemented the program of Perkins' commission.

By the early 1930s Vermonters had begun to appreciate some of the
other economic benefits roads could confer, including access to ex-

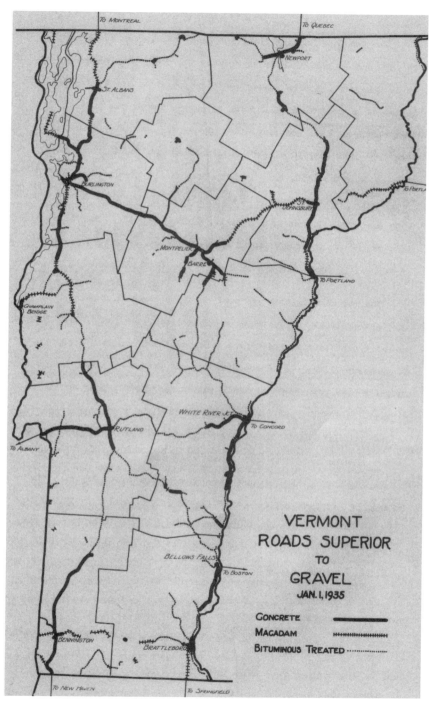

Vermont Roads Superior to Gravel, 1933, showing the major thoroughfares through Vermont. From the 1935 "Graphic Survey: A First Step in State Planning for Vermont," p. 20. Courtesy of the University of Vermont, Special Collections, Bailey Howe Library.

panded recreation. *Rural Vermont* proposed a further expansion of the road system that foreshadowed other proposals for developing the Vermont upcountry. The VCCL's Committee on Summer Residents and Tourism suggested: "Ultimately, after our main trunk lines are hard surfaced, it may be well to consider the possibility of linking up some of our country roads far up on the hills, on either side of the Green Mountains, into a system of scenic highways which afford vastly better outlooks than the valley roads. A scenic highway, well up on the slopes of the Green Mountains, on either side of this range, constructed in semi-permanent form, would appeal strongly to lovers of beautiful scenery."[42] The 1933 proposal for a Green Mountain Parkway would later echo this idea for a ridgeline roadway, using the model of Virginia's Skyline Drive. In the interim, Vermont realized long-discussed plans for a national forest in the Green Mountains.

TOWARD A GREEN MOUNTAIN NATIONAL FOREST
As we have seen, the extensive scale of land abandonment in Vermont, and the growing area of land in forest, meant that state and local resources could not match the demand for forest conservation. In forestry, as in federal-aid highways and flood cleanup, the state eventually reached out to federal partners in order to ensure more effective resource management. This initiative also capitalized on developments on the federal level: beginning in 1911 the U.S. Forest Service had expanded its operations to include the eastern states. The Forest Service had first studied potential national forest sites in Vermont in 1920, but the Vermont parcels were not a high-priority acquisition.[43] As U.S. Forest Service Chief William Greeley observed: "The forest growth in Vermont is very largely thrifty, vigorous, and valuable. . . . One is constantly impressed by the excellent and vigorous condition of the forests and the lack of the denudation and abuse of forest land. . . . In other words, thanks to the natural conditions, the common sense and conservative temper of the people, and the effective work of the State Department of Forestry, Vermont forests are today in splendid shape in comparison with other States."[44] As Greeley's observation suggests, Vermont's early achievements in forestry protected its woodlands more effectively than many other places, thus disqualifying the state from the advantages of federal assistance.

The landscape of federal forest protection changed considerably in 1924, however, when Congress passed the Clarke-McNary Act to amend the guidelines to include timber production in addition to watershed protection. The legislation expanded the Forest Service's acquisition mandate, liberalizing the terms under which the National Forest Reservation Commission (NFRC) could designate new areas as national forests.[45] Seizing upon the opportunity, in February 1925, Vermont passed legislation endorsing the establishment of a national forest within the state.[46] Later that year, the *Vermont State Forest News* encouraged the development of a national forest in Vermont, arguing that it would assure the state of "increased protection of the timberlands from fire, enhanced returns in taxes to the towns over a period of years, more stable wood using industries, and [the valued] biproduct [sic] of increased tourist travel." The state Forest Service suggested that a national forest in the Green Mountains "should help to make Vermont the 'Playground of the Eastern United States.'"[47]

The push for a Vermont national forest began in earnest with the 1925 National Forest Enabling Act. With this statement of support for federal land management Vermont welcomed a new degree of partnership with the United States government, and established a precedent for further cooperation in land use conversion with the administration in Washington, DC. The state Forest Service enumerated the economic advantages of a large-scale forest parcel in the Green Mountain uplands: foremost among them were protecting future hydroelectric developments along Vermont's waterways, maintaining sustained stream flow, and ensuring a stable supply of lumber for the wood products industry.[48] The Enabling Act reflected state officials' awareness that properly managed forest lands could ensure economic development, aesthetics, interstate watersheds, and timber production. Vermonters understood that reliable forest resources were crucial to the state's economic health: "The future welfare of this region depends to a great extent upon the forests, as there is no mining in the region, little farming and little or no grazing. The existence of the wood working industries is dependent upon a continuous supply of logs and lumber." However, as foresters recognized, under current conditions the future of the forest was in no way assured, and the "haphazard methods of lumbering" employed in the state threatened to further

deplete forest resources and thus eliminate the remaining wood products industries from the mountain landscape.[49] The economic pressures
created by the annual tax burden often encouraged landowners to cut all
trees from a farm woodlot—to "wreck it for timber"—en route to farm
abandonment, a common occurrence.[50]

Vermont's efforts to promote the state-sponsored conversion of abandoned or partially abandoned farmlands to public forests offered the best
chance for improved management and the long-term conservation of the
land.[51] In 1928, the Vermont Forest Service presented the National Forest
Reservation Commission with a plan for a national forest comprising
300,000 acres. The plan focused on maintaining healthy watersheds by
stemming soil erosion and reducing flood hazards; cultivating a permanent and prosperous local timber and wood products industry; and providing recreational developments for the people of Vermont and the
"thirty million people within a radius of two hundred miles"—all proposals that served the economic needs of the state as well as the region.[52]

The proposal for a Green Mountain National Forest won immediate
support from all quarters of the Vermont body politic, as the cause of
preserving the state's forest resources was both popular and compelling.
Vermont's fledgling State Commission of Conservation and Development, appointed by Governor Weeks in 1927, attached a resolution to
the proposal, stating: "Whereas the welfare of Vermont depends to a
great extent upon keeping her forest land productive of valuable forest
growth . . . we believe these tracts of land will not be managed along scientific forestry lines while under private ownership."[53] The State Chamber of Commerce's resolution went further to link the devastation of the
flood of 1927 to the urgency of national forest protection.[54] Conservationists' messages about watershed protection and the importance of
proper forest cultivation secured the endorsement of Vermont businessmen and political leaders.

Economic considerations figured large in the calculations of the state
and national governments regarding the creation of a new Vermont purchase unit.[55] The NFRC's *Reconnaissance Report* assessed the status of
conservation projects in Vermont, predicting that the state forest system
would be neglected during the coming years, because the cost of recovery
from the Flood of 1927 was sure to monopolize state funds for the fore-
seeable future. Like many Vermonters, the commissioners linked the

destruction of the flood with the push for a Vermont national forest: "The purchase of additional lands for forest purposes will probably cease . . . for the simple reason that large sums are being spent to reconstruct bridges and rebuild highways which were washed away in the flood of a year ago. This is one of the reasons why the people of Vermont are anxious for the establishment of a National Forest in the state." As an additional rationale, the report suggested that the cost of rebuilding damaged roads and bridges meant that it was "likely that concerns ow[n]ing large tracts of land will be anxious to sell to avoid the payment of higher taxes."[56]

The U.S. Forest Service appreciated the potential value of a Vermont national forest for tourism and forest management. The *Reconnaissance Report* commented on the thriving state of the summer resort industry in the area around the proposed forest unit, observing the range of recreational opportunities within southern Vermont.[57] U.S. Geological Survey surveyor Louis Prindle highlighted the natural connections between recreation and the Forest Service's conservation work: "This portion of the Appalachians has long been noted as a sort of exhibition area. . . . From the viewpoint of beauty, diversity, accessibility and conditions most favorable for forest development, it is most appropriate that such an area be selected as a National Forest."[58] The utilitarian attractions of a Vermont forest unit were equally compelling: securing a reliable, managed timber harvest was good for the state economy and for regional watersheds. In February 1931, the NFRC approved the purchase of the first 31,228 acres in Vermont.[59] The following year, on April 25, 1932, President Hoover proclaimed the creation of the Green Mountain National Forest, and the federal government began to acquire parcels of land. Of the initial 102,000 acre purchase unit, over three-quarters qualified as submarginal for agriculture under the criteria of Vermont Agricultural Experiment Station Bulletin 357.[60]

The national forest program was bolstered by the Forest Service's 1933 Copeland Report, the *National Plan for American Forestry,* which recommended that the federal government embark on a program of purchasing cutover and tax-delinquent land and which spurred a massive expansion in funding for new forests. The creation of the Green Mountain National Forest coincided with the beginning of a massive expansion in the national forest system. Whereas between the passage of the Weeks Act in 1911 and July 1932 the federal government designated twenty-four new eastern national forests, with a total acreage of five million acres, in 1933 and 1934 increased spending doubled that area, and by mid-1935 there were more than sixteen million acres east of the Mississippi River.[61] Overall, between 1933 and 1936, Congress allocated more than forty-five million dollars for land acquisition, a 250 percent increase over the preceding two decades. During the Depression the federal forest initiative was one of few sources of income in Vermont, and so many landowners willingly sold their land to the Green Mountain National Forest. Low land values, an accumulation of delinquent taxes, and a dormant wood products industry meant that there was little market for forest lands during this decade, and the Forest Service surpassed its acquisition goals during its early years in Vermont. By 1935 the federal government had purchased 160,539 acres acres, an impressive beginning to the creation of the Green Mountain National Forest.[62]

Vermont saw great opportunity in the national forest program, and state officials endorsed the U.S. Forest Service's addition of a second unit, the "Northern District" in central Vermont, in March 1934, with a gross area of an additional 205,400 acres.[63] Reflecting the growing attention to recreation, the Vermont Forest Service observed: "This unit is well situated with reference to population, thus making it valuable for nationally developed recreational use. It has reasonably good local markets and good connections with Albany, New York, and Boston outlets." In an economic climate where landowners were struggling to remain solvent, proper forest management frequently lapsed, making "public ownership assuring a wise, far-sighted all-round management program . . . imperative."[64] The Green Mountain Club also endorsed the expansion, welcoming the prospect of shared stewardship over the Long Trail.[65] During the early years of the New Deal, Vermonters clearly recognized the economic value of federal investment in the state, and the national forest project enjoyed wide support. Moreover, this phase of the planning for the Green Mountain National Forest provided a trial for federal-state cooperation in conservation and a model for mutually beneficial land utilization projects.

CONSERVATION PLANNING IN THE NEW DEAL

Throughout the United States, the limited-government mentality of the 1920s was supplanted by the urgency of economic crisis. Even though the role of the federal government in the states had gradually increased

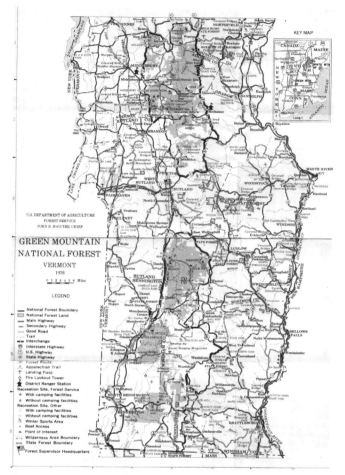

Green Mountain National Forest, 1976 map showing the total boundaries of the Green Mountain National Forest in gray. Produced by the Forest Service, U.S. Department of Agriculture, Green Mountain National Forest headquarters, Rutland, Vermont.

during the first decades of the twentieth century, and the federal presence was felt on roadways and in new parks and forests, the beginning of the Roosevelt administration and the New Deal represented a shift in national political culture. The change, precipitated primarily by the economic dislocations of the Great Depression, occurred in part because of the reformist political philosophy of the new federal policymakers. The economic retractions of the Great Depression stung

Vermonters alongside other Americans; when Roosevelt took office, they were desperate to see some improvement in the regional economy, and eager to share in the benefits of federal assistance. New Deal programs for relief and reform exposed Vermonters to new influences and ideas about methods of local development. The slew of federal agencies that emerged during the early New Deal presented a range of new federal conservation initiatives and an overwhelming number of opportunities for land reform. At times, the proposals resonated with the state's ambitions, while at other moments Vermont recoiled, and a new, increasingly complex dynamic evolved between the levels of government.[66]

The New Deal marked a new phase in Vermont's relations with the federal government. Whereas during the 1910s and 1920s the state had requested federal assistance for roads, flood relief, and the national forest, during the 1930s the federal government often initiated intergovernmental collaborations. No longer did Vermont simply solicit federal aid in the event that local resources proved insufficient to serve state needs. Instead, federal planners descended on Montpelier and other state capitals, flush with optimism and ideas for improving the state; in Vermont, they met a mixed response. The cautious response of Vermont politicians to federal proposals for conservation and social reform resulted from a long tradition of local autonomy, but as the roads, flood reconstruction, and forest projects demonstrate, this independence was less definitive than many have suggested. Particularly during the New Deal, the state sought a compromise between the appeal of federal relief funds and the instinct to retain local control; consequently, Vermont integrated federal programs into state planning in a piecemeal fashion.

Vermont initially suffered little from the low agricultural prices, food shortages, and industrial failures that plagued most of the rest of the nation during the 1930s. Like many other Appalachian workers, most rural Vermonters kept a foothold on the farm, and they were able to fall back on their gardens and woodlots to help them weather the economic crisis. Many touted the part-time farms common in Vermont hill towns as a long-range solution to the economic troubles of the Depression and as evidence of the security of independent production. In 1936 Commissioner of Agriculture Jones acknowledged, "Owing in part to the diversification of Vermont agriculture and in part to the stable and conservative mental attitude of her people, Vermont has probably been less affected . . . than many of her sister states." In fact, whereas the state trailed the nation in per capita income in 1929 (Vermont's mean was $699 compared with the national mean of $715), by 1931 Vermont's per capita income was $78 above the national mean ($503 versus $425).[67]

From the first months of the New Deal, Vermont politicians adapted to the local and national implications of the new federal interventions in production, finance, and community life. In an address to the General Assembly in July 1933, Governor Stanley Wilson expressed his feelings about government assistance. "It has been my belief . . . that Vermont should not put herself in the position of a supplicant for federal assistance unless the time should arrive when we actually need such aid." Yet Wilson also acknowledged that new federal programs would involve tremendous expenditures in all states, to which Vermont would be expected to contribute its share, and he concluded that "since Vermont must bear its share of the cost, Vermont should also take such action as may be necessary to secure its full share of the benefits." Employing this philosophy, Vermonters continued to collaborate with federal agencies on issues of concern to the state.[68]

Beginning in 1933, and especially after 1934, nascent state and federal planning agencies began to articulate a comprehensive vision for Vermont's future. Governor Wilson created the State Planning Board in 1934, which was followed by legislation in April 1935 formally establishing a permanent board. By 1935 Vermont expanded its state planning apparatus, and the Natural Resources Board commissioned the "Graphic Survey: A First Step in State Planning for Vermont" to provide the state board with historical background. Produced by consultants from outside the state, the "Graphic Survey" provided an expansive synopsis of the state of land use planning in Vermont.[69] This report highlighted Vermont's recreational population beyond the decades-old focus on summer homes: "A glance at the map shows Vermont's favorable position for business and for pleasure. Within three hundred miles of Montpelier there is an estimated population of more than thirty millions of people. From the point of view of recreation it may be said that nowhere else in the world is there such an extent of unspoiled wilderness so easily accessible to such a dense mass of urban population."[70] As many Vermonters had recognized for decades, potential profits remained nested in the hills, a prime opportunity for future development.

The CCC represented the high point of federal-state cooperation in Vermont, permitting the state to fulfill much of its conservation agenda and develop recreational resources even during the financially straitened years of the 1930s. In the process, it provided one of the New Deal's most stunning successes in the state. These accomplishments are attributable to the state's pre-existing and robust program of forest conservation, which had been applied for decades to state and municipal forests. Moreover, Commissioner of Forestry Perry Merrill's enthusiasm for the program helped to pull a disproportionately large number of CCC workers into the state. Vermont was initially allotted four camps with 750 men, out of the nation's initial total of 300,000 enrollees. Yet Merrill's expansive blueprint for forest improvement convinced the corps that Vermont was prepared to move beyond this initial allocation, and instead thirteen camps were placed around the state.[71]

Relief laborers initially concentrated on forestry projects, with men working on fire protection, tree planting, road building, pest and disease control, trail cutting, and shelter construction. The U.S. Forest Service managed three camps in the Green Mountain National Forest, and the Vermont Forest Service ran another ten on state forest lands. In all, CCC men planted over a million trees in Vermont.[72] Still other enrollees built ski trails on Bromley Mountain, at Breadloaf, and on Mount Mansfield.[73] Other initiatives took advantage of Vermonters' recently renewed interest in flood control, and thousands of World War I veterans built dams along the Winooski River in order to protect the areas hardest hit by the Flood of 1927. Finally, beginning in 1933 the CCC worked in conjunction with the state government to develop recreational facilities in state parks, including parking areas, campgrounds, bathroom facilities, and water sources, thus adding infrastructure to Vermont's otherwise rudimentary state park system. Parkways to the top of Mount Ascutney and Burke Mountain, as well as beaches at Sand Bar State Park, were designed to offer new opportunities for public enjoyment of the parks' recreational potential.[74] As in Virginia, the results of these efforts paid off beyond Vermont's landscape: by 1934, after six months in the camps, the 2,600 men working in Vermont had gained 35,000 pounds "of good solid flesh," and Merrill observed, "In addition they have been taught how to work, and . . . are now well on their way to learning a trade."[75]

Although scholars have duly noted the state's hesitations about various federal programs, the popularity of the CCC illustrates many Vermonters' willingness to support extensive federal-state cooperation during the early years of the New Deal. Programs in harmony with a pre-existing local ethic of conservation and poor relief brought Vermont both jobs and money during the 1930s. However, as the thoroughness of New Deal conservation planning and implementation became clear, Vermonters confronted the potential implications of an expanded federal presence in the state, and wariness soon accompanied the initial interest in relief funds. In spite of the increased availability of federal construction money, many residents remained skeptical of the vision behind the New Deal. Moreover, the relief programs of the early 1930s succeeded in Vermont partly because they built on pre-existing state-level initiatives, and they did not conflict with the political and economic philosophies of most Vermonters and their elected officials.[76]

Politician George Aiken emerged early in the New Deal as the foremost spokesperson for Vermonters' ambivalence about the expanding national government, articulating a "provincial progressivism" based in the self-reliant leanings of mountain culture.[77] Aiken voiced his concern that "the ownership of and jurisdiction over the natural resources of the United States constitutes the most far-reaching problem of the day. . . . It is brought to a focus by the determination of the national government to acquire control, and even actual ownership, of all natural resources of land and water."[78] This was a refrain he sounded often during his political career. The suspicion that a greedy federal government was poised to gobble up Vermont's patrimony tempered Aiken's position on most natural resource issues as a state and federal official. At a September 1934 speech in Waterbury, while campaigning for lieutenant governor, he suggested, "The most critical problem confronting the people of Vermont is to decide to what extent we shall let the federal government obtain control of land within the state." Aiken was critical of several federal plans for managing Vermont's development: the Green Mountain National Forest, the Green Mountain Parkway, and the Resettlement Administration's submarginal lands program. Explaining his concern about the popular national forest expansion, Aiken suggested that the expanse of the national forest might eventually cover 700,000 acres (12 percent of the state's total), or "the equivalent of 35 fair-sized towns." He argued that the implications of this massive project were severalfold. First, forest expansion had the potential to remove a significant amount of land from the tax rolls, an issue that would later become problematic for several mountain towns. Second, the natural consequence of government ownership, Aiken inferred, was the further depopulation of Vermont's mountains in order to return them to forest, and he implied that this would be done "either with or without the consent of the people," thus raising the specter of forced dispossession. Third, because he was a staunch advocate of summer home development, he feared that the creation of recreation areas would remove land forever from market.[79] Aiken's expansive victory in the 1934 election signaled new challenges for federal-state cooperation on matters of land use policy.

The protection of the mountain forests remained a priority for Vermont voters and policymakers, yet as Aiken's comments suggested, the expansion of the Green Mountain National Forest was also affected by concerns about the federal government's prerogative. The forest project, initiated with such enthusiasm during the 1920s, by the mid-1930s had become intertwined in the public mind with other federal conservation programs, much to the dismay of Forest Service officials. In the recollection of one District Forester, "A major change in National Administration came into being in 1933 and with it an almost revolutionary liberation and expansion in Government activity. This applied to land use and public ownership activities, as well as to economic and social programs. . . . Summing up these and other Federal activities, little Vermont [suddenly] felt that it was about to be swallowed by the Federal Government."[80] Consequently, the once universally popular national forest came to be reexamined as part of a massive expansion in federal conservation projects proposed for Vermont. The discussions about forest policy raised a number of questions concerning local control that were central to Vermonters' perspective on the New Deal.

Ultimately, federal land ownership had assumed a remarkably limited extent by 1935. Of the state's 5,839,360 acres, 98 percent, or 5,714,286, remained in private hands. Various levels of government owned the rest of the state's 125,074 acres: with a little more than half of that acreage (68,080 acres) in federal ownership, another 47,435 acres managed by

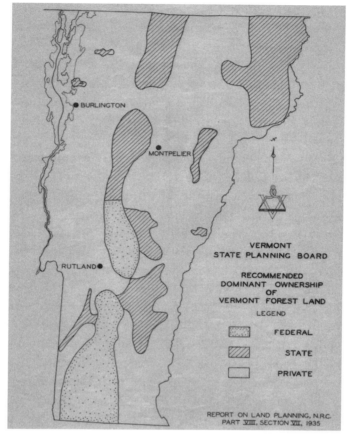

Vermont State Planning Board's *Recommended Dominant Ownership of Vermont Forest Land,* 1935, from the Natural Resources Council's Report on Land Planning, 1935. Vermont Public Records Office, Middlesex, Vermont, PRA 63, Records of the Commissioner of Agriculture; PRA-299; 29407.

the state, and 9,559 owned by town and county governments.[81] The expansion of the Green Mountain National Forest continued during the following years, to around 160,000 acres, but overall these figures contextualize Aiken's exaggeration that the federal government was poised to take over half of Vermont. Nevertheless, the specter of federal control loomed ever larger during the mid-1930s, due in part to the design for a national parkway on the crest of the Green Mountains.

THE GREEN MOUNTAIN PARKWAY

One of the first federal development projects in Vermont was a mountaintop roadway, proposed in 1933 by engineer and adopted Vermonter William Wilgus. Wilgus, the chairman of the Governor's Advisory Committee of Engineers, was tasked with conceptualizing a project that would be eligible for ten million dollars in federal relief funds made available through the National Industrial Recovery Act. Wilgus capitalized upon the idea of a recreational road that would provide construction jobs and open the mountains to visitors.[82] He convinced the executive secretary of the Vermont Chamber of Commerce, James Taylor, of the potential of this proposal, and Taylor, who had successfully promoted the Long Trail, was a valuable ally in the push for the parkway.

Parkway advocates soon reached out to the National Park Service, which embraced the project as part of a plan for a network of ridgeline roads along the Appalachian range, extending out from Virginia's Skyline Drive. During 1934 the National Park Service and the Bureau of Public Roads surveyed the Green Mountains, proposing a roadway consisting of a five-hundred-foot right-of-way on each side, to be expanded in places to include other attractions and views. The resulting *Reconnaissance Survey* described the scope of the parkway: "It will extend the entire length of the State of Vermont through the Green Mountains and their adjacent ranges and foothills, being located so as to embrace as far as possible typical examples of all forms of outstanding natural scenery characteristic of the Green Mountain region."[83] In addition to its aesthetic appeal, the report presented the roadway as a means of reconstructing the long-abused natural features of the mountains, ensuring "the protection and improvement of the forest areas so as to gradually restore the charm and beauty of the original forest," out of what was at the time "mostly second growth forests due to many years of despoliation."[84] Conservation and recreational development were thereby designed to be complementary.

In February 1935 the National Park Service formally presented the state legislature with the blueprint for the Green Mountain Parkway. Like many other New Deal construction projects, the route was intended to provide work relief for unemployed Vermonters as it laid the groundwork for an expanded tourism industry. The road would run 260 miles along the length of the state, and the federal government offered to pay the $18 million cost of construction, provided that Vermont acquire the land, at an estimated price of $500,000. Project advocates argued that the parkway represented an unprecedented opportunity to benefit from federal spending, while critics dreaded the implications of losing control of such a vast territory in the heart of the Green Mountains.[85]

Opponents of the National Park Service proposal observed that by ceding some of the state's most picturesque land for the roadway, Vermonters would lose any chance to develop it themselves, forfeiting control over the mountainous backbone of the state.[86] Five days after the Park Service proposed the Green Mountain Parkway project, the Green Mountain Club presented the state legislature with an alternative to the road. The "All-Vermont Plan" was inspired in part by the Potomac Appalachian Trail Club's failed attempt to influence the path of the Skyline Drive, and the Vermont club pledged not to allow their mountaintop hiking trails to be similarly displaced. The proposal suggested that the state should focus its attention on local needs and recreational development, rather than purchasing land for a roadway that might serve only to bring people on a high-speed thoroughfare through the state. This opposition was rooted in the club's mission to protect the Long Trail, but the logic extended further, and the GMC argued that the parkway "would commercialize a section of the State that has so far been unspoiled."[87]

The All-Vermont Plan reminded legislators that the slopes of the Green Mountains offered ideal sites for summer homes and recreational areas, intermediate uses that would pull tourist money into Vermont from part-time residents and repeat visitors. The GMC celebrated the recent growth in summer home purchases, the fledgling Vermont ski industry at Woodstock and Stowe, and the creation of the state and municipal forest systems as evidence that this type of development was already happening organically. These small-scale projects "would leave Vermont in the possession and control of its own citizens as no National Park scheme can. It would avoid dividing the state by a large area of Federally controlled and tax-free National Park land." In sum, the Green Mountain Club presented its plan as a solution to both the abandonment of Vermont's hill farms and the cession of mountain forests to federal control, as well as a local alternative—based in part on outside investment—to relief projects dominated by the federal government.[88] Unlike Virginia residents' reactive opposition to the Shenandoah National Park, which offered isolated critiques of each argument provided by the federal

Map of the proposed route of the Green Mountain Parkway, 1934. Courtesy of the Vermont Historical Society.

government in favor of the park, or the PATC's belated attempt to re-
route the Skyline Drive, this proposal was delivered by influential Vermonters to the legislature virtually simultaneously with the federal
plans. Prompt, proactive, and comprehensive, like the Vermont Commission on Country Life's research earlier in the decade, the All-Vermont
Plan looked for internal solutions to the state's problems and generated
new ideas about the future development of Vermont.

Opponents of the Green Mountain Parkway envisioned a Vermont
that would remain vital under local control. They cited evidence that during the early 1930s numerous hill farms had been purchased and returned
to use by urbanites who had left the cities seeking a decent standard of
living in rural areas. Lieutenant Governor Aiken, who observed the new
arrivals with pleasure, cited this migration as evidence of a local opportunity for developing rural Vermont. By 1935, Aiken had begun keeping
detailed records of the number of summer home purchases in southern-
most Windham and Windsor Counties, and he coordinated with the
State Planning Board and the Chamber of Commerce to entice more
buyers to the state. Aiken believed that summer homes offered the answer to the hill town problem, and he favored retaining local control over
marketable land. The lieutenant governor argued that summer people,
who had thrown themselves into improving their recently acquired
homes, were the salvation of hill towns and had the potential to revitalize
the towns to which they moved and to further develop local economies—
thus obviating expensive federal or state assistance.[89]

Proponents of the Parkway lauded the federal project as a corrective
to the ad hoc development of Vermont's fragile mountain ecosystems,
stressing the dangers associated with shortsighted private land management. Landscape architect Laurie Davidson Cox, a National Park Service
consultant on the parkway proposal, argued that decentralized local control threatened Vermont's scenic mountain landscape. Cox sounded a
warning about the future of Vermont: "Without the parkway this de-
spoiling of the Vermont wilderness is inevitable and only a matter of
time and probably a rather short time at that . . . spoliation is already on
foot. The area is very largely privately owned and is subject to taxation
and development; it only awaits a market."[90] The rhetoric on both sides
of the Parkway question demonstrated the sharply divergent views of the
dangers posed by federal and individual initiatives.

In March 1935, the General Assembly voted to reject the parkway, 126 to 111.[91] Later that fall, Governor Charles Smith requested reconsideration of the parkway legislation; the legislature responded by calling a statewide referendum for Town Meeting Day, 1936. The months before the March vote found the entire population of the state discussing the road question. Numerous correspondents wrote to Lieutenant Governor Aiken, the presumptive nominee for governor that fall, and his responses reflected ambivalence about the project. Aiken frequently equivocated: "Personally, I do not know whether it would do more good than harm and neither does anyone else."[92] When pressed to take a side, Aiken wrote one constituent "I . . . will tell you frankly that I cannot get excited enough about the Parkway to let either side use my name in any propaganda."[93] Aiken linked the developing summer homes movement to the question of what value the roadway could bring to the state: "While I am not radically opposed to the Parkway . . . the hundreds of people who have come in here and bought homes in Southern Vermont are. . . . I am personally satisfied with the way my own county has developed during the last few years. . . . In one town in this county over a hundred places have been transferred within the last ten years—this one of our smaller towns, too."[94] Aiken's vision for the state entailed continuous independent development, but he also recognized the passion this massive project ignited in many Vermonters, which explains his unwillingness to take a public stance on the parkway question.

Others did not share Aiken's ambivalence. By 1935 some Vermonters voiced concern about the many federal conservation plans that might alienate land from local and state control. For instance, the strongly antiparkway *Rutland Herald* consistently opposed the road. An editorial from September 1934 read, "If money from tourists is desired, it seems to The Herald that much more of it would follow improvement of existing roads, upon or near which are now located those who can benefit by the spending of tourists' money, than would follow the building of a new, remote, mountain road upon which no tourist could spend money even if he wished to do so." An evocative political cartoon, entitled "A Hideous Joke," accompanied the editorial. The caption reinforced the cartoon's message: "To spend ten million dollars for a mountain parkway to encourage tourists while our own citizens are bogged hub-deep

George Long, "A Hideous Joke," political cartoon from *The Rutland Herald*, September 4, 1934.

on the way to their markets, their neighbors or their village store, seems to The Herald to be a hideous joke."[95]

As the debate over the parkway raged, with advocates and opponents each raising a wide range of issues, the largest questions about the future of the state became intertwined in the discussion.[96] Newspapers and public meetings debated the project from 1934 through early 1936, although there was rarely evidence of any definitive majority supporting either side. The referendum appeared too close to predict. Yet ultimately, with an unusually high turnout for Town Meeting Day, the referendum's defeat by 58 percent of voters demonstrated Vermonters' deep interest in maintaining control over their state's development. Although work relief and federal aid offered tempting prospects, Vermonters ultimately rejected the parkway plan, choosing instead to preserve local control over the mountains. This outcome illustrated Vermonters' complex calculus as they considered the merits of federal projects, as well as their abiding concern about control over Vermont's land and resources, and it signaled a new era in relations with the federal government.[97]

The sudden visibility—if not the sudden presence—of the federal government during the mid-1930s attracted the attention of many Vermonters to the potential impact of federal planning on the state. Forestry officials working in Vermont soon became uneasy about the public reaction to the presence of federal agencies in the state. Forest Supervisor M. A. Mattoon warned the Regional Forester in December 1934, "I am disturbed over the situation that is developing in Vermont. There has been and still is considerable confusion in the minds of the people as to the Government's activities in the state." Mattoon related that in spite of the administrative separation between federal projects, "subsistence farming, rural rehabilitation, elimination of submarginal farm land, purchases for parks, forests, parkways, etc. have been poorly presented to the people by the press and are in a very much jumbled up condition in their minds."[98] The state's newspapers and policymakers frequently painted all federal activity with a broad brush. The U.S. Forest Service was the first agency to discern this change, and in early 1935 District Forester R. M. Evans reported to the regional office: "I am not convinced that there is any great amount of opposition to the National Forest program, but there is opposition to the Wilgus Parkway and to the submarginal land purchase program. All Federal purchases are bracketed together and for the average person, it is difficult to distinguish between the submarginal, Parkway and Forest purchases."[99] The Forest Service sought to counteract the bad press by emphasizing its contributions to towns within the national forest, reminding Vermonters that "the stability and permanency of local communities and local industries . . . are the chief aims and object of the National Forest system." Furthermore, the agency also expanded the transportation network within its boundaries, improving roads and building new routes, and in the process, the long-neglected intermountain roads had found a new patron.[100]

In spite of the Forest Service's best efforts, however, public opinion had begun to turn against all federal projects in the state. In late January 1935, the *Rutland Herald,* which was increasingly hostile to the New Deal and particularly to its conservation plans, reported under the headline "Legislators Start Drive to Block Further Federal Land Acquisition in

State. Called Menace . . . Opponents of Government Plans Say Whole Townships Might be Seized and Turned into National Parks." The article elaborated, with a reference to the National Forest Enabling Act: "Those advocating the repeal of the 1925 Act said . . . they anticipated that the contemplated immediate enlargement of National Forests may be 'only the beginning of an attempt to turn a major portion of the State into a National Park.'" One state representative was quoted as warning that the Enabling Act "would permit the Federal Government to take over nine-tenths of the land in the State," without Vermont having any right to restrict the national government's access to its natural resources.[101] The Enabling Act was subsequently amended to restrict the purchase unit boundaries to the forty-five towns already within its designated boundaries.[102] The 1935 forest legislation also created a Vermont Forest Board, composed of Governor Smith, Lieutenant Governor George D. Aiken, Attorney General Lawrence Jones, Commissioner of Forestry Merrill, and Commissioner of Agriculture E. H. Jones, who were charged with approving the management of the national forest. The revision of the Enabling Act demonstrated Vermont's suspicion that the national forest might preclude private development of mountain recreational areas, and District Forester Evans noted in January 1935 that there was "strong sentiment in Vermont against public ownership of hill farms which lend themselves to purchase by out-of-State people for development as summer homes."[103] Ultimately, much of the state's opposition to federal land purchases came to revolve around its desire to protect future recreational development—presciently, as it later turned out.

BACKLASH

The state's rejection of the Green Mountain Parkway development and increased oversight over the national forest appeared well founded, many townships within the national forest began to believe, as the impact of federal ownership became clear during the mid-1930s. As the Green Mountain National Forest project proceeded, its expansion affected both the state and local governments in unforeseen ways. By 1935, towns within the forest began to realize some of the drawbacks of federal ownership.[104] First, because areas within the forest were subject to federal management, forest fires, thinning, and road construction and maintenance all came under the jurisdiction of the Forest Service, leaving towns without complete autonomy over their territory. Second, and more significant, communities were immediately and materially affected by the loss of property tax revenue once the federal government acquired property within their boundaries. Federal property is not taxable, although in compensation for this loss of revenue the Forest Service paid 25 percent of the receipts from timber sales from within national forest boundaries to the towns. However, this money was not immediately forthcoming—and it depended on the annual harvest—while the Forest Service's allotment of another 10 percent to maintaining roads within the towns also entailed a lag due to planning and design.[105] The reduction in taxes was significant: in 1935 R. M. Evans speculated that the returns to the towns from stumpage could amount to more than 31 cents per acre, he observed that such a return was not an "immediately attainable objective." In reality, between 1934 and 1937 the actual return of funds to towns from forest products sales amounted to only 2.3 cents per acre, a far cry from the revenues that the Forest Service had projected.[106] While the disparity was eventually resolved by federal payments to the towns in lieu of taxes, it took several years for the Forest Service to assess harvestable timber on newly acquired lands, and so towns temporarily lost a significant amount of income.

A strong backlash emerged against further forest purchases, as towns feared the detrimental fiscal impacts of federal land ownership. In early March 1936 trouble developed among the poorer mountain towns within the national forest boundaries as the selectboards of the towns of Danby, Chittenden, Mt. Holly, and Ripton all requested a halt to land acquisition. Slow federal payments and the loss of income from taxes were the primary points of contention.[107] Ripton's experience offers a good example of why town officials blanched at the forest program. Of the town's 25,840 acres, by 1936 the Forest Service had taken options on or purchased more than 15,000 acres, which meant a loss of more than half of the town's taxable land— a considerable threat to the town's already limited liquidity.[108] The town's residents' negative reaction against the national forest stemmed from the fiscal reality: "The most obvious result of Federal activity, as far as the town is concerned, has been a loss of tax revenue." National Forest Supervisor Otto Koenig took a long perspective on the fortunes of Ripton and other towns like it along the crest of the Green Mountains in an internal memorandum. "Ripton is a declining town. . . . Its farmland is of poor quality and there are no existing industries of any kind. I can not help but feel that the town constitutes a problem of land use planning, the solution of which is National Forest ownership of all wild land and National Forest employment of local people in the construction and maintenance of improvements, timber management, and other activities. It may be some time before this solution is attainable, and in the interim some means must be found of offsetting the town's tax loss."[109] This assessment was accurate, but for a few years, Vermont towns suffered the immediate effects of this shift in management strategy. Nevertheless, the continued expansion of the Green Mountain National Forest indicated that Koenig's instincts were largely correct.

As the events of the 1920s and 1930s demonstrate, Vermont policymakers and residents welcomed federal conservation planning when it was adapted to the state's conception of the proper role of government and land management. Yet the state kept a wary eye both on its own natural resources and on its federal partner, forever questioning the wisdom of ceding some control over its future to outsiders. Ultimately, the lessons of the 1920s and 1930s proved to Vermonters the utility of federal funding and expertise, even as it reminded them of the intermediate consequences of land use planning. The development of the Green Mountain National Forest and other federal infrastructure projects spurred a further reckoning during the New Deal that balanced competing visions for the state's future.

The 1935 creation of a board to oversee further expansion of the Green Mountain National Forest and the 1936 Green Mountain Parkway vote represented state-level attempts to retain a local veto over federal initiatives in Vermont. During these same years, Vermont also struggled with both the potential for and the consequences of another large-scale federal initiative: the Resettlement Administration's "Farms to Forest" program for reforming the use of submarginal lands in the state. In each instance, Vermont townships' long tradition of independence and their insistence upon managing local developments stood in sharp contrast to the experience of most other Appalachian communities. In many parts of the state the virtually simultaneous proposals for the Green Mountain

National Forest expansions, the Green Mountain Parkway, and land reform through the Resettlement Administration were perceived as one
overarching New Deal initiative, with the potential danger of a federal
landlord controlling the future of the state. Yet the resettlement project,
which had its roots in Washington, rather than in the initiative of leading
Vermonters, faced a far stronger reaction among the state's policymakers.

CHAPTER SIX

Reforming Submarginal Lands, 1933–1938

DURING THE 1930S, as the creation of new eastern national parks and forests transformed the Appalachian landscape, the action agencies of the New Deal proposed other, even more ambitious plans for reforming land use in the mountains. These federal initiatives moved beyond conservation, aspiring instead to implement the full range of social and economic reforms that land use planners had proposed during the 1910s and 1920s. Ultimately, this vision found its fullest expression in the programs of the Resettlement Administration (RA), which briefly embodied the greatest hopes for improved land utilization that had evolved during the previous decades.

The New Deal's land use planning program sought to revitalize struggling rural areas through systematic planning, by integrating conservation, agricultural reform, and social uplift. While planners' impact on federal policy had been relatively limited until economic crisis convulsed the nation, their influence mushroomed following Roosevelt's election and the integration of academics into the federal bureaucracy during the New Deal. These newly minted officials embraced the opportunity to turn their ideas about conservation and agricultural reform into federal policy; like their counterparts who had pushed for the expansion of federal lands in Appalachia, L. C. Gray explained, they believed that "public action is necessary to make the proper use of the land possible."[1]

The agrarian New Dealers believed that there was a moral and economic imperative to help struggling farm families escape an untenable
position on eroded and exhausted land, and they found an avenue in the
Resettlement Administration. The RA's ambitious vision, and wide view
of the problems of rural America, led it to pursue holistic solutions to
age-old problems. The agency integrated mutually reinforcing programs
in conservation, agricultural adjustment, land reform, social uplift, education, and regional planning. The RA designed its resettlement projects
to help subsidize the move of rural farmers from submarginal lands to
more viable farms. Yet it went further, aspiring to convert "unproductive
lands into economic assets—forests, grazing lands, recreation areas and
wildlife refuges—which for those families who remain in the neighbor-
hood will mean new sources of income and opportunities for work," as
Assistant Administrator L. C. Gray explained.[2]

The RA deployed relief funds to achieve long-term relief and economic stabilization. The RA thus offered a means of fulfilling the planning goals of the agricultural economists and land use planners who had
fought for decades to develop a comprehensive solution to the problem of
poor land use. Its programs were dedicated to counteracting the drain
submarginal lands imposed upon society: "Human suffering and social
decay—these costs are the most serious. But there are also costs in higher
taxes. People who live on unproductive land can pay no taxes. Nevertheless, local authorities must provide schools, roads, and usually some form
of relief for these people." Rationalizing settlement and services appealed
to the economists and sociologists who staffed the agency, representing a
simple and effective step toward better land utilization. An early brochure summed up this approach to problem areas: "The Resettlement
Administration has been established on the theory that it is wasteful and
useless to distribute temporary relief—food and clothing—in such areas
because there is little hope that the people living there will ever be able to
support themselves. It is therefore using the funds which would be
spent for temporary relief over a period of a year or two to buy these
lands and help these people move to good farms." The program thereby
addressed questions that had defied generations of local officials: tax
rates, schools, road maintenance, and relief.[3]

The traditional interpretation of New Deal land policy typically pres-
ents the Resettlement Administration as a failed agency. Some scholars

have acknowledged its expansive potential: Paul Mertz described it as the New Deal's comprehensive rural anti-poverty program, while Grant McConnell called it the "greatest innovation in agricultural policy since the passage of the Homestead Act."[4] Indeed, during its brief existence the RA marked the possibility—albeit unfulfilled—of a holistic reform program within the federal government. As such, it was the culmination of the farsighted vision of the future of American land use articulated during the early twentieth century, and it represented an attempt to promote a sensible model of land use planning as the nation shifted from a predominantly rural to an urban and suburban nation.

A closer look at the achievements and failures of the Resettlement Administration helps to contextualize the larger vision behind the New Deal. The RA embodied— more fully than most other New Deal programs—a range of social, land use, and economic reforms that aspired to reshape the rural American landscape. Moreover, whereas some have argued that the county land use planning program of 1938 was the most significant agrarian program of the 1930s, the RA presaged the ideas of this initiative and it launched itself even more fully into comprehensive land use reform.[5] In the neglected history of this agency we can trace the evolution of a federal blueprint for applying sophisticated ideas about centralized planning to the nation's most challenging landscapes.[6] In limited places the RA achieved the goals that the Tennessee Valley Authority initially designated for its regional plan—and jettisoned in the flurry of political negotiations over electrical generation and flood control.[7]

The history of the 1930s often includes a litany of political fortunes made and broken by the politics of relief. Herbert Hoover's failed bid for reelection in 1932 was an indication of the people's frustration with his hands-off approach to the economic crises convulsing the country.[8] Whereas Hoover's interpretation of federal prerogative limited his willingness to intervene in the national economy, Franklin Roosevelt's economic and social policy actively confronted the economic downturn and the social problems of the depression. The new president seized this opportunity to enact long-considered social and economic reforms. The Roosevelt administration's experimentation during the mid-1930s, born as a reaction to the crisis of the Great Depression, spawned a number of innovative answers

JUS' MINDIN' HIS BUSINESS AND GOIN' ALONG!

Clifford Berryman, "Jus' Mindin' His Business and Goin' Along!" *Washington Star*, March 25, 1933.

to long-standing rural problems. It signaled, moreover, the beginning of a new era in American government. Land use planning in the federal government burgeoned after 1933, and the scope of the New Deal's initiatives, which evolved from the planners' ideas from the 1920s and early 1930s, demonstrates the administration's expansive view of reform.

Various initiatives for federal land use planning emerged almost simultaneously during the first year of the Roosevelt presidency. The new administration's focus on land use reflected both the president's interest in land utilization and the scale of the rural economic crisis. In particular, three national initiatives of the First New Deal integrated plans for land use reform into their rural relief programs. The Agricultural Adjustment Administration (AAA), the most influential New Deal agricultural agency, created a Land Policy Section to coordinate its approach to land use, while the Federal Emergency Relief Administration (FERA) developed two branches to manage land policy, the Land Program and

Rural Rehabilitation Divisions. Meanwhile, the Department of the Interior's Division of Subsistence Homesteads (DSH) began to plan for rural resettlement communities after Congress passed legislation facilitating the relocation of stranded populations into planned rural communities.[9]

These agencies' early programs laid the groundwork for the Resettlement Administration's holistic agenda. The RA concentrated on social and economic uplift for the "lower third," including provisions for education, conservation, and efficient production. It was also one of the most controversial of Roosevelt's programs, drawing the ire of both conservative Southern Democrats and liberal Republicans who reacted with hostility to the expanding federal government during the New Deal. On the local level, the RA's ambitions for wholesale reform of impoverished communities sometimes discomfited those accustomed to fending for themselves. Consequently, the RA's grand national plans for reordering rural land use met with challenges in the mountains of Appalachia that mirrored the larger New Deal nationwide.

BEHIND THE AGRARIAN NEW DEAL

As the experiences of national park and national forest planners in Virginia and Vermont have illustrated, the successes and failures of land use planning in these states were closely tied to each state's history with the federal government. During the mid-1930s, the trajectories of RA projects in the Blue Ridge and Green Mountains were affected by the federal conservation projects already under way. The states' mountain landscapes, which shared ecological, economic, and cultural features, thus became the objects of very different land use planning programs.

In Virginia, federal resettlement and rural rehabilitation programs focused on solving a problem that had been plaguing the Shenandoah National Park project for over a decade: the removal of residents from within the boundaries of the park. By 1934 Virginia and the National Park Service were at an impasse, because they could not agree on how to resolve the disposition of park landowners and squatters. Mountain residents sat in limbo for years while the state and federal governments argued over their fate. Into the breach stepped the Division of Subsistence Homesteads, which designed the Shenandoah Homesteads, a rural community program meant to resettle the poorest mountain people onto fertile valley farms. Ultimately, many of the residents of the Blue

Ridge hollows moved into Subsistence Homesteads communities, although between 1932 and 1938 no fewer than seven state and federal agencies cooperated on this project.

By contrast, in Vermont land use planners focused on converting submarginal lands, taking a programmatic approach to reordering the rural landscape by identifying poor-quality farms that were better suited to other uses. The New Deal land program in Vermont, called "Farms to Forest," proposed to consolidate settlement in the most viable areas of the state, converting submarginal farms to conservation and recreation areas. This project echoed successful local initiatives, and yet state officials rejected it in the turbulent middle years of the 1930s as the scale of federal planning in the state caused them to withdraw their cooperation from new federal initiatives. The failure of this project in Vermont mirrored the growing discomfort with federal planning nationwide, and it signaled the integral importance of local support for federal programs.

Both Virginia and Vermont were perceived as likely sites for the New Deal's planning efforts. Agrarian New Dealers, principally L. C. Gray, M. L. Wilson, Rexford Tugwell, and Henry A. Wallace, saw Appalachia as an ideal location for implementing the multi-faceted conservation agenda that they believed was capable of solving the age-old dilemma posed by submarginal land. These scholar-policymakers shared the vision expressed in an early RA brochure: "We have seen that these barren farms cannot be made to grow crops. But that does not mean that there is no profitable use to which they can be turned. The land on many of these farms . . . can be converted into game preserves or public parks where the general public can camp, hike, fish, and enjoy the out-of-doors." Although the study of land types and analyses of the optimal use of the land were no longer new in the 1930s, the federal government's promotion and sanction of this program was both novel and controversial, as the discussions over the project in Appalachia would reflect.[10]

Conservation and land reform converged during the New Deal as the Agricultural Adjustment Administration, Federal Emergency Relief Administration, and Division of Subsistence Homesteads, and later the Resettlement Administration adapted land utilization and agricultural advancement programs to the Appalachian uplands. In the Green Mountains and the Blue Ridge, federal land use planning took two trajectories: the submarginal land program in Vermont and the rehabilitation of

Ben Shahn, "Years of Dust," Resettlement Administration, 1937. Library of Congress Prints and Photographs Division, LC-USZC4-430.

impoverished farmers through subsistence homesteads in Virginia. The Resettlement Administration motto, "Rescues Victims, Restores Land to Proper Use," was accurate in both states, but each project privileged different aspects of this dualism.

The submarginal lands program was initially proposed for the State of Vermont by the Agricultural Adjustment Administration's Land Policy Section, and it sought to reconfigure the use of "land that, under

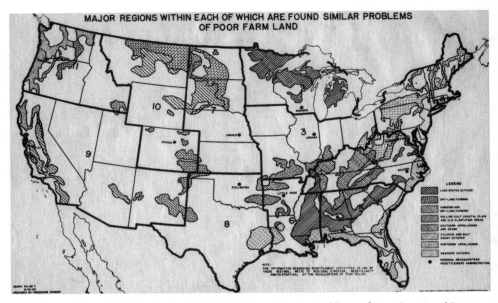

"Major Regions Within Each of Which Are Found Similar Problems of Poor Farm Land,"
Resettlement Administration, 1935. From National Archives and Records Administration, College Park, 83/157/10/ 1.

proper conditions of utilization, it will not pay to cultivate according to the normal standards of return to labor and capital that tend to prevail throughout the competitive field."[11] Federal plans for Vermont sought to remove farmers from poor land and place them on more viable farms, turning unprofitable fields and pastures into managed forests and recreational areas. This program focused primarily on the health of the land.

The second program, intended to create stable agricultural communities, coalesced around subsistence homesteads, which entailed developing small, diversified farms on good land and moving poor farmers into centralized communities where they could benefit from federal assistance and expertise. This program was designed to serve the mountain farmers slated to be evicted from the Shenandoah National Park. In Virginia, the focus was on the people; land, both the territory conserved within the park and those farms improved for production in the valley communities, was secondary in importance.

PLANNING AGENCIES AND THE PEOPLE

In 1933 the federal agencies concerned with land policy merged a long-held vision for improving the land and the people with the funding and expertise for realizing the planners' ambitions. The FERA and the AAA, both created on May 12, 1933, initially coordinated the programs for injecting cash into rural America. Congress tasked these agencies with combating the economic dislocations caused by the Depression, and their planning arms worked to reform land use and improve the rural landscape so that it would be better aligned with the national economy and the continent's natural resources.

Although the AAA primarily targeted production control, in December 1933 it created a land program that focused on the problems associated with inefficient land utilization, the Land Policy Section.[12] This division oversaw conversion of poor farmland to alternate uses, encouraging struggling farm families to try their hand at more suitable land. Administrators reassured farmers that they would profit from this program, which sought to "hasten and render less painful" much-needed rural reorganization. This process simultaneously furthered the acquisition of land for state parks and forests. From the outset, AAA land use planners sought to assist communities by lowering the expenses of town governments, adapting lands to their most productive and beneficial uses, and improving the situation of farm families, all part of the government land utilization program. Yet the unflinching focus of most of the AAA's resources on production control undermined its land policy work, to the frustration of Secretary of Agriculture Henry A. Wallace and Assistant Secretary Rexford Tugwell. In 1934 Wallace described the urgency of pushing the federal land program further, so as to achieve the highest ambitions of land use planning. While praising the early stages of federal land policy, he pushed the agency to move further. Commiserating with the hundreds of thousands of farmers on relief, he argued that they had been "trying to accomplish the impossible, but they didn't know it until their endurance was sapped, and their case made plainly hopeless by the depression." Within the USDA Wallace promoted the rapid implementation of initiatives meant to assist these farmers in attaining a more viable existence.[13]

The early stages of the land planning program in FERA were coordinated by the Surplus Relief Corporation, to which Congress had appropriated twenty-five million dollars to purchase poor land, retire it from farming, and add it to the public domain. This land purchase initiative was designed, as Tugwell described it, as a "temporary and emergency measure, to be replaced in time by a long-time plan for land use which amounts to . . . 'a national re-settlement of America.'" With this reservoir of funds the Surplus Relief Corporation sought to facilitate the "selective retirement of marginal land, not piecemeal, patch by patch, but by whole farms, tracts and areas." Yet the implementation of proposed purchases lagged, in part because of complications in land acquisition.[14] The AAA and FERA sought complementary ends, but they lacked the administrative coordination to operate most effectively.

The AAA Land Policy Section in Vermont laid the groundwork for the Farms to Forest project. The plan for reorganizing the Green Mountain landscape dates to early 1934, when federal officials approached the Vermont legislature with a program designed to withdraw submarginal lands from production and concentrate farms on the most productive and accessible land available. The federal government proposed to assist the state with coordinating the resettlement of families from their farms, intending to convert depleted farmland to recreational and conservation projects. This proposal found common ground with the land use planning already underway in Vermont at the time. The AAA, however, sought to implement a plan both broader and more comprehensive than these local precedents.

In 1934 AAA and FERA planners collaborated on a submarginal lands project in Vermont. Building upon the research conducted for C. F. Clayton and L. J. Peet's 1933 report *Land Utilization as a Basis for Rural Economic Organization* (Bulletin 357), which had been co-sponsored by the BAE, these agencies promoted the establishment of a coordinated state-federal planning program for the Vermont mountains. Governor Stanley Wilson was intrigued by the proposal, and he named a committee to investigate local problem areas for conversion in the summer of 1934. The committee identified several mountainous areas as ideal for purchase under the federal submarginal lands program.[15] The committee outlined six areas for purchase and proposed converting the land to forests, wildlife reserves, and recreational areas. The report described the conditions that made these areas eligible for federal relief funds, and it proposed a purchase program in ten of the thirteen towns Clayton and Peet had analyzed as well as another thirty-six towns with "similar economic and social conditions." The committee emphasized the benefits that would accrue to the state from farmland withdrawal: the converted land would supplement state forest holdings and create new recreation areas, including locations already deemed too expensive for purchase for state parks. Furthermore, it concluded that virtually all affected families could be relocated within their towns, to "well-located, small places and partially-operated well-located farms" outside designated purchase units. This proposal envisioned that the reallocation of land use would permit towns to retain their population and their tax base at the same time that the least productive areas were vacated, much as had occurred at the township level a decade earlier in Sheffield.[16]

Little would be visibly different in these towns, Wilson's committee stressed. The AAA and FERA would oversee a careful reshuffling of land use, with families relocated from the poorest and most outlying farms onto better land. The tangible benefits were many: towns could improve recreational opportunities, ensure a sustainable timber harvest, and operate more efficiently, with fewer roads and schools to maintain and a more concentrated population, while farmers would find their chances for agricultural success improved and the towns would preserve local self-determination and personal investments. Finally, society would benefit from the "economic and social rehabilitation of individual families," with the "consequent strengthening of the entire economic and social organization."[17]

Wilson's committee prepared its proposal amid increasing economic woes, as the cumulative effects of years of economic depression menaced Vermont farmers. Reflecting the zeitgeist of these lean years, Commissioner of Agriculture E. H. Jones began his 1934 annual report by reminding readers: "My report in 1932 opened with these words 'the biennial period just closed has been an extremely trying time for Vermont farmers.'" Yet, "during the period to be covered by this report these conditions have been intensified rather than diminished." As Jones was well positioned to observe, the poor agricultural situation had ramifications throughout the state's economy. It hurt not only farmers and businessmen but also local governments, which suffered defaults on tax payments and an increase in calls for emergency relief. When the AAA requested a more extensive proposal for Vermont land use planning, Wilson's committee selected a preliminary 20,000 acres for retirement, highlighting conditions in the mountains. The proposal observed that there were "practically no modern conveniences" and that some families were "struggling helplessly against the effects of vanishing incomes," in urgent need of relief. With this document, the committee publicized the political, economic, and social potential of this program, identifying areas that were in particular distress and promoting their reorganization. This proposal encouraged the federal purchase of privately owned land, and outlined both the necessary interagency cooperation and a general budget for the project; it also foreshadowed the state's concern about local autonomy with a request for information about future control over recreation and conservation lands.[18]

Subsequent discussions about the future of Vermont's hill towns illustrated both the enthusiasm and the discomfort generated by New Deal relief programs. Governor Wilson approved the commission's report, paving the way for further state action, even as other Vermonters were divided over the plans for submarginal farmlands. As early as 1934, Lieutenant Governor George Aiken and Speaker of the House Ernest Moore had pronounced that the federal purchase of private lands was antithetical to American principles of self-determination, local autonomy, and states' rights. Aiken in particular bristled at the assumption that the mountains around his home were valuable only for timberland and recreational areas. Other Vermonters, including author and public intellectual Dorothy Canfield, Commissioner of Agriculture Jones, and the leaders of the state Grange and Chamber of Commerce actively supported the federal government's goal of turning underproductive farms into forests and parks. Proponents of land use reform embraced the opportunity to ensure a scientifically managed and sustainable timber crop, to protect the soil at high elevations, and to ensure the quality of agriculture in the state. To them, the valuation of these mountain lands depended on how they could best serve the community and the region, rather than on how a change in their use might affect the lives of individual farmers and their communities. Vermonters' discussions of land use planning took place as almost a philosophical exercise, and they considered the benefits and advantages of the federal project with no real urgency. The consequence was a methodical approach to the federal proposal, much like the discussions that took place virtually simultaneously over the Green Mountain Parkway.[19]

Virginians enjoyed no comparable time for thoughtful reflection on the implications of land conversions for the mountain region; federal plans for the creation of the Shenandoah National Park had been under way for a decade by the time the AAA and FERA proposed a resettlement project for the Blue Ridge. Moreover, the park project had already been imperiled by the state's inability to coordinate with the federal government on the disposition of mountain residents. Therefore, a very different scenario unfolded surrounding the New Deal planning proposal for the Shenandoah Homesteads.

In 1925, when Virginia committed itself to acquiring the northern Blue Ridge and turning it into a national park, the National Park Service insisted that the Commonwealth of Virginia coordinate the removal of the residents of the region. Many residents left, buying land elsewhere or moving to new communities, but those who still remained in the mountains in the mid-1930s were virtually stranded, either because they possessed no title to their land, and thus received no money for their farms, or because they owned a small, low-value parcel, and the condemnation award provided insufficient funds to allow them to move to a new farm. Moreover, the new park rules outlawed many traditional means of generating an income, including lumbering and grazing, and mountain families confronted an economic crisis. L. Ferdinand Zerkel, a former realtor who had worked to promote the park for years, elaborated on the financial predicament of the mountain residents in 1930: "With their small land holdings and homes in the area under construction for the Park, these people not only cannot sell their land (as I am in an excellent position to know) but there is no opportunity for them to borrow money against their real estate security—the only actual asset they have as a basis for loans." Local banks refused to loan money when the only security was property located within the park area, and so many people found their hands tied. The mechanisms of land condemnation thus further compounded the effects of the nationwide economic downturn and the regional droughts that had ruined crops in the early 1930s.[20]

In 1934, as Virginia and the National Park Service appeared locked in a stalemate over how to deal with remaining residents, the Division of Subsistence Homesteads stepped into the vacuum, offering money and expertise to resettle mountain residents. The resulting Shenandoah Homesteads designated seven communities in the surrounding valleys to serve the people displaced by the national park. Consequently, and in spite of the Park Service's repeated attempts to separate the federal government from the removal of mountain residents, the Shenandoah National Park project appeared destined to be shaped by the land programs of the New Deal.

The Division of Subsistence Homesteads employed many of the rural sociologists and agricultural economists who moved into government during the early days of the New Deal. These planners found eager allies in politicians from rural states, like Senator John H. Bankhead, Jr. (D-AL), who had long argued that only a back-to-the-land movement could lead to the "restoration of that small yeoman class which has been the backbone of every great civilization." Building upon the ideas of progressive agricultural planners, the subsistence homesteads program sought to help struggling Americans attain self-sufficiency during the darkest days of the Great Depression. Director M. L. Wilson had worked as an extension agent, county agent, and agricultural economist in Montana before moving to pursue a career in Washington. Wilson had spent his career promoting agricultural efficiency and the development of combined agricultural and industrial communities, and he first proposed the idea of subsistence homesteads as early as 1931. As he began his tenure at the Division of Subsistence Homesteads, Wilson envisioned that the program would offer its clients fresh opportunities and a stable form of community, a "locale for a new way of life." Just as the CCC promised to broaden the horizons of the youth of American cities and the AAA offered a new model of agricultural production, projects in agricultural and community development like the Subsistence Homesteads encompassed a new vision for the redevelopment of rural America.[21]

The Division of Subsistence Homesteads launched its programs with an expansive programmatic mandate embodying the various elements of land use planning. Wilson proclaimed: "There are thousands of farm families marooned on eroded and worn-out lands or on lands inherently too poor on which to make a living, trying to carry on a hopeless struggle for existence. . . . Such completely dislocated rural communities must be reorganized and rehabilitated. The poor lands should be put into forests or grass or other vegetative cover and the farm families given a chance to get out of the rural slums onto better lands where they will have an opportunity to become self-supporting and to achieve a decent standard of living."[22] This program faced a number of challenges in its attempt to provide for families, including the reality that prospective residents of the Shenandoah Homesteads hesitated to move into a federal community located outside the mountains.[23]

At the outset, the DSH and FERA's Virginia organization co-sponsored the program for Shenandoah National Park residents. Subsistence Homesteads could not provide for direct relief, yet its guidelines required that families entering the program possessed adequate resources, and so FERA money provided the funding necessary to establish these families on homesteads. In February 1934, during the early stages of planning for the Blue Ridge resettlements, the Shenandoah Homesteads office set out to determine what type of relief residents would require and how their needs could be met most effectively. The resulting enumeration supplemented the localized family survey Miriam Sizer had conducted for the National Park Service in 1932, reconfirming earlier predictions that that there would be significant demand for financial assistance and social programs.[24] Over half of the approximately 550 families who remained in the mountains in 1934 possessed equity in their land that was sufficient for them to relocate. Of those, 200 eventually moved into new homes independently, and another 125 households received enough money from the condemnation payment to make initial payments on new farms. But 225 of the families living in the mountains did not have a legal land claim, and they received no payments from the state to reimburse them for the loss of their homes. Most of these families could not afford to move from the park, and so they remained, dependent on the goodwill of the state and federal governments.[25]

The first step in developing the Shenandoah Homesteads involved selecting land for the new communities; in June 1934 a committee of state and federal officials identified potential sites, evaluating land for its agricultural viability as well as for ease of purchase. The prospective parcels had a history of poor management, yet the committee agreed, "The productivity of this soil can be quickly and cheaply restored by the use of a sound farming program." Improving the fertility of this soil fulfilled one of the central missions of land use planning—to return farmland to its highest potential—and the purchase area contained "some of the best farming land in the Valley and Piedmont sections of Virginia." As throughout the various iterations of the New Deal land program, the planners for the Shenandoah Homesteads endeavored to exchange poor land for good.[26]

Secretary Wallace described New Deal land policy with this larger vision in mind: "Under the leadership of Franklin Roosevelt, the whole land problem has received an emphasis such as it never had before. . . . As President, he soon saw the foolishness of spending millions in public works money to irrigate new land while at the same time, the AAA was taking land out of use."[27] Although a comprehensive plan for land management remained to be developed, Wallace acknowledged the historic failure of the nation's land policy: "In the past, our land policies have often contradicted and cancelled each other. The government had no agency to unify such policies. Both the land and its people have suffered. . . . This year we are really beginning to build on the foundation nobly laid by the forest acquisition policy of Theodore Roosevelt and Gifford Pinchot. The report submitted by the natural resources committee to Congress in January of 1935 will, in all probability, if the Congress and the American people are willing, furnish the blueprint for putting our lands in order."[28] As Wallace foreshadowed, the National Planning Board, a product of the first Hundred Days, encouraged states to establish their own planning boards and conduct conservation and development surveys; it and its successor agencies simultaneously laid a framework for the future of national planning.[29] In spite of the enthusiasm at the federal level, however, and the comprehensive vision that national officials were able to express, land use planning often ran into complications at the local level—as in Vermont and Virginia.

CHALLENGES TO THE FEDERAL VISION

In the early months of the Farms to Forest and Shenandoah Homesteads programs in Vermont and Virginia, the possibilities seemed endless. Throughout 1933 and most of 1934 the major relief and reform programs of the first New Deal were congealing; meanwhile, Congress supported these new government initiatives, and the American public voiced its approval of proactive planning in a landslide congressional victory for the Democrats in November 1934.

The Shenandoah Homesteads confronted a major hurdle, however, in November 1934 when the Department of the Interior's solicitor reviewed the program for resettling rural dwellers and determined that it was inconsistent with the mandate contained in the National Industrial Recovery Act, under which it had been funded.[30] Therefore, in late 1934, the Division of Subsistence Homesteads, which had been the principal architect of the resettlement program, terminated its support for the Shenandoah Homesteads. In the meantime, the status of those families still living in the mountains remained uncertain, and a new stalemate ensued as neither Virginia nor the National Park Service could conceive of a way for the mountain residents to vacate the park on terms acceptable to all parties. For several months in early 1935 it appeared that the project would be abandoned without further institutional support, likely derailing the entire Shenandoah National Park project.[31]

L. Ferdinand Zerkel, the director of the Shenandoah Homesteads, feared that money for the further development of the homesteads would thereafter have to come from the cash-poor and relief-averse Virginia counties, and he anticipated this would doom the project to failure. Zerkel felt keenly the insecurity of the Shenandoah Homesteads projects. His voluminous correspondence with the administrators of the Virginia State Conservation and Development Commission, the Virginia Division of Public Welfare, the National Park Service, and the Federal Emergency Relief Administration chronicles both the energy and the instability of land use planning in the early New Deal.[32] Desperate to find alternate funding for the project, in early April 1935 Zerkel sent a file on the Shenandoah Homesteads program to Secretary of the Interior Harold Ickes. Capitalizing on his history of collaboration with federal officials, Zerkel alluded to his personal ties to the Ickeses, suggesting in his note that if the secretary found the file too time-consuming to peruse, he might pass it along to his wife, "who knows the problem down here from our conversations about these Shenandoah Park Area residents." Zerkel expressed concern for those who had been slated for homes: the Shenandoah Homesteads were a huge undertaking, and the project required unprecedented planning and funding.[33]

In spite of the advocacy of local administrators like Zerkel and his counterpart in Vermont, W. E. Bradder, plans for a seamless land conversion in both Virginia and Vermont faltered in late 1934 and 1935. In Vermont, the ideological conflicts associated with the withdrawal of submarginal lands from production quickly began to emerge among state officials. The first plans for Vermont land conversion were for a recreational project of between 3,000 and 8,000 acres in the lakes region surrounding Lake Bomoseen in central Vermont. The project called for the purchase of lake and pond frontage, budgeting $330,000 to develop fifteen Vermont lakes and ponds for use as public parks. As an incentive for state cooperation, the federal government proposed to put Vermont's unemployed to work building roads and facilities in the parks as part of the work relief program.[34]

In Vermont, as elsewhere, federal officials sought to work with people already in state government to ensure the most effective coordination. During September 1934 the AAA appointed Vermont commissioner of forestry Perry Merrill as the project manager for the state's program. Merrill, one of the members of Wilson's submarginal lands committee, retained his position as Vermont commissioner of forestry and as the state Civilian Conservation Corps director while doing preliminary work with the AAA. In early 1935 Merrill appointed W. E. Bradder, one of his subordinates in the Vermont Forest Service, as the project manager for the AAA (and later the RA), while Merrill continued to serve on the state advisory boards. Bradder inherited a politically sensitive project. In 1934, Vermont elected a new governor, Charles Smith, who took office in January 1935. Under Smith, the land reform was evaluated with increasing rigor, as federal officials, following the recommendations of Wilson's commission, began to develop plans for purchase areas. However, Smith's administration was less receptive than his predecessor's to the submarginal lands program, a reaction partially attributable to George Aiken, a critic of the federal Farms to Forest program, the new lieutenant governor—and a dynamic figure in the new administration.[35]

The submarginal lands debate ultimately framed the argument for Aiken's opposition to the federal government's encroachment on Vermonters' autonomy. Similar in popular and political appeal to Virginia Democrat Harry Flood Byrd, and sharing Byrd's distinctly limited vision of government intervention, by the mid-1930s Aiken had come to dominate the political life of his state. A native of the southeastern town of Dummerston, and born on an upcountry farm, the young Aiken had adapted to the constraints of the land and became a horticulturalist, quickly establishing his reputation as one of the state's foremost experts on trees and plants. Between 1928 and 1938 he ascended from speaker of the General Assembly to lieutenant governor, governor, and U.S. senator, building his political career upon the promise to protect and empower rural Vermont.[36] Aiken argued that Vermonters had demonstrated the intelligence and force of will to survive in the mountains and that they were capable of doing quite well without federal handouts.[37]

The idea of resettling farmers from their family lands did not appeal to politicians like George Aiken, who maintained that Vermont farmers were "healthy and well-nourished, comfortably warm and self-supporting—'statistically bankrupt' . . . but actually solvent." Aiken proposed that the question presented by the submarginal lands program was not whether society could be bettered by transfer of ownership, but rather whether Vermont's cherished spirit of independence and self-sufficiency could be maintained after federal intrusion into its hill towns.[38] Economic arguments provided Aiken with his primary critique of federal purchase under the submarginal lands program: it had the potential to fix land prices at low levels and would, he argued, forever limit the potential for growth in the hill towns. A 1934 state policy document evaluating the costs and benefits of the submarginal land program had also voiced this concern, asking: "Is it not the duty of the state to see that this natural resource of the towns is preserved for its best use, especially so as it may in the future provide the financial salvation of many of our towns?" These arguments raised the question of immediate versus eventual economic security, because it seemed possible to some Vermonters that, by guarding the land resource within the towns, the profits from future recreational development might accrue to Vermonters rather than the distant national government. Building in part on the vision articulated a few years earlier by the authors of *Rural Vermont*, Vermont policymakers entertained hopes for a brighter economic future in the hill towns, particularly after seeing how the work of the CCC camps had added value to the state parks and forests. In the mid-1930s it was still unclear exactly how mountain communities might be developed, but many of the towns that had long caused state planners the greatest concern would later develop into flourishing ski areas and thriving summer resorts; in this case, prosperity was virtually around the corner.[39]

Aiken was typical of many Vermonters in embracing the fiscal conservatism of old-line Yankee Republicanism to argue against many of the social programs of the New Deal. He was skeptical of New Deal relief and construction programs and loath to relinquish local control over the mountains and valleys of Vermont. Pay-as-you-go held wide appeal in Vermont, and Aiken capitalized on Vermonters' ambivalence toward the federal government to encourage them to reject the expansion of federal power. Asking whether "the New Deal . . . and F.D.R. desire to take over the state," Aiken argued that the alienation of mountain lands from local control would inevitably hinder local development—whether in agriculture, summer homes, or some other yet unforeseen type of economic growth. Thus, when he took office in January 1935, the new lieutenant governor's resistance to the submarginal lands purchase program had an increasing influence on other state officials, and a series of subtle challenges to the FERA-AAA program began to emerge.[40]

THE AGE OF RESETTLEMENT: 1935–1937

As the programs of the New Deal matured, the federal officials coordinating emergency relief increasingly reoriented their work away from stopgap measures and toward more systemic reforms. This reflected a new mentality that contributed to the consolidation of rural rehabilitation and land use programs, and it temporarily ensured the survival of both the Shenandoah Homesteads and Farms to Forest programs.

Although the programs begun during the first Hundred Days had been successful in taking away some of the worst pressures of unemployment, the banking crisis, and low crop prices, they did not resolve the economic upheaval in rural America. Yet the return of a modicum of economic stability led conservative Democrats like Virginia's Senator Harry Flood Byrd and Republicans like George D. Aiken to chafe at the continuing proliferation of federal programs and the consequent growth of government. Roosevelt, meanwhile, sought to keep the momentum of his reforms going, and he pushed planning projects to move into new areas of relief and reform, sometimes without congressional sanction. Meanwhile, Congress and the courts began to express their disapproval of the executive branch's expansive vision of the role of the federal government.

In April 1935, President Roosevelt directed that all activities relating to rural resettlement and submarginal lands be reorganized and consolidated into the Resettlement Administration, which would oversee the program for the conservation of human and natural resources. With this action the president sought to end stopgap relief measures and reorient federal policy around long-term planning through rehabilitation and conservation measures. Later, RA Administrator Rexford Tugwell reflected, "We both thought it must surely succeed. . . . It had logic because it brought together agencies complementary to each other. . . . It was necessary because it would stop a disastrous wastage of people and of natural resources. And it seemed sufficiently feasible because the consciousness of the problem was very general and because the funds were available for emergency use."[41] The Resettlement Administration combined the functions of the Division of Subsistence Homesteads, the Land Policy Section of the AAA, and the Land Program and Rural Rehabilitation Divisions of FERA to coordinate all government work serving chronically impoverished farm families. The consolidation of these divisions liberated the agency from the conservative, procedurally minded bureaucrats in the Department of Agriculture who had formerly derailed planning for long-term rural reform. Like other emergency agencies, the RA was thus freed from the precedents in the USDA, and it was allowed to shape its mission to solve the "new and complex problems" of the age.[42] With the creation of the Resettlement Administration, the most progressive rural relief and land reform programs of the day were combined into one agency, which had the potential to be at once more streamlined and efficient. This reorganization also exposed RA programs to greater visibility, and more criticism, especially since it lacked legislative sanction.[43]

The RA was charged with administering rural rehabilitation, providing relief in stricken farm communities, and resettling impoverished rural and urban families at the same time as it coordinated projects to combat soil erosion and stream pollution, and to facilitate reforestation, flood control, and other conservation measures. It added a conservation component to the already innovative rural reform programs of the Division of Subsistence Homesteads and Federal Emergency Relief Administration community projects: as Tugwell described it, a "simultaneous attack on the wastage of people and the inefficient use of resources."[44] L. C. Gray, assistant administrator of the RA, described the agency's mission: "As distinct from that of any other branch of the Federal Government, [it] is to convert misused and unproductive land now largely in farms, to conservational uses as a means of improving the local economy and living standards in rural communities, while retiring from cultivation lands poorly adapted to arable farming."[45]

The Resettlement Administration combined the functions of pre-existing organizations, merging authority over these programs into the new agency over the course of the summer. Within the new RA the Division of Land Utilization was charged with coordinating submarginal land conversions, and the Rural Resettlement Division assumed responsibility for rehabilitation and resettlement projects from the DSH and the FERA community programs.[46] Roosevelt funded the agency out of a discretionary appropriation designated for relief under the Emergency Relief Act of 1935, and this permitted RA administrators to remake once-independent divisions with the benefit of two years of administrative experience; this reorganization facilitated a more coordinated nation-wide planning process. This was a useful evolution, because although the AAA, FERA, and DSH had been cooperating in developing their land programs, they had always been operating under the mandates of different departments. Thus, early in the summer of 1935 the new Resettlement Administration offered both centralized direction and the dynamic leadership of Rexford Tugwell, which seemed to suggest that more uniform and dramatic progress on rural reform and rehabilitation would follow.[47] Tugwell had been a professor of economics at Columbia University and a forceful advocate of economic and agricultural reform, and he collaborated closely with Roosevelt during the 1932 campaign. Beginning in 1933 as undersecretary of agriculture he became intimately involved with formulating the administration's economic and agricultural policy, and took a personal interest in the lower third being served by the RA.[48]

Resettlement officials presented farmers with an explanation of their mission through a series of articles published in the agricultural and popular press, featuring the agency's purpose and its activities. The most lasting aspect of the agency's early outreach was the Historical Division, which housed the famous documentary photographers Walker Evans, Dorothea Lange, and Ben Shahn, and filmmaker Pare Lorentz, among others. Yet the publicity program extended beyond the visual arts and into a robust system for distribution of print material as well. Strategically placed articles and widely disseminated pamphlets highlighted the work of the Land Utilization Division and the Rural Resettlement Division, two branches of the RA that were designed to assist small-scale farmers living on poor land, like the mountain farms of Virginia and Vermont. Throughout its public relations campaign, the RA pledged to improve the condition of "land too poor or too poorly located to earn a living for those who till it." This agenda went beyond removing farmers, however, and the RA maintained that it was committed to finding "a profitable use for this land. It may be forestation, reforestation, wild life preservation, recreation, or something that will serve a twofold purpose; that of getting this land into useful production and preventing waste of human effort on land that cannot make profitable returns on the labor expended." Generally, once the Land Utilization Division had designated an area for withdrawal from production, the Rural Resettlement Division would help interested farmers find new land, or provide technical assistance and loans for farm rehabilitation. A farmer in the rehabilitation program would be assisted in improving his facilities and moderating his debt burden, thereby benefiting from coordinated technical and managerial assistance from the experts in the Resettlement Administration and the state Extension Service. RA publications stressed the desire to work with farmers to improve all aspects of their household economy, and with the states to ensure the most effective allocation of services and planning expertise.[49]

FARMS TO FOREST: RESETTLEMENT REJECTED

In spite of this coordinated publicity program, Vermont's consideration of the proposal to withdraw submarginal farms from production continued to grow more guarded. Whereas in the summer of 1934 the prospect of federal funding to move poor families off failing farms had tempted state officials, by the middle of 1935 they had begun to focus on the drawbacks of such extensive federal involvement in state matters. Vermont policymakers began to focus on leases and usage rights, voicing concerns about losing control over any federally purchased lands.

Unlike Virginia, where the Shenandoah Homesteads program had been retrofitted into a solution for those people who needed to be moved out of the Shenandoah National Park, the Farms to Forest program in Vermont was expected to justify its existence and convince people of its value. As an uncontaminated expression of the vision behind land use planning, it also provided a test case for the ideas embodied in the Resettlement Administration and remained true to the agency's mission: to ameliorate local conditions, rectify the decades-old poverty of disadvantaged American farmers, and strengthen the communities in which they lived.

By the middle of 1935, consultants to the National Resources Planning Board in Vermont prepared a statement encouraging the state to
proceed in land use planning along the lines recommended by *Rural
Vermont* and *Land Utilization as a Basis of Rural Economic Organization.*
The resulting report, "Graphic Survey: A First Step in State Planning,"
recommended:

> *An Adequate Land Program for Vermont and Methods by Which It
> May Be Developed.* . . . There is need for a definite land program
> in Vermont. This program should enable properly qualified
> men to survey, analyze, and prepare a plan of procedure by
> which this State could put its land to maximum use under
> optimum conditions. Two hundred enlightened Vermont
> spokesmen have made a definite plea for proper land utiliza-
> tion. The United States Department of Agriculture, cooperat-
> ing with the University of Vermont, has vitalized the plea by
> making topographic and soil surveys of the State and has
> actually surveyed land-use conditions in Thirteen Hill Towns.
> In continuity of the programs suggested by Vermont, the
> Federal Government has made funds available by which this
> State can actually participate in the realization of its desires as
> regards land use.[50]

The authors of the "Graphic Survey" stressed the continuity in planning
for improved land use in Vermont, highlighting the contribution of state
institutions toward the FERA, AAA, and RA plans in an attempt to encourage support for a comprehensive statewide program of land use
planning.

In April 1935 the Vermont state legislature passed an act giving preliminary approval to the purchase of submarginal lands under the federal Farms to Forest program. It included, like the Green Mountain
National Forest legislation of the month before, the appointment of a
new state board to oversee the program. This board was composed of
Lieutenant Governor George Aiken, Speaker of the House Ernest Moore,
Attorney General Lawrence Jones, and Auditor of Accounts Benjamin
Gates. As Aiken related in *Speaking from Vermont,* "There was a bit of
irony in this legislative action, which made your author chairman of the
board. There was a bit of irony in that the legislators knew that he lived

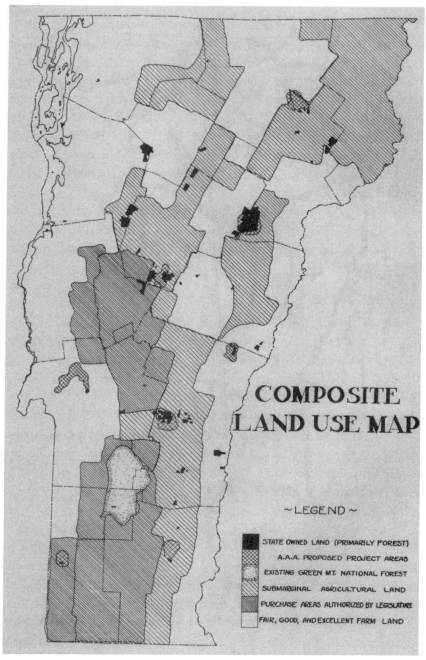

COMPOSITE
LAND USE MAP

~ LEGEND ~

STATE OWNED LAND (PRIMARILY FOREST)
A.A.A. PROPOSED PROJECT AREAS
EXISTING GREEN MT. NATIONAL FOREST
SUBMARGINAL AGRICULTURAL LAND
PURCHASE AREAS AUTHORIZED BY LEGISLATURE
FAIR, GOOD, AND EXCELLENT FARM LAND

"Composite Land Use Map" showing the recommendations for best land use management regimes for Vermont's upcountry land. From the 1935 "Graphic Survey: A First Step in State Planning for Vermont," p. 16. Courtesy of the University of Vermont, Special Collections, Bailey Howe Library.

on a very submarginal farm. There was a bit more irony in . . . making the Speaker of the House a member of the Board, for the legislators knew that the Speaker lived comfortably in an area which was rated as a hundred percent submarginal for twenty miles in all directions from his home." Of course, Aiken made his living as a nurseryman, not as a farmer, and Speaker Moore was a lawyer, but these men's combined political acumen made them a potent force in the state capitol, and they dominated the machinations of the state board on the submarginal lands question.[51]

As part of Vermont's Submarginal Lands Act (Act 3 of 1935), the legislature endeavored to protect the State of Vermont against federal manipulation, directing the submarginal lands board to investigate plans for land transfers to the federal government. The legislation stipulated that the federal government must agree to lease to the State of Vermont "any or all of such real property" that was purchased for use as state forests, parks, game reserves, and game sanctuaries for 999 years at an annual rental of $1. During that 999-year period the state also sought to retain the option to buy the land back from the federal government—at the original purchase price. Moreover, land purchases required approval not only from the submarginal lands board and the governor, but also from the selectmen of the towns in which property was to be purchased. The towns, after all, would lose tax revenues from public ownership of the lands, even as they gained access to new recreation and conservation areas. Unlike the national forests, recreational areas developed by the federal government would not return a profit comparable to timber receipts, meaning a net loss in town property taxes.[52]

The restrictions posed by the state government signaled at best a tenuous cooperation with the federal land use program. The submarginal lands board met on May 7, 1935 with Vermont project manager Bradder to discuss the withdrawal of submarginal lands. Bradder had worked for years to promote the conservation of Vermont's forests, and in this meeting he sought to convince the board of the benefits of conveying submarginal farms to the federal government. He reminded them that other states had already authorized the sale of submarginal lands, much to their satisfaction; moreover, he encouraged them to consider how much the consolidation of settlement could contribute to reducing town expenses and lowering local tax rates. Yet this federal emissary

addressed an unenthusiastic audience; Auditor of Accounts Gates reported that the consensus in the Vermont legislature was that it did not
"want the Government to own all this land." The board then unanimously
agreed that no federal agency should take further options on submarginal
land until the matter of permanent control was resolved to the satisfaction
of state officials. This meeting ended after what must have been a tense
fifteen minutes, in striking contrast to a meeting earlier the same day,
when the Vermont national forest board, composed of the same members, agreed to a 250,000-acre expansion of the purchase area for the
Green Mountain National Forest.[53]

In August, Bradder wrote to Governor Smith describing his growing concern over the future of the submarginal land program in Vermont. He encouraged the governor to send L. C. Gray, the acting director
of the Land Utilization Division of the RA, a telegram "assuring him of
the desire of the people of Vermont for the purchase and development
of lands investigated by his Division and the wholehearted cooperation
of State Officials in aiding the Project." Smith eventually sent the letter,
and yet his support for the submarginal lands project remained tenta-
tive. In spite of the pressure applied by federal officials for a decision to
accept or reject federal funds, Vermonters hesitated to commit to a program to cede local control to federal managers.[54] Federal officials were
sensitive to the political situation in Republican Vermont, and the RA's
regional information officer reported: "We had to be very careful not to
stir up the inherent antagonism of the Vermonters toward any sem-
blance of dictation by . . . Washington, and other such fine points, and I
think we got away with it fairly well. It so happens that we had nothing
to sell. We were . . . merely defining the terms upon which we would
proceed. . . . saying, 'Take it or leave it,' in a nice way."[55] Yet federal officials grew increasingly frustrated by state officials' recalcitrance. There
appeared increasingly little room for negotiation, as one RA employee
noted, once "the state legislature decided it did not want to do business
with us because, as the speaker of the House put it, we were an 'alien
government.' "[56]

By fall, any consensus that had existed between of state and federal
officials about the submarginal lands program had virtually dissolved.
The minutes of an October submarginal lands board meeting illustrate
that the details of any land transfer were increasingly contested. The

board had refused in July to finalize options for purchasing the recreational demonstration area lands near Lake Bomoseen, which disquieted RA administrators. In October Bradder informed the board that unless it cleared options soon, the money appropriated for Vermont would be reallocated to similar projects in New York. Bradder reminded the committee that recreational opportunities in Vermont remained noticeably limited; in 1935 the state government owned land on only two bodies of water in the state. He observed: "Without trespassing or crossing somebody's land the people of the state cannot camp or go bathing or enjoy the advantages of the lakes of Vermont." The RA administrator attempted to push the board toward action, stressing not only the humanitarian benefits of providing public access to the lakes in this region, but also the economic and ecological value of conservation. Bradder explained that the project required only the board's approval to proceed.[57] Submarginal lands board member George Aiken's tongue-in-cheek account of this stage in the negotiations evokes the conflict between the Vermont board and the Resettlement Administration: "The committee then asked upon what terms the land would be turned back to the State. Federal Hands were thrown in the air in horror. Why, the very idea! No other State in the Union had even asked to know upon what terms this land would be returned to them. They all trusted their Uncle Sam. They knew that whatever terms were submitted would, of course, be to the advantage of the States, with Uncle playing the rôle of benefactor. . . . Federal eyes wept with sadness to think that Vermont should even want to know the terms. But the Vermont committee, surrounded by submarginal land which had supported generation after generation, was adamant. We would either know the terms that the Federal government proposed to make in this matter, or there would be no sale."[58]

Shortly thereafter the federal government discontinued work on the Vermont project. Not all Vermonters were pleased with this outcome. Brattleboro newspaper publisher Alfred Heininger editorialized on the rejection of submarginal lands program, exploding: "It cost the people of Vermont the loss of about one and one-half millions of federal money. . . . This attitude seems pinched in the head, atrocious blundering, coagulated stupidity."[59] By late October, the RA had begun to shut down the Rutland office for the Lake Bomoseen project. Meanwhile, leaving Vermonters the possibility of a rapprochement, federal administrators continued to extend their options on surveyed properties wherever possible, hoping to reach an eventual accommodation with the state. Nevertheless, the stage seemed set for an RA defeat, as the responses of state officials to the agency's national and local representatives made clear. Aiken wrote to Speaker of the House Moore with a frank description of his perceptions of the different agencies working in Vermont during the New Deal: "The Forest Service men have been pretty open and above board with us and I believe have constituted a pretty good line of defense against the submarginal outfit. . . . I do think that the Forest Service has more consideration for the welfare of the towns and local industries than the Tugwell crew would ever have." This perception ultimately exercised a significant influence on the fate of land use planning in Vermont.[60] When the Vermont legislature met in a special session in December 1935 it chose not to modify the submarginal lands legislation. The vote of 121 to 108 spoke for itself—there would be no further negotiation with the federal government on the submarginal lands project.[61]

In early 1936 Aiken expressed his opinion on the land use controversy in a letter to the editor in the *Rutland Daily Herald*. The lieutenant governor observed: "With chaotic conditions prevailing in Washington and the probability that many federal projects will be ruled out by the Supreme Court, it appears to me to be a good time for Vermont to sit tight and live within our means. A little later the land utilization program will either be on a sounder basis than at present or will be abandoned."[62] Given the political climate of early 1936, with the recent Supreme Court ruling in *Schechter Poultry Corp. v. United States* overturning the NIRA, and the growing complaints of both Republicans and conservative Democrats in Congress about the sweeping landmark legislation of 1935, it seemed plausible that the action agencies of the New Deal might fade into oblivion.[63] Aiken continued by outlining the conditions he thought should restrict Vermont's collaboration with federal planners: "If, then, we can cooperate with the federal government in the establishment of wild life preserves and recreational areas without sacrificing the rights of the state it will probably be advisable to do so. As for the proposition to put over half the land in the state under federal ownership and to remove the people there from, we should never consent to this."[64] By then, the last chance for federal-state cooperation on withdrawing submarginal lands from production in Vermont failed.[65] Years later, Commissioner of Forestry Merrill lamented Vermont's failure to create a vast public park at no cost to the state, noting that Congress returned possession of all recreational demonstration areas to the states in 1942. Vermont may have lost an opportunity to create new parks and forests in the state, but few state-level politicians voiced any regret for the failed RA recreation program.[66]

SHENANDOAH HOMESTEADS: THE REALITIES OF RESETTLEMENT

The abortive negotiations over the Farms to Forest program in Vermont never reached the level of complexity that accompanied the implementation of the Shenandoah Homesteads project in Virginia. From 1934 to 1938, the challenges of land purchase, site planning and construction, and resettlement consumed the attention of dozens of Subsistence Homesteads, FERA, RA, and later FSA staffers. Reflecting in part the sympathy with which officials in these agencies approached the plight of poor farmers, their project reports portrayed a very different image of the residents of the Blue Ridge than those from other federal agencies. In 1937 the director of the Rural Resettlement Division, John O. Walker, displayed a far greater sensitivity to the needs of the people than his counterpart in the National Park Service, writing, "Despite the economic and social limitations of their lives, these mountain people are capable of much more. . . . They are known for their shrewdness, self-reliance, physical hardiness, and honesty."[67] The progressive optimism of RA officials, coupled with the necessity of providing for stranded park residents, generated ample motivation for this community project.

Ultimately, the Shenandoah Homesteads consisted of seven settlements totaling 6,796 acres, with communities ranging in size from 450 to 1,625 acres: Ida Valley, with twenty families (875 acres); Greene, with sixteen families (575 acres); Madison, with sixteen families (450 acres); Wolftown, with twenty-six families (1,600 acres); Washington, with nineteen families (700 acres); Flint Hill, with forty families (1,625 acres); and Elkton, with thirty-eight families (1,175 acres). Of the 404 families who remained in the park in 1934, 175 were ultimately provided with houses in the Shenandoah Homesteads.[68]

The Shenandoah Homesteads used FERA and RA funds to establish families in the valleys, providing the necessary livestock and tools, as well as land and buildings. Families who moved to the homesteads

possessed only a few basic farm tools and had little experience with market production, so the RA supplied them with almost an entire farm's
worth of equipment. A description of the homesteads from 1938 explained: "Families will be encouraged to adopt a live-at-home plan; that
is, to raise and can the major portion of their own food supply, and keep
enough chickens, hogs and milk cows to serve at least their own needs.
The principal crops will include corn, barley, clover, berries, truck garden crops, cattle, hogs and chickens."[69] Shenandoah Homesteads staff
envisioned that project farmers would engage in a wide range of agricultural activities, and stocked each household with one cow, twenty-five
chickens, and two young pigs, in addition to tools. With these supplies,
and the expert advice of RA staff and their county agents, project farmers
were expected to adapt to the diverse tasks of maintaining a farm. Facilities within the communities were designed according to the RA's standards of efficient housekeeping. The three- to four-room houses were
built of frame construction placed upon a rock foundation, and had water
provided from springs or wells. Farm buildings included a stable, poultry
house, pigsty, and sanitary privy, and each property was surrounded with
fences.[70]

As was the case in other areas of New Deal emergency funding, these
project plans reflected the mandates of different agencies as well as the
political philosophies of individual administrators. In September 1935,
once the RA had assumed responsibility for the Subsistence Homesteads
projects, an administrative order mandated that all houses contain inside
toilets, baths, and electric wiring. By early 1937, however, after the RA
was merged into the Farm Security Administration, however, the standards for these houses changed once again. Partially in response to legislative criticism, led in the U.S. Senate by Virginian Harry Byrd, and in
part because of the expense of experimental building techniques, by the
late 1930s high costs had become a central target of the New Deal community programs. The transfer of the Subsistence Homesteads to the
FSA in 1937 marked a return to more conservative administration. In
that year, expenditures for the construction of houses in the South were
limited to $1,200, which required eliminating luxuries like baths and
indoor plumbing and necessitated the design of smaller and cheaper
buildings.[71] The Shenandoah Homesteads ran considerably above the
FSA guidelines, both before and after retrenchment. Shenandoah

Marion Post Wolcott, *Homes on FSA (Farm Security Administration) project. Ida Valley Farms, Shenandoah Homesteads, near Luray, Virginia,* May 1941. Farm Security Administration, Office of War Information Photograph Collection, Library of Congress. LC-USF34-057543-D

Homesteads properties averaged $6,357 for each of the 172 units, versus the $1,225 originally estimated. Congress and the media were attracted by the stories about the extraordinary cost of these resettlement communities so close to the nation's capital, and these overruns proved a matter of considerable complaint and speculation both in Richmond and in Washington.[72]

The Shenandoah Homesteads received most of its public censure from Senator Byrd, who called the project "a permanent monument to a waste and extravagance such as has never before been known in a civilized country." He decried the inclusion of such luxuries as bathtubs and indoor plumbing, as well as the purchase of furniture for the homes of "simple mountain people." With uncommon hostility for an official describing a program that directly benefited his state, Byrd sharply attacked the Shenandoah Homesteads project as a wasteful example of New Deal mismanagement. His frustration with what he saw as a misappropriation of funds led him to call for congressional inquiries into the expenditures for the Shenandoah Homesteads, and resulted in a lengthy battle with both Secretary of Agriculture Wallace and the Resettlement Administration (and later Farm Security Administration). Although Byrd did not succeed in stopping construction of the communities, his attacks drew media attention to the project and generated negative press for the resettlement program.[73]

Press coverage of resettlement varied considerably. Some articles evoked sympathy for the displaced mountain people, while others, including a 1936 *Washington Post* article written by *Hollow Folk* co-author Thomas Henry, expressed support for the state's attempt to improve the lives of those who had lived in the park. "A year ago the State started clearing them out. The legal process was to condemn their miserable shanties and gardens and pay for them—at the most a few hundred dollars. They had no titles, but the State bent over backwards to be fair. What was to become of them? They had nowhere to go. They could, so far as the law was concerned, have been escorted bodily to the nearest county roads and told to shift for themselves." Henry's article featured the federal government's benevolence, suggesting that the planners' recognition that these farmers "had nowhere to go—no money, no tools, no plans," led the RA to assist in their resettlement. Observing that there was no statutory obligation on the part of either the Commonwealth of Virginia or the National Park Service to recognize the needs or claims of squatters, Henry commended the federal government for generosity toward the mountain residents.[74]

Articles covering Shenandoah Homesteads in the national press included a range of critiques in their coverage. An editorial in the *Baltimore Sun* in June 1936, "Resettlement," challenged the assertion that the mountain people were capable of improving themselves, even with the sustained assistance of the federal government. The *Sun* focused on the impracticality of federal uplift efforts: "There is no law that has kept these people in the mountains for generations," adding that "there is nothing in the record . . . which suggests that any great deal of attention was given to the possibility that . . . the problem might be simply that they had made and would make very little use of chances, however bountiful the outlay of a Government bent on making them over." In this reading, the poor conditions in the mountains were attributable to the inadequacy of the people themselves. The editors criticized the RA's eagerness to offer these people new opportunities, predicting that this project would ultimately be undermined by the inadequacy of the people it sought to serve. By judging that the community programs of the New Deal were misguided in their attempt to integrate marginal citizens into the mainstream of American life, this interpretation also implied that federal relief programs misallocated the precious economic resources of Depression-era governments.[75]

While critical legislators and journalists found ample opportunities to question the design and financing of the homestead communities, the land use planners were consumed with the task of ensuring that the families chosen for homesteading would be able to afford, and eventually own, their new farms. The RA and FSA aimed to smooth the transition to farm management for project families, and took a long view of the accomplishments of homestead families. The first homesteads were rented on an annual basis to FSA clients, which allowed project staff to retain some control over the fate of the Subsistence Homesteads experiment. Eventually, resettled families were expected to attain a greater degree of financial security and the ability to purchase their homes.[76]

Construction on the Shenandoah Homesteads communities had begun in September 1935, and after two years and tens of thousands of dollars in cost overruns, the first families arrived from the park in fall 1937. The Shenandoah National Park superintendent's report for October 1937 heralded the transition for these new residents: "The first families . . . were moved to the new Ida Valley settlement. This marks the beginning of the exodus of the mountain Park residents." Federal workers gradually moved people from the mountains, and all of the families slated for resettlement had moved by the early spring of 1938. The stage was set, therefore, not only for the restoration to forest of the farms these families had once inhabited, but also for the rehabilitation of these farmers and their integration into valley society—in effect, the culmination of the Shenandoah Homesteads had been achieved.[77]

THE PROJECTS END

By the election of 1936 the most activist parts of the agrarian New Deal, including its land utilization programs had become increasingly vulnerable. In the final tally, the RA lacked both the support and the infrastructure to facilitate the considerable transfers of population from submarginal lands. Thus, as occurred in Virginia, the RA's range of influence extended primarily to those areas already disturbed by economic dislocation, among them the Shenandoah National Park, the Lower Mississippi Valley, and the Dust Bowl of the Great Plains. Where the social order remained intact, even in other economically depressed areas of the country, communities showed little interest in larger-scale social planning.[78]

Ultimately, the urgent relief needs of the nation's workers and the economic imperatives for alleviating the fiscal emergency precluded the implementation of the New Deal reformers' largest ambitions. By the end of the 1930s, efforts to promote long-range planning, workers' rights, and social justice all remained incomplete. The most comprehensive reform programs suffered from local conservatism and the divided attention of the federal government during the latter half of the Great Depression.[79]

In places like Vermont, where economic conditions had remained relatively stable, the most vocal local residents concluded that federal intervention in land management was undesirable, believing instead that the state needed to protect its potential for future economic development. The opponents of the Farms to Forest program wanted to retain to eventual profits from the land, and the right to safeguard the priority of private over public management of the land and its resources. Many in the state—like conservatives elsewhere—had also come to fear the dramatic expansion of the federal government under the Roosevelt administration. In Vermont, demand for the relief and infrastructure measures of the New Deal meant that several programs, including the Civilian Conservation Corps and the Rural Electrification Administration, achieved great successes in the Green Mountains. Yet the state's independence simultaneously undercut federal efforts to coordinate large-scale planning by subsuming its territory into a national system of land management. Ultimately, proponents of the submarginal lands program were outgunned by Vermont's political establishment, which used its influence to oppose the RA program.[80]

Vermonters articulated two distinct visions of the future during the mid-1930s. The first, represented by George Aiken, the Green Mountain Club, and a majority of state legislators, endorsed local control and incremental development, and individual initiative instead of government planning. The second, embodied in RA land use planning, proposed federal assistance in reshaping the state's landscape, thus paving the way for a more egalitarian and managed Vermont. Ultimately, federal intervention and the cession of local control that it entailed proved unacceptable to the majority of Vermont policymakers and citizens. Economic assistance helped the state navigate the Depression, and it contributed to preserving the state forests and the Green Mountain National Forest, but its influence was ultimately limited by the alternative vision for the future shared by leading Vermonters. In the end, Vermont emerged from the Great Depression far less altered by federal programs than many other states.[81]

The rejection of New Deal programs, and particularly of the Resettlement Administration's plan for reorganizing the state's agricultural landscape, was not based solely upon ideological opposition to federal ownership of land, as many politicians at the time claimed. Opposition to the submarginal lands program congealed even as other conservation measures, including the work of the CCC and the expansion of the Green Mountain National Forest, enjoyed widespread support in Vermont. The latter programs did not arouse the discomfort of state officials in the same way as the federal land use planning program.

There was more nuance in the acceptance and rejection of federal assistance than Vermont officials were willing, or able, to articulate. First, Vermont agricultural economists, foresters, and town selectboards had been recommending the rearrangement of settlement in mountain townships for decades, often using the same logic as the federal planners who sought to promote alternative land use. Vermont officials had long suggested that only government intervention could ensure economic improvement, and although this idea originated in the townships, it later moved to the state and federal level as the availability of limited resources for conservation became clear. Second, the discomfort with the RA program emerged primarily as a question of intent: the state welcomed federal funds for programs with local antecedents, but the management of the submarginal lands project proved too top-down for state officials to support. And third, the economic development generated by summer homes and skiing had already begun in Vermont by the 1930s, so some Vermonters opted to put their faith in the future expansion of this industry, rather than depend on the federal government. The removal of submarginal farms from private ownership seemed likely to limit the number of properties ideal for purchase by the professors and doctors from the cities who were the primary audience of state promotional publications including *Vermont Farms for Sale* and *Vermont Summer Homes.* As a consequence, Vermonters gambled that the long-term limitations on economic development represented by federal ownership outweighed the immediate gain from land purchases and relief spending by the government.[82]

Meanwhile, in Virginia, the New Deal Subsistence Homesteads program proved integral to the success of the Shenandoah National Park project, which remained a centerpiece of the commonwealth's economic development projects. As a result, the compromises surrounding the land planning programs of the mid-1930s were objectionable to many state officials, yet Virginia did not draft any alternative vision that might have limited federal influence within the Blue Ridge region. The assertive uplift mentality of the DSH, RA, and FSA helped to rehabilitate the reputation of the mountain people in the public perception. By the late 1930s, the denigration that once characterized descriptions of mountain communities had changed to empathy, with newspaper reports focused on the heartbreak of people forced to leave their homes by the federal government. Ultimately, the necessity of dispersing the residents in order to ensure the creation of the Shenandoah National Park drove the Subsistence Homesteads project to completion. In part, because the Shenandoah project focused on serving the needs of the people directly, it promised immediate, tangible consequences; by contrast, the Vermont project aspired to bring order to the mountain landscape, without presenting the shift in land use or the uplift of communities as either urgent or imperative.

The final difference between these planning trajectories is rooted in the political makeup of these two states: in Vermont, with officials closely linked to their neighbors in small political units, community interests were integrated into the process of governing. Meanwhile, Virginia mountain communities hovered at the fringes of large and diverse counties, so the people living in the upcountry were largely excluded from decisions about local politics. In the end, the fate of these communities during the 1930s proved dependent on how well they could argue their case to the federal government. Individual Virginia residents of the Blue Ridge made an admirable case for remaining in their mountain homes, but without the sanction of local political organizations they failed to affect the planning process.

By 1936, the Resettlement Administration had over ten million acres of marginal land under option, including 250 projects in 470 counties nationwide. In mid-1937, as it concluded operations, it reported total expenditures of over $260 million, and it had purchased over nine million acres of land.[83] As small parts of the operations of this action agency, the RA projects in Virginia and Vermont represent two trajectories within New Deal federal planning—one based in the need for practical solutions and the other designed to promote the adjustments in land use endorsed by federal planners.

During the mid-1930s the states were briefly subsumed within the federal orbit, yet as the New Deal dissipated they began to reassert their prerogative over regional affairs. However, the lasting consequences of these land acquisition and community programs were far more enduring than many of the other emergency relief efforts of the era. From the 1930s through the present, Appalachian states and their residents have continued to debate the effects of federal assistance, management, and control on marginal landscapes. In places where state governments accepted federal aid, as in Virginia and Vermont's Green Mountain National Forest, the new, national, mountain commons transformed both the landscape and the people. Where federal aid was refused, as in the Vermont Farms to Forest program, mountain lands continued to be shaped by private interests. The implications of these two models of land management continue to resonate into the twenty-first century. The imprint of the New Deal agenda, with its successes and its failures, remains clearly marked on the Virginia and Vermont landscapes and on the memory of the American people.

Epilogue

CELLARHOLES AND WILDERNESS: THE RETURN OF THE
APPALACHIAN FOREST

THE LEGACY OF EARLY TWENTIETH-CENTURY land use planning left a prominent mark on the Appalachian Mountain landscape—creating vast swaths of public lands "in the very heart of civilized America," as Hubert Work once observed. This prioritization of adjusted land use spurred significant economic and cultural changes, turning a landscape of small subsistence farms and forests into a managed federal landscape. Today, the Appalachian forests are as fully integrated into modern life as the cities a few short hours away—Skyline Drive pulloffs are frequented by both hikers and automobilists checking email, while Vermont's ski areas employ the most cutting-edge ski and snowboard technology. The Appalachian wilderness is indeed a playground, and no longer used much for farming.

It has been a short century since these mountains were still a mystery to many Americans. In the 1910s and 1920s the people of the Blue Ridge and Green Mountains remained on the margins; curiosities for the denizens of the Jazz Age, a living relic of a distant past. Although these regions were never nearly as far removed from modern society as local colorists suggested, they did represent a counterpoint to the quickly urbanizing East, and because of their economic and social marginality they were some of the first American landscapes to be swept up in the nationalizing project of the expanding nation-state.

Land use planning played a central role in altering both the ecology and the political economy of these Appalachian landscapes. Between the efforts of the National Park Service, the U.S. Forest Service, and the Resettlement Administration, the transition from private land to public management was effected with varying degrees of success. It is in large part due to the activism of the federal government that so much valuable forestland remains intact and accessible to tourists and recreationists, protected within an expanded public domain. Ultimately, the policy decisions of the 1920s and 1930s prepared the groundwork for the regeneration of "wilderness" in Appalachia.

The mountains eventually reassumed the appearance of the primeval forest, with large areas that now seem untouched by human culture. Conservationists, who began to call themselves environmentalists, shifted their attention to protecting significant parts of Appalachia as wilderness, in recognition of the mountains' successful rehabilitation to what was seen as their natural state. The planners who had sought to remove marginal farms from the mountains would have found in wilderness designation the fulfillment of their most cherished goals.

Scattered in the thick twenty-first-century Appalachian forest are abundant reminders of the human history of land reform. In Vermont, hikers encounter old cellarholes and the ubiquitous stone wall, even at improbably high elevations in the Green Mountains. Although the stonework carries no sign explaining who once lived there, springtime blossoms among the ancient lilacs and apple trees hint at what was once a hopeful season on those mountain farms. The stories of former residents of the Blue Ridge are better known, due to a rich local sense of history and the resurgence of interest in the people displaced by the Shenandoah National Park. Residual fragments of homesites offer a mute reminder of lives long since past, and the National Park Service coaxes visitors to look for evidence of former habitations, while warning them not to disturb the artifacts that remain.

These tangible reminders of the history of these mountains bear witness to the long history of land use in the mountains, and to the success of the Appalachians' reversion to forest. They testify also to the effects of federal intervention in land management. By the mid-1930s, the ambitions of agricultural economists, conservationists, and rural sociologists for improving land use were culminating in parts of the mountains of Virginia and Vermont. Although the planners' vision was never fully realized either in Appalachia or elsewhere, the conversion of sub-marginal land from farms to forest did result in the creation of a vast protected space in the eastern mountains. As the decades passed, once-cleared parts of the mountains reverted to forest.

As the previous chapters have demonstrated, these land use changes were not inevitable, and beginning in the 1920s federal agencies battled to assert control over their mountain territories. Particularly during the New Deal, social and environmental reforms came together as the fed-eral government aspired to restore the natural landscape and to uplift disadvantaged mountain communities. The Civilian Conservation Corps continued laboring to regenerate the mountain forests into the early 1940s, after the Shenandoah National Park had been dedicated. During its years in the park the corps assisted in moving the neediest families into resettlement communities in the valleys. By 1940 only a few dozen elderly residents remained in the park, where they were allowed to end their days in their Blue Ridge homes.[1] In the meantime, the resettled mountain people had begun to farm new land in the neighboring Shenandoah Homesteads. As rural sociologists had hoped, homestead-ers received advice from the county and home demonstration agents, their children attended county schools, and their standard of living increasingly resembled the national average. In Vermont, the political fallout from the state's rejection of the submarginal lands and the Green Mountain Parkway projects had dissipated by the end of the 1930s, as CCC workers developed recreational facilities in state parks and im-proved forestland in the Green Mountain National Forest. In the mean-time, Vermont's mountain farms continued to be abandoned and the fields returned to forest. Soon, however, the expansion of tourism and the burgeoning ski industry attracted new investment in rural property and led to a slow but steady rural revival.

By 1975 much had changed in the mountains of Virginia and Ver-mont. The National Park Service aggressively managed the Shenandoah National Park, promoting the redevelopment of its forests and wildlife population and cultivating the attractions of the Skyline Drive. Conse-quently, after the park was created, the mountain environment and its flora and fauna were considerably altered, with the reintroduction of large mammals and the planting of tens of thousands of new trees intended to

ꜱeed the return to forest of the small clearings that had once surrounded mountain farms.[2]

In Vermont under the U.S. Forest Service the removal of pre-existing
uses was neither so thorough nor so coordinated. The Green Mountain
National Forest, like others nationwide, has been managed to provide
sustained yields of timber, and it continues to be logged periodically. Furthermore, former landowners retained the right to lease their property
back from the federal government, which led to the continued use of
camps and hunting areas throughout the region. As a consequence, the
imprint of federal management on the national forest closely resembles
that of the surrounding private property—these areas look today much
like those that had once been designated for purchase under the Resettlement Administration. Simultaneously, many privately owned parts of the
Vermont mountains have continued to revert to forest, even as summer
homes and ski areas have expanded across the landscape. Vermonters
remain committed to promoting a strong tourist industry.

The return of the forest has been celebrated as a testament to the
successes of conservation planning. With the passage of the Eastern
Wilderness Areas Act in 1975, the Virginia and Vermont mountains
once again became the focus of a regional debate over the place of the
federal government in regulating land use. Discussions about the implications of this new management regime consumed the communities
surrounding the Shenandoah National Park and the Green Mountain
National Forest, even as sizeable portions of the Appalachian Mountain
chain were designated as federally protected wilderness areas.

Wilderness areas represented a new stage in the protection of the
Appalachian landscape. Because there had been little federal land in the
East before the 1920s, the eastern wilderness areas were remarkable in
that few of them had been federally protected for longer than fifty years.
Therefore, these forests, swamps, rivers, and mountains were still recov-
ering from former uses. Senator Frank Church of Idaho celebrated the
wilderness proposal for the Shenandoah National Park in 1972, pro-
claiming: "One of the great promises of the Wilderness Act [is] that we
can dedicate formerly abused areas where the primeval scene can be restored by natural forces, so that we can have a truly National Wilderness
Preservation System."[3]

The wilderness legislation was triggered by concerns about the over-development of federal lands, and it attempted to establish a balance between the recreational uses favored by car campers and the quest for solitude expressed by people seeking unmechanized leisure. Although environmentalists embraced the Eastern Wilderness Areas Act, critics saw it as unreasonably restricting their use of landscapes that they considered common property. In the Shenandoah National Park, for example, there was considerable backlash against the wilderness designation around Old Rag Mountain, which rises just above Nicholson and Corbin Hollows. Neighbors of the park protested against adding this area to the wilderness preservation system on the grounds that the interests of those who used the park the most, day hikers and local residents, were not served by the legislation. Jim Graves, head of the Madison County Planning Commission and the owner of property abutting the park, observed, "A lot of people feel the government is coming in again and saying this is the way it's going to be and if you don't like it, move out." Expressing a residual hostility against national park policy typical of the area, Graves noted "We've lived here and worked here all our lives and our answer this time is if you don't like the way things are now then go somewhere else." Opponents of the wilderness designation also argued that homes and businesses would be threatened by the exclusion of motorized vehicles, which meant that fire prevention would likely be suspended. Still others argued that a wilderness area would restrict further tourist growth for the counties surrounding the park, areas that had come to rely on tourism and related industries for a significant proportion of their income. As Graves observed, "Backpackers don't buy things."[4]

Ultimately, the Park Service and local critics reached a compromise: fire roads would remain, and the boundaries of the wilderness area would be adjusted to permit the continuation of fire prevention. The Shenandoah Wilderness was designated in 1976, and it now clusters in the areas of the park farthest from the traffic of Skyline Drive, covering 79,699 of the park's 193,538 acres. Similar wilderness areas also cover Vermont's federal lands, including one-quarter of the total acreage within the Green Mountain National Forest. After a 2006 expansion under the New England Wilderness Act, Vermont's acreage in the Wilderness Protection System totaled nearly 101,000 acres.[5]

Meanwhile, Vermonters' concern about the implications of the wilderness designation paled in comparison with contemporary debates over the regulation of private development in the Green Mountains. During the 1950s and 1960s, the growing attractions of Vermont's ski industry had spurred the construction of expansive ski areas in many of the most remote mountain communities—including Waitsfield, Sherburne, Jamaica, and Ripton—areas that during the 1920s had been identified as the most vulnerable to decline. By the late 1960s, ski towns had begun to worry Vermont policymakers. The ecologically vulnerable slopes of the Green Mountains were increasingly turning into densely packed vacation resorts without any long-term vision for future growth. Most immediately, the expansion of new residential developments had begun to threaten public water supplies through soil erosion and the overloading of rural septic systems.[6]

Responding to a groundswell of concern about the growing scale of development and pollution, in 1969 Governor Deane C. Davis tasked a new Commission on Environmental Control with determining the best course of action for preserving the state's rural landscapes. The commission assessed the implications of the lack of oversight and regulation at the township level, acknowledging that Vermont was at a crossroads: "We still have more unspoiled resources than do most parts of the Eastern United States. Once destroyed or lost, these resources may never be retrieved." Recognizing the economic lucre associated with Vermont's tourism industry, it proposed, "Vermont is now enjoying the benefits of a substantial economic development. The function of its government must be to build upon that economic opportunity while making full use of what has been learned from the failures and consequences of unplanned development elsewhere."[7] The commission proposed a new legislative framework for managing land use statewide.[8]

Governor Davis signed Vermont's Land Use and Development Law (commonly known as Act 250) in 1970, stipulating that non-agricultural or forestry-related developments over ten acres in size must meet certain planning and environmental criteria. With this legislation, Vermont stepped in to regulate land use, altering the scale of development in the state. Act 250 propelled Vermont to the forefront of environmental regulation, thus solidifying its reputation as a state committed to managed growth. The long-term impact of this new planning paradigm has slowed the pace of new construction and forced developers to abide by the physical constraints of the area's ecology and local services.[9] This form of environmental regulation was more expansive than any policy proposed during the 1930s, and it represented the continued concern in Vermont with ensuring the viability of vulnerable upcountry areas. Due to Act 250, the uses of Vermont's private mountain lands are in some ways more restricted than those within the neighboring national forests.

Today the Appalachian Mountains are a mixed-use, multiple-regime landscape. After a century of negotiations over the fate of the land and the people, many of the ambitions of state policymakers and federal planners appear to have been achieved. Today the Appalachian Trail through the Shenandoah National Park remains a popular destination for hikers. Harry Flood Byrd, who every year until his death hiked challenging Old Rag Mountain, would be pleased by the easy access to the park—and by the likelihood of encountering dozens of other visitors, many of whom have come from outside the state—in fulfillment of his dream of developing a tourist economy around Virginia's natural areas. Skyline Drive remains a primary attraction, and on many days a long line of cars waits to pay the fee so that they might coast along the mountain ridgeline. The road bisects the long, narrow park, so visitors often happen across wild turkey, black bears, and white-tailed deer along the roadside. These animals, which populate the National Park Service's Blue Ridge museum of nature, provide a thrilling photo opportunity as they share with hikers the effects of fragmented habitat.

To the north, Vermont's Long Trail runs for two hundred and seventy miles along the ridges of the Green Mountains, and it remains largely untouched by road development. Running through private property, ski areas, state forests and parks, and national forests, this path guards the mixed uses that George Aiken sought for the mountains.[10] The range is now covered with a mixture of small and large private holdings, national and state forests, and a variety of forms of recreation. Vermont, like the Shenandoah, has become a playground for the region, and the state has developed a tourist industry that would gratify the state's early boosters. In 1973, 22 percent of Vermont towns received more than a quarter of their annual property taxes from vacation properties, and most of these second homes were clustered in the mountains and the lakes regions, where economic prospects had seemed most dim during the 1920s.[11]

The return of the Appalachian Mountains to forest has occurred under a variety of management regimes, even in the parts of the region that remain in private hands. Nevertheless, the transition from farms to forest that was promoted beginning in the 1920s and 1930s by local, state, and federal officials has been the most important causal force in reordering the mountain landscape, creating a new, largely recreational, forest commons. Federal land use planning led to fundamental changes in the approach of government to private lands, signaling that expert, long-term management provided unprecedented protection for vulnerable landscapes and the people who inhabited them. This awakening within the federal bureaucracy, by extension, spurred the expansion of the American nation-state. The modern administrative boundaries within Appalachia illustrate how completely the land use initiatives of the 1920s and 1930s have altered the region. Today, the mountains are covered with a patchwork of federal, state, and private lands. A new ecology of mixed-use development dominates the region, as roads and wilderness areas, trailers and ski trails, and fast food chains and organic farms cohabit the mountains. Appalachia remains a locus for conflicts over nature protection, outdoor recreation, and economic development in its mountain forests. Although the forms of land use are markedly different from the farms and forests of the early twentieth century, the Appalachian Mountains remain a closely managed landscape, reflecting both the diverse needs of their residents and the greatest ambitions of the nation's land managers, past and present.

NOTES

INTRODUCTION

1. Karl Jacoby, *Crimes Against Nature: Squatters, Poachers, Thieves, and the Hidden History of American Conservation* (Berkeley: University of California Press, 2001); Mark David Spence, *Dispossessing the Wilderness: Indian Removal and the Making of the National Parks* (New York: Oxford University Press, 1999); Louis S. Warren, *The Hunter's Game: Poachers and Conservationists in Twentieth-Century America* (New Haven: Yale University Press, 1997).
2. See, for example, L. C. Gray, ed., *Economic and Social Problems and Conditions in the Southern Appalachians* (Washington: Government Printing Office, 1935); John Gaventa, *Power and Powerlessness: Quiescence and Rebellion in an Appalachian Valley* (Urbana: University of Illinois Press, 1980); Appalachian Land Ownership Task Force, *Who Owns Appalachia?* (Lexington: University Press of Kentucky, 1983); Ronald D. Eller, *Miners, Millhands, and Mountaineers: Industrialization of the Appalachian South, 1880–1930* (Knoxville: University of Tennessee, 1982); Ronald L. Lewis, *Transforming the Appalachian Countryside* (Chapel Hill: University of North Carolina Press, 1998); Paul Salstrom, *Appalachia's Path to Dependency: Rethinking a Region's Economic History, 1730–1940* (Lexington: University Press of Kentucky, 1994); and more recently, Ken Fones-Wolf, *Glass Houses: Industry, Labor, and Political Economy in Appalachia, 1890s–1930s* (Urbana: University of Illinois Press, 2007).
3. James Scott, *Seeing Like a State* (New Haven: Yale University Press, 1998), 2, 5.
4. Andrew E. Nuquist, *Town Government in Vermont* (Burlington: University of Vermont Government Research Center, 1964), 5–6.

5. These data come from the University of Virginia's Historical Census browser, taken from the GeoStat Center website. http://fisher.lib.virginia.edu/collections/stats/histcensus/php/county.php (accessed on 18 February 2008).

CHAPTER 1. A HARVEST OF SCARCITY

1. Mandel Sherman and Thomas R. Henry, *Hollow Folk* (New York: Thomas Y. Crowell, 1933), 1, 209.
2. Sherman and Henry, *Hollow Folk*, dust jacket.
3. Two rail lines crossed the Blue Ridge in this region, the Southern Railroad's Manassas Gap crossing (completed c. 1854) and the Chesapeake and Ohio's line crossing through Rock Fish Gap (the tunnel through the mountain ridge was completed in 1858). Moreover, the Shenandoah branch of the Norfolk and Western Railroad traveled along the mountain range, a few miles west of the Blue Ridge. The closest stations to the mountain ridges, however, were miles distant from the hollow communities. R. Clifford Hall, Forest Examiner, "Report on the Reconnaissance of the Blue Ridge in Virginia Between Simmons and Manassas Gaps," Reservation Evaluation Commission (R. E. C.) Report No. 1, September 1914, pp. 2–3, National Archives and Records Administration, College Park, MD (hereafter abbreviated as NARA), Record Group 79, Entry 10A, Box 25, Folder 11 (hereafter abbreviated as 79/10A/25/11).
4. E. A. Ross, "Pocketed Americans," *The New Republic* 37 (1924), 170, as cited in Rupert Vance, *The Human Geography of the South* (Chapel Hill: University of North Carolina Press, 1932), 242.
5. Work Projects Administration, *Virginia: A Guide to the Old Dominion* (New York: Oxford University Press, 1940), 414–15.
6. Gene Wilhelm, Jr., "Fire Ecology in the Shenandoah National Park," in *Proceedings: Tall Timbers Fire Ecology Conference* (Tallahassee: Tall Timbers Research Station, 1973), 454–55; Donald Edward Davis, *Where There Are Mountains: An Environmental History of the Southern Appalachians* (Athens: University of Georgia Press, 2000), 192. Keever suggests that the chestnut represented 40 percent of the overstory trees in the climax forest. Catherine Keever, "Present Composition of Some Stands of the Former Oak-Chestnut Forest in the Southern Blue Ridge Mountains," *Ecology* 34 (June 1953): 44. Russell cites sources that suggest 50 percent of the rocky ridges in western Maryland were covered by chestnuts, with another 30 percent in red and white oaks, and these figures could translate to the Shenandoah region, because of its proximity to this study area. Emily W. B. Russell, "Pre-blight Distribution of *Castanea dentate* (Marsh.) Borkh." *Bulletin of the Torrey Botanical Club* 114 (1987): 185. Ralph Lutts estimates that a total of 3.5 billion trees were killed by the chestnut blight. Ralph H. Lutts, "Like Manna from God: The American Chestnut Trade in Southwestern Virginia," *Environmental History* 9 (July 2004): 497.
7. Vance, *Human Geography of the South*, 28; Michael Williams, *Americans and Their Forests: A Historical Geography* (New York: Cambridge University Press, 1989), 77.

8. Hall, "Reconnaissance of the Blue Ridge," 3.

9. The forest examiner noted the potential for continued use of the local forest resources: "There is not much timber left on the west slope, but the east slope, which is more inaccessible, contains enough timber to maintain the industry for some years." Hall, "Reconnaissance of the Blue Ridge," 3.

10. Descriptions of the various foods and medicines gathered from the woods abound in accounts of Blue Ridge life and culture. See, for example, Dorothy Noble Smith, *Recollections: The People of the Blue Ridge Remember* (Verona, VA: McClure, 1983), and Ted Olson, *Blue Ridge Folklife* (Jackson: University Press of Mississippi, 1998). Some Appalachian scholars, including Durwood Dunn in *Cades Cove,* have described people's use of the fruits of the forest as "waste and excessive consumption," there is little evidence in the Virginia Blue Ridge of a pattern of devastation of the "seemingly inexhaustible" resources of the mountains. Quotations from Durwood Dunn, *Cades Cove: A Southern Appalachian Community* (Knoxville: University of Tennessee Press, 1988), 34.

11. Stephen Nash, "The Blighted Chestnut," *National Parks* 62 (July–August 1988): 16, as cited in Davis, *Where There Are Mountains,* 194–95; Lutts, "Like Manna from God," 498, 509.

12. Claude Lindsay Yowell, *A History of Madison County* (Strasburg, VA: Shenandoah, 1926), 155, 157.

13. Davis, *Where There Are Mountains,* 197–98; Yowell, *History of Madison County,* 155, 157.

14. Wilhelm, "Fire Ecology," 454–57; Keever, 44, 53.

15. One of the most concise accounts of this self-sufficient economy is found in Mary Beth Pudup, "The Limits of Subsistence: Agriculture and Industry in Central Appalachia," *Agricultural History* 64 (Winter 1990): 61–89.

16. Julia Davis, *The Shenandoah* (New York: Farrar & Rinehart, 1945), 319.

17. Edwin E. White, *Highland Heritage: The Southern Mountains and the Nation* (New York: Friendship Press, 1937), 30.

18. For other accounts of the economy of mountain communities see Elvin Hatch, "Delivering the Goods: Cash, Subsistence Farms, and Identity in a Blue Ridge County in the 1930s," in *Journal of Appalachian Studies* 9 (Spring 2003): 6–48; Paul Salstrom, *Appalachia's Path to Dependency: Rethinking a Region's Economic History, 1730–1940* (Lexington: University Press of Kentucky, 1994); Ronald Eller, *Miners, Millhands, and Mountaineers* (Knoxville: University of Tennessee Press, 1982).

19. Work Projects Administration, *Virginia,* 5.

20. "A self-sufficing farm, according to the census definition, is one from which the value of the products used directly by the farm family is equal to or greater than the value of all the crops, livestock, livestock products, and forest products sold or traded." H. W. Hawthorne, "Farm Organization and Management," in *Economic and Social Problems and Conditions in the Southern Appalachians,* ed. L. C. Gray (Washington: Government Printing Office, 1935), 41. Although some historians dispute the use of the term "self-sufficiency,"

its utility for the social scientists of the 1920s and 1930s makes it desirable for the purposes of this study. For a discussion of the terminology, see Wilma Dunaway, *The First American Frontier* (Chapel Hill: University of North Carolina Press, 1996), 123–24, and Pudup, "Limits of Subsistence," 61–89.

21. Numbers of subsistence farms rose significantly during the 1930s, when the economic upsets of the Great Depression forced millions of Americans to depend on their own agricultural production to feed themselves. Gray, *Economic and Social Problems*, 46. Paul Salstrom puts the number of self-sufficing farms at 166,000 in *Appalachia's Path to Dependency*, 101.

22. "Names of Park Area Families," Shenandoah National Park Archives, Luray, VA (hereafter SNPA), Resource Management Records, box 100, folder 1. There were 2,301 individuals in those 465 families: "Summary Statement concerning Families in the Shenandoah Park Area (B. L. Hummel)—Basis for S.H. and F.E.R.A. Co-operation," SNPA, Resource Management Records, box 99, folder 7.

23. In 1880, an average of 25 percent was cultivated, 20 percent was in pasture, and the remainder comprised forested woodlands. Davis, *Where There Are Mountains*, 179; Gray, *Economic and Social Problems*, 16.

24. Other scholars have demonstrated the correlation between high rates of re-production and the movement of farm families up Appalachian hollows throughout the region. See Dwight B. Billings and Kathleen M. Blee, "Agri-culture and Poverty in the Kentucky Mountains, Beech Creek, 1850–1910," in *Appalachia in the Making*, ed. Mary Beth Pudup, Dwight B. Billings, and Altina L. Walker (Chapel Hill: University of North Carolina Press, 1995), 256–61.

25. See Brian Donahue, *The Great Meadow* (New Haven: Yale University Press, 2004); K. Lockridge, "Land, Population, and the Evolution of New England Society, 1630–1790," *Past and Present* (April 1968): 69; Billings and Blee, "Agriculture and Poverty," 262.

26. Miriam Sizer, "Habitation," in "Final Report," NARA, 79/10A/422/7. Another 1934 population survey determined that 56 percent were engaged as tenants or were squatting on their farms, and thus had no legal equity in the land. "Names of Park Area Families," SNPA, Resource Management Records, box 100, folder 1.

27. Andrew H. Myers, "The Creation of the Shenandoah National Park: Albe-marle County Cultures in Conflict," *Albemarle County History* 51 (1993): 62; Audrey Horning, *In The Shadow of Ragged Mountain* (Luray, VA: Shenandoah National Park Association, 2004), 102.

28. Francis J. Marschner, "Rural Population Density in the Southern Appala-chians," USDA Miscellaneous Publication No. 367 (Washington: Govern-ment Printing Office, 1940), 4–5; H. H. Bennett, "Adjustment of Agriculture to Its Environment," *Annals of the Association of American Geographers* 33 (December 1943): 163–98.

29. Marschner, "Rural Population Density," 18.

30. Gifford Pinchot, *Breaking New Ground* (New York: Harcourt Brace Jovanovich, 1947), 61. For more on Pinchot's attitude toward scientific management and the dangers of private ownership, see Williams, *Americans and Their Forests,* 418–20.
31. Marschner, "Rural Population Density," 4.
32. *Hollow Folk*'s interpretative framework demonstrates its sympathy with the analytical norms of its period and echoes other classics of sociology published during the period, including Florence Danielson and Charles Davenport's 1912 *The Hill Folk,* Robert and Helen Lynd's 1929 *Middletown,* and Caroline Ware's 1935 *Greenwich Village.* These studies attempted to make sense of the American condition through close analysis of discrete communities, and they were inspired in part by the intellectual project of defining American culture and identity.
33. The hollows named in *Hollow Folk* were thinly veiled pseudonyms for some small eastern Blue Ridge mountain communities, which facilitates corroboration of the research. Sherman and Henry, *Hollow Folk,* 4.
34. Late twentieth-century scholars Charles Perdue and Nancy Martin-Perdue, who have closely examined the families displaced in the 1930s by the Shenandoah National Park, are foremost among the critics of *Hollow Folk.* They articulated a common critique: "This book purports to be a work of social scientific scholarship. . . . But the authors were unable to view the mountain people in anything resembling an objective manner and the result is at best insensitive reporting and at worst falsified data." Charles L. Perdue, Jr., and Nancy J. Martin-Perdue, "Appalachian Fables and Facts: A Case Study of the Shenandoah National Park Removals," *Appalachian Journal* (Autumn/Winter 1979–80): 92.
35. Having spent a considerable portion of her career observing the mountain people and teaching in local schools, Sizer was deeply concerned about the fate of the mountain residents. Her interest in the hollow communities, which appears to have exasperated both mountain families and the National Park Service at times, was sustained and sympathetic, although tinged by social-scientific bias. The data sheets gathered for Sizer's report contain innumerable details that complement Sherman and Henry's published work and contribute significantly to the development of a sketch of this subsistence landscape. Many of the stories cited in the NPS data sheets match almost verbatim the anecdotes in *Hollow Folk.* It is, however, unclear whether she submitted to the Park Service her work on the families that had been done for the book, or whether she copied some of the information from one project to the other. Sizer's appointment came about as part of the NPS's effort to lend "voluntary assistance" to the State of Virginia as it sought to accomplish the removal of families from the park. Memo for Mr. Cammerer from Brooks, Chief, Land Division, 22 August 1932, NARA, 79/10A/442/1. Sizer was employed by the NPS as a "collaborator-at-large (special adviser)" from June 3 to August 29, 1932, "for the purpose of conducting a census of the indigent

mountain people residing in SNP and gathering sociological data concerning
them." Letter from J. Atwood Maulding, Chief, Division of Appointments, to
A. M. Jarman, Bureau of Appointments, UVA, 21 April 1938, NARA College
Park, 79/10A/442/3.

36. Sherman and Henry's work examined Corbin, Nicholson, Weakley, and Richards Hollows (listed according to their assessment of the hollows' levels of
cultural sophistication), in an attempt to gauge how distance from roads,
landscape, productivity, and the presence of churches and schools affected
the level of civilization in the isolated communities. Sizer's research for the
National Park Service took a different approach, concentrating instead on the
viability of the communities and on the future prospects for the mountain
families, and she studied the families in Corbin, Nicholson, Weakley, Richards, and Dark Hollows. Sherman and Henry, *Hollow Folk*, 4–9; Miriam
Sizer, Family Data Sheets, Shenandoah National Park Survey, 1932, NARA,
79/10A/442/7.

37. The patterns within the Blue Ridge demonstrate a clear relation between
quality of the land and production, and it is clear that farmers were as responsive to the characteristics of their soils and terrain as they could afford to be.
While there are not adequate data to prove a carefully delineated pattern of
land use, it appears likely that these farmers practiced a form of mixed husbandry similar to that discussed in Brian Donahue's *The Great Meadow* (New
Haven: Yale University Press, 2005).

38. Sizer records, summary, "Taken from three-year report of Washington Child
Research Center, 1928–1931: Mountaineers, by Mandel Sherman," NARA,
79/10A/442/1.

39. U.S. Geological Survey topographic map, Stony Man, Virginia, quadrangle,
published in 1933 from surveys conducted in 1928–29, sheets at the University of Virginia; Sizer survey, Family Data Sheets.

40. According to part of Sizer's records, 35 of 75 families (47 percent) owned only
hilly land. Her classification system is not defined, and it appears that she
accepted the description of the families of the character of their property.
Sizer survey, Family Data Sheets.

41. Hall, "Reconnaissance of the Blue Ridge," 2.

42. Stony Man, Virginia, quadrangle.

43. Margaret Hitch, "Life in a Blue Ridge Hollow," *Journal of Geography* 30
(November 1931): 312.

44. All of the farms in the Madison County hollows had small gardens adjoining
the house, supplemented by an open field of row crops, cultivated each year,
and an outfield, which was periodically rotated, though not fertilized by farm
animals. Livestock was grazed in the surrounding forest. Some of the hollow
farms used terracing to extend the space for crops, and farmers grew their
field crops in strips along the fertile alluvial soils of the streams. Hitch, "Life
in a Blue Ridge Hollow," 314; Gene Wilhelm, Jr., "Folk Settlements in the
Blue Ridge Mountains," *Appalachian Journal* 5 (Winter 1978): 222–23, 226.

45. Smith, *Recollections*, 12; Roy Edwin Thomas, compiler, *Southern Appalachia, 1885–1915* (Jefferson, NC: McFarland, 1991), 39–40; see also another account of diversified food production in central Virginia in Michael M. Gregory, "Exploring 250 Years of Land Use History in Western Virginia: Viewing a Landscape through Artifacts, Documents, and Oral History," in *Culture, Environment, and Conservation in the Appalachian South*, ed. Benita J. Howell (Urbana: University of Illinois Press, 2002), 62.

46. Letters from George Freeman Pollock, 20 November 1930, and Roy Lyman Sexton, MD, 22 December 1930, to WE Carson, 79/10A/444/1. For more information on preserving fruits, vegetables, and meats, see Eliot Wigginton, ed., *The Foxfire Book* (New York: Anchor, 1972); for general information on food in the South, see Sam Bowers Hilliard, *Hog Meat and Hoecake: Food Supply in the Old South, 1840–1860* (Carbondale, IL: Southern Illinois University Press, 1972); Audrey J. Horning, "Beyond the Shenandoah Valley: Interaction, Image, and Identity in the Blue Ridge," in *After the Backcountry: Rural Life in the Great Valley of Virginia, 1800–1900*, ed. Kenneth E. Koons and Warren R. Hofstra (Knoxville: University of Tennessee Press, 2000), 153; White, *Highland Heritage*, 32–33; Smith, *Recollections*, 31.

47. Rupert Vance quoted E. C. Brooks, *The Story of Corn*, p. 134, on the difference between corn and wheat: "A reflective Tennessee pioneer has written: '. . . Corn will produce four times as much as wheat per acre and requires only one tenth of the seed to seed it down and only one third of the time from planting till it can be used as food. Wheat must have prepared soil, and be sown in the fall and watched and guarded for nine months before it is even ready to harvest; whereas a woman can take a 'sang hoe' in April and with a quart of seed plant a patch around a cabin and in six weeks she and the children can begin to eat roasting ears; and when it [sic] gets too hard for that she can parch it. She needs to gather only what she uses for the day, for it will stand all winter, well protected by its waterproof shuck. Not so with wheat. It must be all gathered at once when ripe, and thrashed, cleaned, and garnered. And even then it is hard to get bread out of it without a mill." Vance, *Human Geography of the South*, 415; J. Russell Smith, *North America: Its People and the Resources, Development, and Prospects of the Continent as an Agricultural, Industrial, and Commercial Area* (New York: Harcourt, Brace, 1925), 209, 218; Virginia Lee Warren, "Blue Ridge Families Get a Transfer—From 19th to 20th Century," *Washington Post*, 3 November 1935, NARA, 79/10B/1654/1.

48. Donald E. Davis claimed (without citation) that a family of seven consumed approximately 100 bushels of corn in a year. Davis, *Where There Are Mountains*, 139–40.

49. These agricultural patterns were replicated across the upland South. Open-range herding was a mainstay of the local economies of mountain families in both the Southern Appalachians and the Ozarks. Andrew H. Myers, "The Creation of the Shenandoah National Park: Albemarle County Cultures in Conflict," *Albemarle County History* (1993): 59; Alvin E. Peterson, "Some

Nicholson Hollow Notes," *Bulletin, Potomac Appalachian Trail Club* 23 (July–September): 76; John Solomon Otto and Augustus Marion Burns III, "Traditional Agricultural Practices in the Arkansas Highlands," *Journal of American Folklore* 94 (April–June 1981): 178, 180, 185.

50. Gene Wilhelm, Jr., "Shenandoah Resettlements," *Pioneer America* 14 (1982): 15–17; White, *Highland Heritage*, 6–22; Davis, *Where There Are Mountains*, 99–100; Audrey J. Horning, "Myth, Migration, and Material Culture: Archaeology and the Ulster Influence on Appalachia," *Historical Archaeology* 36 (Winter 2002): 141.

51. Sizer reported that the crop fields were plowed, implying the use of livestock, although the numbers indicate inequitable ownership and there is no evidence that families swapped labor or livestock during planting or harvest season. Among the thirty-two families in Nicholson Hollow, who owned fifteen horses, at least four families owned two horses, while at least six owned no horses. The mules, of course, would have to have been procured from outside the communities, since there were no donkeys listed in the records and mules do not breed. Sizer survey, Family Data Sheets.

52. White, *Highland Heritage*, 61.

53. Gray, *Economic and Social Problems*, 67–68; Sizer survey, Family Data Sheets.

54. Smith, *North America*, 217; see also Mary French Caldwell, "Change Comes to the Appalachian Mountaineer," *Current History* 31 (February 1930): 961–67.

55. "Summary Statement concerning Families in the Shenandoah Park Area (B. L. Hummel)—Basis for S. H. and F. E. R. A. co-operation," SNPA, Resource Management Records, box 99, folder 7.

56. "Names of Park Area Families," p. 1, SNPA, Resource Management Records, box 100, folder 1.

57. L. Ferdinand Zerkel, report, "Survey Data on 465 Shenandoah National Park Families," no date. SNPA, Resource Management Records, box 101, folder 5; L. C. Gray, "Economic Conditions and Tendencies in the Southern Appalachians as Indicated by the Cooperative Survey," *Mountain Life and Work* 9 (July 1933), 9.

58. On the topic of wheat, according to Sizer, "difficulties of harvesting and threshing prevent this crop," instead of other alternatives like the unsuitability of the soil and terrain to sufficient acreages. After a growing season during which relatively little time was devoted to grain crops, harvesting corn was the largest late-summer task on most farms. At harvest time, using the ubiquitous corn knife, the entire family "cut, shucked, and hauled in on slides" the ears of corn. Farmers harvested the small grains like rye, buckwheat, and oats with scythes or cradles, hauled to the barn on slides, and threshed with a hickory flail. All members of the family participated in this phase of the agricultural cycle: children joined their parents in the field, often by the age of seven, working in the fields and orchards, hoeing corn, and picking apples. Sizer, "Work Habits," 56.

59. Farmers throughout Europe and the United States had begun implementing a rotational system of agriculture beginning in the mid-eighteenth century, but the Norfolk system of crop rotation that prescribed planting nitrogen-rich crops after soil-depleting grains apparently went unimplemented in mountain farming. Sizer, "Work Habits," 56; Williams, *Americans and Their Forests*, 60–63.

60. Wilhelm, "Shenandoah Resettlements," 17 Gene Wilhelm, Jr., "Appalachian Isolation: Fact or Fiction," *in An Appalachian Symposium: Essays Written in Honor of Cratis D. Williams*, ed. J. W. Williamson (Boone, NC: Appalachian State University, 1977), 83–85; Sizer survey, Family Data Sheets.

61. In the 1850s, Pollock's father had participated in a speculative copper venture in the mountains and had become a partial owner of a 5,731-acre tract of mountain land that had proven worthless as a mineral investment.

62. George Freeman Pollock, *Skyland (The Eaton Ranch of the East): Situated on High Plateau in the Blue Ridge near Grand Old Stony Man Peak, Overlooking Famous Shenandoah Valley* (Roanoke, VA: The Stone Printing and Mfg. Co., 1920), 8, 10; G. Freeman Pollock, "Why Skyland?" *Potomac Appalachian Trail Club Bulletin* 4 (October 1935): 76–77.

63. George Freeman Pollock, *Skyland: The Heart of the Shenandoah National Park*, ed. Stuart E. Brown, Jr. (n.p.: Chesapeake Book Company, 1960), 88–89, 157.

64. Horning, *In the Shadow of Ragged Mountain*, 72.

65. Eleven families residing in Nicholson Hollow received a cash settlement for their property, and these landowners were paid between $30 and $3,460 by the State of Virginia, for an average of $1,322.55 (Sizer attributed ownership to at least thirteen of the Nicholson Hollow families). Corbin Hollow, in which Sizer counted only one landowner (though four cases of possession right), had eight families who received cash settlements for their land, ranging from $60 to $932, for an average of $570.

66. Hall, "Reconnaissance of the Blue Ridge," 4.

67. Davis, *Where There Are Mountains*, 101, 130.

68. Myers, "Creation of the Shenandoah National Park," 65.

69. Sherman and Henry, *Hollow Folk*, 184.

70. The accounts of George Corbin, a resident of upper Nicholson Hollow, show that he kept three hundred leghorn chickens and sold his eggs to the shopkeeper of the Nethers store each week. Local shopkeepers then sold these eggs, which comprised a significant part of his family's cash earnings, to other farmers or to traveling egg brokers who subsequently transported them to towns and cities within the region. Smith, *Recollections*, 18; Vance, *Human Geography of the South*, 431. On eggs, see interview by Lu Ann Jones with Fredda Davis and Ruby Byers, in Smithsonian Institution, *Oral History of Southern Agriculture*, pp. 12, 13, 74, as cited in Lu Ann Jones, *Mama Learned Us to Work: Farm Women in the New South* (Chapel Hill: University of North Carolina Press, 2002), 72.

71. Peterson, "Some Nicholson Hollow Notes," 78; Pollock, *Skyland* (1960), 67; Smith, *Recollections*, 13.

72. Other scholars have identified the limited purchase patterns of communities on the margins of market agriculture, including Michael Gregory, who in "Exploring 250 Years of Land Use History," p. 66, cites David Bowen, "The Moore/Dunlap Account Book Analysis," manuscript on file, Washington and Lee Anthropology Laboratory, Lexington, Virginia; Hatch, "Delivering the Goods": 6–49; "Menus in three adjoining hollows in late summer when the people have the most plentiful supply of food," in Sherman and Henry, *Hollow Folk*, 45–46.

73. Horning, *In the Shadow of Ragged Mountain*, 29–97.

74. White, *Highland Heritage*, 62.

75. This pattern was widespread in Appalachia. Missionary John M. Moore related that a mountain man once said to him, "You come with your cameras and photograph our worst houses and our lowest people and then throw them on the screens to be seen. You never tell of our good people nor of the substantial things of the community." John M. Moore, *The South Today* (New York: Missionary Education Movement of the United States and Canada, 1916), 132, as quoted in Vance, *Human Geography of the South*, 244. Similarly, Durwood Dunn asserted the same thing about the community known as Chestnut Flats, which during the late nineteenth and early twentieth centuries was the most often discussed of the settlements in the cove. He critiques local color writers, like Robert Lindsay Mason, author of the 1927 *Lure of the Great Smokies*, who depended extensively on the stories of residents of Chestnut Flats for his stories about mountain culture. Dunn, whose family came from a more stable and affluent area of Cades Cove, believed that "by presenting information gathered from only a tiny outcast subcommunity, [Mason] totally distorted the lifestyle and customs of the much larger cove community." Durwood Dunn, *Cades Cove* (Knoxville: University of Tennessee Press, 1988), 195–99.

76. In fact, evidence from the late 1920s suggests that Sherman and Henry's team had a secret agreement to cooperate with the National Park Service from the outset, which suggests another, even less impartial, rationale for their economic survey and the publication of *Hollow Folk*.

77. After the 1.03 inches of rain that fell on June 17 in the Shenandoah Valley the only significant rainfall until August 26 was .43 inches in late July. Compounding the dry weather, temperatures remained in the high 90s and low 100s for forty-three of fifty days in July and August. Fire statistics for 1930, according to Wilhelm, list the total acreage burned in the southern part of the park as 38,810 acres, as per L. Y. Berg and R. B. Moore, "Forest Cover Types of Shenandoah National Park," unpublished report, 1941, SNPA, as cited in Wilhelm, "Fire Ecology," 472, 486; Myers, "Creation of the Shenandoah National Park," 67; Virginia State Climatology Office, "Summer of '30: A Harbinger of 2002?" http://climate.virginia.edu/advisory/advisory.htm (accessed on 22 May 2002).

78. As a result the available labor supply in Virginia in 1930 exceeded demand by 44 percent, in comparison with the more typical 3 percent in 1929. The crop

failures of the nearby valley and piedmont had an effect on the mountain families as well, because some workers traveled seasonally to harvest corn and apples. Virginius Dabney, "Drought in Virginia Worst in 40 Years," *New York Times*, 28 September 1930; Letter from W. E. Carson to Louis C. Cramton, member of the House of Representatives, 31 December 1930, NARA, 79/10A/444/1; Carson to Albright, 3 November 1930, NARA, 79/10A/444/1.

79. Virginius Dabney, "Virginia Farmers Seek More Dry Aid; Commonwealth Suffered More From Drought Than Any Other State," Editorial Correspondence, *New York Times*, 11 January 1931; L. Ferdinand Zerkel to William Carson, 5 December 1930, NARA, 79/10A/445/6.

80. As Zerkel explained, the failure of these crops was particularly hard for the mountaineers, because "canning crops, particularly tomatoes and beans, are their usual best ones, along with the corn that provides meal, feed for stock and some money from the sale of such as is not used by the mountain and foothill farmer." L. Ferdinand Zerkel to William Carson, 5 December 1930, NARA, 79/10A/445/6.

81. Letter from Carson to Cramton, 31 December 1930.

82. The only supplement to the mountain people's meager crops during the difficult winter came from relief work through a federal-aid road law proposed by President Hoover in 1931. This relief legislation is discussed in chapter four. There is an interesting literature on the history of natural disaster relief, including Nan Woodruff, *As Rare as Rain: Federal Relief in the Great Southern Drought of 1930–31* (Chicago: University of Illinois Press, 1985), 145; Michele L. Landis, "Fate, Responsibility, and 'Natural' Disaster Relief: Narrating the American Welfare State," *Law and Society Review* 33 (1999): 257–318.

83. "A School Equalization Fund; Being a Series of Articles Appearing in the *Richmond News Leader,* October 7–10, 1929," The Richmond News Leader Reprints (Richmond: The Richmond News Leader, 1930), 9.

84. However, Estabrook reported that as many people in the Virginia mountains paid income taxes as those across the rest of the state, excepting the cities of Richmond and Norfolk. Vance, *Human Geography of the South,* 245, citing Arthur H. Estabrook, "Is there a Mountain Problem?" *Mountain Life and Work* 4 (April 1928), 5–13.

85. The Virginia constitution of 1901–1902 had instituted a poll tax, which required payment three years in advance of eligibility to vote. This provision had the consequence of eliminating poor whites and blacks from the electorate. Alden Hatch, *The Byrds of Virginia* (New York: Holt, Rinehart & Winston, 1969), 423; Miriam M. Sizer, "A Virginia Mountain School," *Childhood Education* 8 (January 1932): 252–55; Miriam Sizer, "Shenandoah National Park Area, Notes on County Government—Madison County," Sizer Report, NARA, 79/10A/442/1, 67–68.

86. Gladys Baker, *The County Agent* (Chicago: University of Chicago Press, 1939), xiv–xv.

87. Sizer, "Shenandoah National Park Area," 68; Sizer, "County Agents," Final Report, 60, NARA 79/10A/442/1.

88. "The necessity of pleasing the dominant economic and political leaders because of dependence upon county appropriations . . . has resulted in service by the county agent primarily for the more prosperous farmers. The neglect of the 'lower third' of farm people has also been due partially to the indifference as well as to the inability of this class to follow the county agent's advice. Government agents receiving substantial funds and direction from the county government tend to be responsive to the dominant economic and political groups within the county." Baker, *County Agent*, xv–xvi.

89. Sizer, "County Agents," 60.

CHAPTER 2. CUSTOMS IN COMMON

1. Henry C. Taylor, "Introduction," in Vermont Commission on Country Life, *Rural Vermont: A Program for the Future, by Two Hundred Vermonters* (Burlington: Vermont Commission on Country Life, 1931), 2.

2. The population of Vermont only grew from 314,120 in 1850 to 352,428 in 1920. Samuel B. Hand, Jeffrey D. Marshall, and D. Gregory Sanford, " 'Little Republics': The Structure of State Politics in Vermont, 1854–1920," *Vermont History* 53 (Summer 1985): 5–6.

3. Hand, Marshall, and Sanford, " 'Little Republics,' " 5; U.S. Census, "U.S. Population: 1790–1990, Population and Housing Unit Counts," http://www .census.gov/population/censusdata/table-4.pdf (accessed on 4 December 2009).

4. Elbridge Churchill Jacobs, *The Physical Features of Vermont* (Montpelier: Vermont Geological Survey, 1950), 73. Other sources give the width of the mountains as between ten and twenty miles, and as between twenty-five and fifty miles: S. Axel Anderson and Florence M. Woodard, "Agricultural Vermont," *Economic Geography* 8 (January 1932): 14; Thomas C. Vint, Laurie D. Cox, John Nolen, and George Albrecht, *The Green Mountain Parkway: Final Report by the Landscape Architects of the National Park Service,* large bound manuscript, p. 4,University of Vermont Special Collections (hereafter UVMSC), Green Mountain Parkway files.

5. Robert Shalhope uses the terms "uphill" and "downhill" to differentiate between the types of towns, arguing that the cultural differences were influential in the state's political development. Robert Shalhope, *Bennington and the Green Mountain Boys: The Emergence of Liberal Democracy in Vermont, 1760–1850* (Baltimore: Johns Hopkins University Press, 1996). This terminology was appropriated in a book by Paul M. Searls, *Two Vermonts: Geography and Identity, 1865–1910* (Hanover: University of New Hampshire Press, 2006), 10.

6. J. Russell Smith, *North America* (New York: Harcourt, Brace, 1925), 146.

7. "Rough stony land occupies about 20 percent of the area of the state. It is almost entirely in forest and should remain so for it has little or no agricultural value. There are also extensive areas, approximately 20 percent, covered by the stony types of the Berkshire, Becket, Hermon and Hollis groups that

should remain in forest unless there is a far greater demand for pasture than at present." Vermont Commission on Country Life, *Rural Vermont*, 52–56; John Nolen, Philip Shutler, Albert La Fleur, and Dana M. Doten, "Graphic Survey: A First Step in State Planning for Vermont," report submitted to the Vermont State Planning Board and National Resources Board, 1935, p. 7, UVMSC.

8. Charles W. Johnson, *The Nature of Vermont: Introduction and Guide to a New England Environment* (Hanover, NH: University Press of New England, 1980), 35.

9. In 1882, sales from the Burlington lumber market totaled one hundred and seventeen million board feet, which ranked the city third nationally in the volume of lumber sold. Walter H. Crockett, *Vermont: Its Resources and Opportunities* (Rutland, VT: Marble City Press, 1916), 60; Christopher McGrory Klyza and Stephen Trombulak, *The Story of Vermont* (Hanover, NH: Middlebury College Press, 1999), 87–114; Hiram A. Cutting, "The Forests of Vermont," in *Ninth Vermont Agricultural Report of the State Board of Agriculture for the Years 1885–1886* (Montpelier: Vermont Watchman & State Journal Press, 1886): 204–5.

10. E. R. Pember, "Our Hill Farms," *Eighth Vermont Agricultural Report* (Burlington: State Department of Agriculture, 1884), 364, as cited in Harold Fisher Wilson, *The Hill Country of Northern New England: Its Social and Economic History, 1790–1930* (New York: Columbia University Press, 1936), 129.

11. Anderson and Woodard, "Agricultural Vermont," 39; Vermont Commission on Country Life, *Rural Vermont*, 108–9.

12. Smith, *North America*, 149; Clayton and Peet, *Land Utilization*, 25.

13. George F. Wells, "The Status of Rural Vermont," in *Vermont Agricultural Report 1903* (St. Albans, VT: The Cummings Printing Company, 1903), 72.

14. Vermont State Publicity Department and State Department of Agriculture, *Homeseekers' Guide to Vermont Farms* (St. Albans, VT: St. Albans Messenger Company, 1911), 13.

15. Ryden dates the celebration of fall foliage to the period after World War II, when the hardwoods had grown to significant size. "The foliage that people see today when driving on the back roads of northern and western New England appeared only in the twentieth century, the result of at least two waves of forest clearance activity. Even while it represents a flight from history, fall foliage itself is a product of history, the literal outgrowth of an era when New England forests were seen as prosaic resources and not inviolate, timeless icons." Kent C. Ryden, *Landscape with Figures* (Iowa City: University of Iowa Press, 2001), 261–62; Tom Wessels, *Reading the Forested Landscape* (Woodstock, VT: The Countryman Press, 1997), 73–74.

16. Jan Albers, *Hands on the Land: A History of the Vermont Landscape* (Cambridge, MA: MIT Press, 2000), 112.

17. While statewide population increased by almost 30,000 residents between 1850 and 1900, the number of Vermonters who lived in rural towns (population

under 2,000) declined by 64 percent. The numerical decline within towns under 2,000 residents was from 289,472 to 186,991. Wilson, *Hill Country*, 107–8. As a result the median population of a Vermont township dropped from 1,224 residents in 1850 to 935 residents in 1900, a net loss of 290 people and roughly 60 taxpayers. Hand, Marshall, and Sanford, "'Little Republics,'" 6.

18. Herbert Corey, "The Green Mountain State," *National Geographic Magazine* 51 (March 1927): 366–67.

19. J. H. Putnam, "The Depopulation of Rural Districts," *Report of Vermont Board of Agriculture*, 1878, 132.

20. Vermont Commission on Country Life, *Rural Vermont*, 16.

21. Elevations in the towns ranged from approximately 900 feet to over 3,800 feet. C. F. Clayton and L. J. Peet, *Land Utilization as a Basis of Rural Economic Organization: Based on a Study of Land Utilization and Related Problems in 13 Hill Towns of Vermont*, Vermont Agricultural Experiment Station Bulletin 357 (Burlington: Free Press, 1933), 7–8, 11, 23–25; Clayton and Peet, *Land Utilization*, 11.

22. Anderson and Woodard, "Agricultural Vermont," 18, 28; Clayton and Peet, *Land Utilization*, 59.

23. Report of the Vermont Forest Service, "Proposed Northern Extension of National Forest Purchase Unit in Vermont," 1933, p. 6, Green Mountain National Forest headquarters, Rutland Office, history files (hereafter GMNF).

24. Roland B. Greeley, "Part-Time Farming and Recreational Land Use in New England," *Economic Geography* 18 (April 1942): 148.

25. Wilson, *Hill Country*, 226–27; [Elin Anderson], *Selective Migration from Three Rural Vermont Towns and Its Significance*, Fifth Annual Report of the Eugenics Survey of Vermont (Burlington: University of Vermont, 1931), 28.

26. [Anderson], *Selective Migration*, 69–70.

27. Of the land in crops on these farms, 3.7 percent was dedicated to corn for silage, 2.7 percent to potatoes, 2.6 percent to oats cut for hay, 1.9 percent to oats cut for grain, 0.7 percent in garden crops, with another 2.7 percent in other uses. Much like the situation elsewhere in rural America, however, farm families ate a monotonous diet, spare on fresh produce, and the commentary by farm visitors testifies to the disconnect between rural realities and the urban idealization of country living. Journalist Alvan Sanborn wrote in *The Atlantic Monthly* about the beleaguered town of Dickerman, Massachusetts, describing the foodways of the town as representative of its general maladaptation to the regional economy: "The sanitary, not to mention the epicurean possibilities of the meats, vegetables, mushrooms, and fruits within easy reach, either are not known or are ignored." Regarding meat, Sanborn echoed the critiques of other commentators on rural food throughout the nineteenth and early twentieth centuries: "Pork in one form or another is its staple,—'meat' and pork, 'hearty food' and pork, are used as synonyms; and pork is supplemented mainly with hot cream-of-tartar and saleratus biscuit, doughnuts, and pies." This is in contrast to the value placed upon "plain

country fare" by visitors to Vermont, who envisioned an idealized country cuisine characterized by freshness: in dairy products, eggs, vegetables, and fruits, as well as by a diversity of fruits and vegetables. Brown notes: "In reality, visitors hoping for fresh, seasonal simplicity had to contend with the monotonous, high-fat diet of most farmers. Urban reformers recorded with repugnance the endless round of pork, biscuits, doughnuts, and pies the average farmer ate. One writer described her former boarding experience as 'a bad dream,' recalling the 'tough beef,' 'blue milk,' and 'the ubiquitous prune and pie' (that is, dried fruit and dried fruit pie) she had endured." The solution, as the farm press suggested, was that farm families who took in boarders should plan on devoting more attention to the garden, planting a greater variety of fruits and vegetables, and ensuring a constant supply of fresh produce for their guests. Dona Brown, *Inventing New England: Regional Tourism in the Nineteenth Century* (Washington: Smithsonian Institution Press, 1995), 159, 161; Alvan F. Sanborn, "The Future of Rural New England," *The Atlantic Monthly* 80 (July 1897): 75–76; Clayton and Peet, *Land Utilization*, 64, 67.

28. Dorothy Canfield Fisher, "Vermonters," in *Vermont: A Guide to the Green Mountain State*, Written by Workers of the Federal Writers' Project of the Works Progress Administration for the State of Vermont (Boston: Houghton Mifflin, 1937), 7.

29. Report of the Vermont Forest Service, "Proposed Northern Extension," 6. Noteworthy are the tone and language used by those who wrote about the conditions in upcountry Vermont. Unlike the sociologists who studied the Virginia Blue Ridge, these researchers were far more likely to describe their subjects as neighbors and equals, rather than as an inferior "other" as occurred regularly in the Virginia reports. Wilson described the conditions leading to abandonment in the area around Bethel, Vermont, just to the east of Granville, in *Hill Country*, 360–62, 373–74.

30. Some of the most explicit examples are Rollin Lynde Hartt, in "A New England Hill Town I and II," *The Atlantic Monthly* 83 (1899): 561–74 and 712–20; Clarence Deming, "Broken Shadows on the New England Farm," *The Independent* 55 (13 April 1903): 1018–20; and Charles C. Nott, "A Good Farm for Nothing," *The Nation* 49 (1889): 406. More recent scholarly treatments of this literature include Brown, *Inventing New England;* William F. Robinson, *Abandoned New England* (Boston: New York Graphic Society, 1976); and Blake Harrison, *The View from Vermont* (Burlington: University of Vermont Press, 2006).

31. The study was conducted by George Wells, a student at the University of Vermont who wrote his senior essay on the problem of rural Vermont. Wells grew up in Bakersfield, Vermont, in dairy-rich Franklin County. His report was published in the state agricultural report for 1903. Wells, "Status of Rural Vermont," 65–66.

32. Town meetings are the annual gathering held in early March at which the affairs of the town are discussed and a plan and budget approved by all the voters registered in the town.

33. Throughout its history Vermont has had a high rate of land ownership, and in many towns even the poorest farmers often had a degree of economic autonomy. The rate of tenancy in Vermont in 1940 was 9.5 percent, and the rest of the inhabitants were landowners. John D. Black, *The Rural Economy of New England* (Cambridge, MA: Harvard University Press, 1950), 162; Hand, Marshall, and Sanford, " 'Little Republics,' " 5; Klyza and Trombulak, *Story of Vermont*, 92.

34. Other scholars have suggested that road maintenance was a low priority and a local concern in rural communities during the late nineteenth century, and that road reforms were overlooked as a consequence. See Christopher W. Wells, "The Changing Nature of Country Roads: Farmers, Reformers, and the Shifting Uses of Rural Space, 1880–1905," *Agricultural History* 80 (Spring 2006): 146, 150; Wells, "Status of Rural Vermont," 78–81.

35. "Since a tax rate is high because of the large economic needs of the public which they are able to cover and because there is a limited amount of taxable property, such data as given above indicate that the economic status of many rural communities in Vermont is extremely low, while the average status for these towns is below for desirable communities." Wells, "Status of Rural Vermont," 82. As an example of how the tax rate fluctuates in relation to taxable property within a locality, by 1920 the tax rate for Ripton had fallen to $2.00 per $100.00 of property, though in 1940 it had risen again to $2.15 plus $.85 for schools, for a total of $3.00. During this same period, the grand list (one percent of the total value of real and personal property within the town), declined from $3,065.44 to $2,298.36. *Walton's Vermont Register for Farmers, Business and Professional Men, State Year Book with Map and Almanac 1920* (Rutland: The Tuttle Company, 1920), 387; *Vermont Year Book, Walton's Register 1940* (Chester: The National Survey, 1940), 274.

36. Wells, "Status of Rural Vermont,", 156–57.

37. Andrew E. Nuquist and Edith W. Nuquist, *Vermont State Government and Administration* (Burlington: University of Vermont Government Research Center, 1966), 383.

38. For example, in 1934, the town of Jamaica had a grand list of $3,547.38 and a tax rate of 390 cents, for a total tax payment to the state of $13,834.38. Ripton had a grand list of $3,215.79 and a tax rate of 225 cents, and paid $7,235.53. By comparison, the city of Montpelier, the state capital, had a grand list of $81,900.15 and a tax rate of 325 cents, for a total payment of $266,175.49. *Biennial Report of the Commissioner of Taxes of the State of Vermont for the term ending June 30, 1934* (Springfield, VT: Springfield Printing Corp., 1934), 20–23.

39. Clayton and Peet, *Land Utilization*, 102.

40. Genieve Lamson, *A Study of Agricultural Populations in Selected Vermont Towns, 1929–1930* (Burlington: Vermont Commission on Country Life, 1931), 62.

41. In 1930, 67 percent of Vermonters lived in rural areas, but only 31 percent lived and worked on farms (or were farmers first and foremost). Richard

Munson Judd, *The New Deal in Vermont: Its Impact and Aftermath* (New York: Garland, 1979), 8–9, cites *State Planning, Vermont, 1936, Progress Report Submitted to the Vermont State Planning Board and the Natural Resources Committee* (Montpelier, 1936), 29.

42. Putnam, "Depopulation of Rural Districts," 134–35.

43. Putnam, "Depopulation of Rural Districts," 136–37.

44. As noted geographer J. Russell Smith observed in a survey of northern New England in 1925, "The agriculture of the Vermont upland has survived better than that of New Hampshire. The land is richer and the grass is better. Corn is grown on some of the land and is utilized by means of the silo. Root crops must be used at the higher elevation. The city markets to the southward give a good price for milk, and express trains carry the produce of the Green Mountain pastures of Vermont to Boston." Smith, *North America*, 149.

45. E. H. Jones, "Personal Report of the Commissioner of Agriculture," in *Agriculture of Vermont: Seventeenth Biennial Report of the Commissioner of Agriculture of the State of Vermont, 1933–1934* (Montpelier, 1934), 6.

46. Robert McCullough, *The Landscape of Community: A History of Communal Forests in New England* (Hanover, NH: University Press of New England, 1995), 116–17.

47. Nuquist and Nuquist, *Vermont State Government and Administration*, 341.

48. Governor Urban M. Woodbury, "1894 State of the State Address," as cited in John Aubrey Douglass, "Prospective for a National Forest: Economic Influences on Vermont's Efforts to Manage Forest Resources," *Vermont History* 54 (Spring 1986): 73.

49. Ultimately, the first significant acquisition for the Green Mountain National Forest came from the Hapgood Estate. Marshall J. Hapgood, in *The Vermonter*, (November 1907), as cited in Arthur F. Stone, *The Vermont of Today: With Its Historic Background, Attractions and People* (New York: Lewis Historical Publishing Company, 1929), 327.

50. McCullough, *Landscape of Community*, 118; Douglass, "Prospective for a National Forest," 76.

51. The first state forester was Austin Hawes, appointed in 1909. Stone, *Vermont of Today*, 329; Perry H. Merrill, *The Making of a Forester: An Autobiographical History* (Montpelier: Perry H. Merrill, 1984), 50.

52. "State Forests and Their Value to Vermont," *Green Mountain State Forest News*, v. 2, n. 3 (March 1926): 5; Stone, *Vermont of Today*, 332; Merrill, *Making of a Forester*, 126.

53. Nancy Gallagher, *Breeding Better Vermonters* (Hanover, NH: University Press of New England, 1999), 48, citing Wilson, *Hill Country*, 346–80.

54. Clayton and Peet, *Land Utilization*, 36.

55. "Jamaica" and "Ripton" in *Walton's Vermont Register* (Rutland, VT: The Tuttle Company, 1926), 183–84, 267–68.

56. Samuel Damon, "Ripton," in *Vermont Quarterly Gazetteer, A Historical Magazine, Embracing a Digest of the History of Each Town, Civil, Educational, Religious,*

Geological and Literary, ed. Abby Maria Hemenway (Boston: Press of Geo. C. Rand & Avery, 1860), 86.

57. "Ripton" in *Walton's Vermont Register and Farmer's Almanac for 1880* (Rutland, VT: H. A. Sawyer & Co., 1880), 137.

58. "Ripton" in *Walton's Vermont Register, For Farmers, Business & Professional Men, State Year Book with Map and Almanac, 1920* (Rutland, VT: The Tuttle Company, 1920), 387.

59. "Ripton" in *Walton's Register—1940* (Chester, VT: The National Survey, 1940), 274.

60. "Ripton," in *Walton's Register, 1871*, and *Walton's Register, 1924*. 1850 estimate from the Vermont Department of Forests, Parks and Recreation, cited in Klyza and Trombulak, *Story of Vermont*, 92–93; Clayton and Peet, *Land Utilization*, 13–14, 19.

61. [Anderson], *Selective Migration*, 7.

62. Worksheets on Jamaica, in [Anderson], *Selective Migration*.

63. The town's population appeared to be in decline, as the proportion of residents over the age of fifty in Jamaica was 29.8 percent, whereas the average in Vermont was 22.5 percent, and in the United States as a whole it was 15.3 percent. [Anderson], *Selective Migration*, 61, 70.

64. Gallagher, *Breeding Better Vermonters*, 98–104, 114–15.

65. The ESV was a principal sponsor of "An act for human betterment by voluntary sterilization," Vermont's sterilization law, which was signed by Governor John Weeks on 1 April 1931. Kevin Dann, *Lewis Creek Lost and Found* (Hanover, NH: Middlebury College Press, 2001), 201.

66. Foreword to the manuscript finding aid, Vermont Public Records Office, Middlesex, VT, Box PAA-22, p.2. The research of the VCCL was ultimately funded by the Social Science Research Council and the Laura Spelman Rockefeller Memorial Fund. Henry F. Perkins, "The Comprehensive Survey of Rural Vermont," in *New England's Prospect: 1933*, Special Publication of the American Geographical Society, n. 16, ed. John K. Wright (New York: American Geographical Society, 1933), 207; Gallagher, *Breeding Better Vermonters*, 92.

67. It is worth noting, considering the considerable disfavor eugenic thought currently enjoys, just how intertwined the two projects were. The 1928 report of the ESV included plans for future studies, including community studies, a survey of demographic change, and a before-and-after analysis of an area affected by the 1927 flood. As *Rural Vermont* described: "In all of its work since the beginning of the comprehensive survey by the Vermont Commission on Country Life the Eugenics Survey has operated as an integral part of that Commission. Its detailed findings have been published in the form of annual reports and its main conclusions are embodied in the present volume." Vermont Commission on Country Life, *Rural Vermont*, 11; Gallagher, *Breeding Better Vermonters*, 87; Kevin Dann, "From Degeneration to Regeneration: The Eugenics Survey of Vermont, 1925–1936," in *Vermont History* 59 (Winter 1991): 14.

68. A review of the book commented: "It speaks well for 'Vermont conservatism' that two hundred representative Vermonters can subject their state to such candid self-analysis as is revealed in 'Rural Vermont' and with so little of the booster spirit creeping in." Review of *Rural Vermont* in *Geographical Review* 22 (July 1932): 504.

69. Editor's note, in Perkins, "Comprehensive Survey of Rural Vermont," 206.

70. "Henry C. Taylor," obituary in *American Journal of Agricultural Economics* 51 (August 1969): 732–33.

71. Vermont Commission on Country Life, *Rural Vermont*, 4.

72. Taylor's mentor at the University of Wisconsin, Richard T. Ely, described his own political beliefs as "progressive conservatism," which was certainly an influence on Taylor's phrasing of this description. See Gilbert and Baker, 290. Henry C. Taylor, "The Vermont Commission on Country Life," *Journal of Farm Economics* 11 (January 1930): 164–65.

73. Editor's note, in Perkins, "Comprehensive Survey of Rural Vermont," 206.

74. Taylor, "Vermont Commission," 168.

75. Although Anderson was listed as the principal field worker, and although she was described as the primary author of the report, the publication does not credit her as the author. This is consistent with other ESV reports, and other historians have noted that the ESV rarely credited its researchers with their work; see, for example, Dann, "From Degeneration to Regeneration," 12, n. 19. Quotation from [Anderson], *Selective Migration*, v.

76. Anderson had obtained a master's degree from the New York School of Social Work before the ESV hired her as its principal field worker in 1929. Gallagher, *Breeding Better Vermonters*, 111.

77. Tellingly, this attitude did not translate into *Rural Vermont*'s chapter on "The People" that was derived from this study. See Vermont Commission on Country Life, *Rural Vermont*, 30–32; [Anderson], *Selective Migration*, 13–14.

78. [Anderson], *Selective Migration*, 42, 58, 77; Gallagher, *Breeding Better Vermonters*, 110.

79. [Anderson], *Selective Migration*, 78.

80. Taylor, "Vermont Commission on Country Life," 168.

81. "Annual Report of the Director to the Executive Committee of the Vermont Commission on Country Life for the fiscal year July 1, 1928 to June 30, 1929," 7, Reference folder, "Vermont Commission on Country Life," UVMSC.

82. Bulletin 357 was based upon data collected in 1929, before the culmination of the economic slowdowns of the Great Depression. Like *Hollow Folk*, these data were compiled in the late 1920s, and the report was published in 1933, just in time for those charged with designing the programming of the New Deal to take notice. The thirteen towns Bulletin 357 studied extensively were, moving south, Fayston, Warren, Roxbury, Granville, Ripton, Goshen, Pittsfield, Stockbridge, Sherburne, Shrewsbury, Plymouth, Mount Holly, and Wardsboro. Vermont Commission on Country Life, *Rural Vermont*, 142. Clayton was an agricultural economist within the BAE Division of Land Economics, and in 1935

the co-editor of the important study of the Southern Appalachians *Economic and Social Problems and Conditions of the Southern Appalachians* with L. C. Gray, the director of the Division of Land Economics. Peet was a graduate student at the University of Vermont, with a 1930 dissertation entitled "Problems of land utilization in the hill towns of Vermont based on a study of thirteen towns in 1929." Peet was employed by the Vermont Agricultural Experiment Station, but by 1933 he had joined the BAE Division of Land Economics as well. Clayton later worked for the Resettlement Administration.

83. The total acreage of the 87 towns was 1,719,524, and that of the 13 towns that were studied intensively was 343,370 acres. Clayton and Peet, *Land Utilization*, 6, 45.

84. Clayton and Peet, *Land Utilization*, 5, 15, 21, 31, 33; Vermont Commission on Country Life, *Rural Vermont*, 144.

85. Forest cover was 77.2 percent. Klyza and Trombulak, *Story of Vermont*, 89, 93; Clayton and Peet, *Land Utilization*, 13.

86. See, for example, an account of the impact of summer tourism in the Department of Agriculture's *Report on Summer Travel for 1894* (Montpelier: Watchman Publishing Company Press, 1894); Brown, *Inventing New England*, 155; Nuquist and Nuquist, *Vermont State Government and Administration*, 507; Deborah Pickman Clifford and Nicholas R. Clifford, *"The Troubled Roar of the Waters": Vermont in Flood and Recovery, 1927–1931* (Hanover, NH: University Press of New Hampshire, 2007), 164.

87. The 1891 *Vermont, Its Resources and Attractions, With a List of Desirable Homes for Sale,* was the first publication by the State Board of Agriculture to target potential landowners, and it was followed by many other publications promoting farms and homes for sale. The names of publications within this series varied, with titles including *Good Homes in Vermont, A List of Desirable Farms for Sale* (Montpelier: Watchman Publishing Co., 1893); *Vermont: Its Fertile Farms and Summer Homes* (Montpelier: Watchman Publishing Co., 1895); *Vermont, Its Opportunities for Investment in Agriculture, Manufacture, Minerals, Its Attractions for Summer Homes* (Board of Agriculture, 1903); *Beautiful Vermont, Unsurpassed as a residence or a playground, For the Summer Resident, The Summer Visitor, The Tourist, The Capitalist and the Workingman* (State Board of Agriculture, 1907); *Homeseeker's Guide to Vermont Farms* (St. Albans: St. Albans Messenger Co., 1911); *Vermont Farms: Some Facts and Figures Concerning the Agricultural Resources and Opportunities of the Green Mountain State* (Essex Junction: Vermont Bureau of Publicity, n.d.); Vermont Bureau of Publicity, *Vermont Farms and Residential Properties for Sale* (Montpelier: Capital City Press, 1916); Vermont Bureau of Publicity, *Summer Homes in Vermont, Cottage Sites and Farms For Sale* (Montpelier: Capital City Press, 1917, 1920, 1923, 1929); Vermont Bureau of Publicity, *Vermont Farms and Summer Homes for Sale* (St. Albans: The Messenger Press, 1929, 1931, 1932, 1934, 1942, 1943); Dorothy Canfield, *Vermont Summer Homes* (Montpelier: Vermont Bureau of Publicity, 1932). For a period around the turn of the century, Vermont rail-

roads published their own guides to Vermont, including the Central Vermont's *Summer Homes among the Green Hills*. In 1927 the Summer Homes in Vermont Corporation published *Your Summer Home in Vermont* (New York: Summer Homes in Vermont Corporation, 1927), which had a similar format to the state publications but appears to have been produced by a different organization, oriented around customer service: "For those who seek country life we furnish the last word in summer homes service. Scattered throughout the State, over a hundred representatives of ours are glad to show our properties and give the home seeker the benefit of their intimate knowledge of surroundings and property values in their respective localities."

88. Crockett, *Vermont,* 108.

89. Crockett, *Vermont,* 100–101.

90. This Committee, unlike most of the others involved with the VCCL, had paid field workers who produced studies on the potential for development in Vermont. Only the Committee for the Human Factor, the Committee on the Care of the Handicapped, and the Committee on Summer Residents and Tourists benefited from non-volunteer labor. Dann, "From Degeneration to Regeneration," 19, 22; Vermont Commission on Country Life, *Rural Vermont,* 2, 130.

91. Clayton and Peet, *Land Utilization,* 50–51.

92. Vermont Commission on Country Life, *Rural Vermont,* 118, 133.

93. This tactic was borrowed from the 1917 *Summer Homes in Vermont,* which had claimed: "Cottage sites may be purchased at a very small price and often a lot may be purchased and a bungalow built for the price of a comparatively cheap automobile." "Address of Governor Stanley C. Wilson of Vermont on Summer Homes in Vermont," broadcast from Station WBZ, Boston, 25 April 1931, *Radio Address of Governor Stanley C. Wilson* (Montpelier: Vermont Bureau of Publicity, 1931), 6. Vermont Bureau of Publicity, *Summer Homes in Vermont: Cottage Sites and Farms for Sale* (Essex Junction: Office of the Secretary of State, 1917), 3.

94. Stone, *Vermont of Today,* 878, quoted from Mortimer R. Proctor and Roderic M. Olzendam, "The Green Mountain Tour" (1917).

95. [Anderson], *Selective Migration,* 8.

96. Warren E. Booker, ed., *Historical Notes, Jamaica, Windham County, Vermont* (Brattleboro: E. L. Hildreth & Company, 1940), 152–53.

97. Anderson continued along a eugenic track: "There is lacking in the environment the stimulus that is necessary to bringing out the best inherent capacities of the citizens and to encouraging the children to greater effort. In the words of a critical newcomer, 'The people seem to be dormant.' This suggests deterioration, and is, in consequence, a challenge to the State to pursue a line of action, for the sake of its future welfare, that will prevent deterioration from taking place in the quality of the stock of the citizens yet to be born in such of its rural communities." [Anderson], *Selective Migration,* 74–75.

98. "Towns Suggested for Study—Information About Towns: Cornwall, Waitsfield, Jamaica," ESV Papers, as cited in Gallagher, *Breeding Better Vermonters*, 111.

99. The Nearings later fled from Jamaica, as the ski industry boomed at the nearby Stratton Mountain resort, disgusted with the transformation of this once-bucolic town into a seasonal resort for outdoor enthusiasts.

100. L. P. S. (from a newspaper advertisement), "Hill Farms," frontispiece to *Vermont Farms and Summer Homes for Sale, 1931* (St. Albans: The Messenger Press, 1931).

101. Vermont Commission on Country Life, *Rural Vermont*, 147.

102. Wells, "Status of Rural Vermont,", 91.

103. Vermont Publicity Service, *Industrial Vermont: The Mineral, Manufacturing, and Water Power Resources of the Green Mountain State* (Montpelier: Capital City Press, 1914), 48.

104. Smith, *North America*, 153.

105. Clayton and Peet, *Land Utilization*, 5–6.

CHAPTER 3. ACADEMICS AND PARTISANS

1. Historians have recently begun to correct this oversight. See Neil Maher, *Nature's New Deal* (New York: Oxford University Press, 2008); Sarah T. Phillips, *This Land, This Nation* (New York: Cambridge University Press, 2007); and Paul Sutter, *Driven Wild* (Seattle: University of Washington Press, 2002).

2. Hal Barron, *Mixed Harvest: The Second Great Transformation in the Rural North, 1870–1930* (Chapel Hill: University of North Carolina Press, 1997), 8, 19.

3. Arthur M. Hyde, "The Past Year in Agriculture," in *Yearbook of Agriculture, 1931* (Washington, DC: Government Printing Office, 1931), 38.

4. Historians have acknowledged the influence of ecology on the programs of the 1930s, particularly thanks to Donald Worster's pathbreaking history of ecological thinking, *Nature's Economy: A History of Ecological Ideas* (New York: Cambridge University Press, 1977). The literature on land use planning has been less familiar to historians, although Richard Kirkendall's *Social Scientists and Farm Politics in the Age of Roosevelt* (Columbia: University of Missouri Press, 1966) and Sidney Baldwin's *Poverty and Politics: The Rise and Decline of the Farm Security Administration* (Chapel Hill: University of North Carolina Press, 1968) both address this genre of scholarship, as does Ben Minteer's *The Landscape of Reform: Civic Pragmatism and Environmental Thought in America* (Cambridge, MA: MIT Press, 2006).

5. Nevertheless, historians tend to overlook the history of these conservation initiatives. Donald Worster suggested in *Dust Bowl:* "In the thirties . . . the conspicuous need was for agricultural conservation. The new task involved safeguarding, with public power, privately owned and privately worked land. It demanded, according to the planners, fresh thinking about traditional property rights of the individual where they threatened the community's

welfare. Among the goals of this new agricultural conservation were removing excess and marginal acreage from crop production, preventing soil erosion through improved agronomic practices, rural zoning and other
grassroots regulatory action, solving chronic farm poverty, and bringing the
science of ecology into resource management." Donald Worster, *Dust Bowl:
The Great Plains in the 1930s* (New York: Oxford University Press, 1979), 186.
Sarah Phillips repeated the oversight: "For the first time, national administrators linked conservation with agricultural programs, and considered environmental planning vital to the nation's economic renewal and long-term
vitality." Phillips, *This Land, This Nation,* 3. Others, however, like Ben Minteer
in *Landscape of Reform,* have acknowledged the complex thinking about conservation and regional planning during the 1910s and 1920s.

6. See Samuel Hays, *Conservation and the Gospel of Efficiency* (1959; revised ed.,
Pittsburgh: University of Pittsburgh Press, 1999); Louis Warren, *The Hunter's
Game: Poachers and Conservationists in Twentieth-Century America* (New Haven:
Yale University Press, 1997); Karl Jacoby, *Crimes Against Nature* (Berkeley:
University of California Press, 2001); Barron, *Mixed Harvest;* Jack Temple
Kirby, *Rural Worlds Lost* (Baton Rouge: Louisiana State University Press, 1987).

7. Hays, *Conservation and the Gospel of Efficiency,* 69, 127.

8. Roosevelt, in *Conservation* (January 1909), 15, 5, as quoted in Hays, *Conservation and the Gospel of Efficiency,* 130.

9. Hays, *Conservation and the Gospel of Efficiency,* 271.

10. Neil Maher suggests that the broadening of conservation to include soils as
well as parks was new during the CCC era, but in reality these ideas had
cross-fertilized long before the 1930s. Maher, *Nature's New Deal,* 75.

11. The Country Life Movement has received abundant scholarly attention, re-
cently in a slew of journal articles that foreshadow additional monographs.
See Minteer, *Landscape of Reform;* Scott Peters, "'Every Farmer Should be
Awakened': Liberty Hyde Bailey's Vision of Agricultural Extension Work,"
Agricultural History 80 (Spring 2006): 190–219; and William L. Bowers, *The
Country Life Movement in America* (Port Washington, NY: Kennikat Press,
1974).

12. Liberty Hyde Bailey, *The Country Life Movement in the United States* (New
York: MacMillan, 1911).

13. A number of studies of the National Park Service offer a significant literature
on the mentality behind the park program, particularly Richard West Sellers,
Preserving Nature in the National Parks (New Haven: Yale University Press,
1998) and Horace Albright's memoirs, with Marian Albright Schenck, *Creating the National Park Service: The Missing Years* (Norman: University of Okla-
homa Press, 1999) and, with Robert Cahn, *The Birth of the National Park
Service: The Founding Years* (Salt Lake City: Howe Bros., 1985). Mark David
Spence's *Dispossessing the Wilderness* (New York: Oxford University Press,
1999) places into context the removal of Native Americans from the western
parks under the auspices of the National Park Service, as Daniel Pierce's *The

Great Smokies (Knoxville: University of Tennessee Press, 2000) does for another group of southern mountaineers.

14. Glenn Frank, quoted in George D. Pratt, "Land Utilization and Conservation," in *Proceedings of the National Conference on Land Utilization*, Chicago, IL, November 19–21, 1931, called by the Secretary of Agriculture and the Executive Committee of the Association of Land-Grant Colleges and Universities (Washington, DC: Government Printing Office, 1932), 84.

15. A cadre of national figures promoted the creation of a national park service, and they oversaw drafting and promotion of the 1916 Organic Act. National parks advocate Frederick Law Olmsted, Jr., wrote the critical paragraph of the enabling act, which has been the source of inspiration for ninety years of debates over the meaning and purpose of the national park system. Albright and Schenck, *Creating the National Park Service*, 145.

16. Stephen Mather, *Annual Report of the National Park Service, Fiscal Year Ended June 30, 1925* (Washington, DC: Government Printing Office, 1925), 2; National Park Service, *The National Parks: Shaping the System* (Washington, DC: U.S. Department of the Interior, 2005), 18–19, 26–27.

17. Sellers, *Preserving Nature*, 68; Albright and Cahn, *Birth of the National Park Service*, 83–84, 189; John Ise, *Our National Park Policy: A Critical History* (Baltimore: Johns Hopkins University Press, 1961), 268.

18. Committee on Public Lands, "Report to accompany H. R. 11980," 68th Congress, 2d Session, Report No. 1320, 29 January 1925, 2.

19. Hubert Work, Secretary of the Interior, speech at Richmond, Virginia, 31 January 1928, NARA, 79/10A/440/4; Stuart Chase, *Rich Land, Poor Land* (New York: Whittlesey House, 1936), 326.

20. A few months later, the president "gave organized form to the enthusiasm for regaining contact with the outdoors," by calling for a National Conference on Outdoor Recreation. Coolidge declared: "The physical vigor, moral strength, and clean simplicity of mind of the American people can be immeasurably furthered by the properly developed opportunities for life in the open. . . . From such life much of the American spirit of freedom springs." Roderick Nash, *Wilderness and the American Mind* (New Haven: Yale University Press, 1957, 1982), 190.

21. As a consequence, the area of national parks and monuments was extended by almost three million acres, more than 40 percent, during Hoover's four years in office. Work, speech at Richmond, Virginia, pp. 1–2; Herbert Hoover, *The Memoirs of Herbert Hoover, 1920–1933* (New York: Macmillan, 1952), 241.

22. Michael Williams, *Americans and Their Forests: A Historical Geography* (New York: Cambridge University Press, 1989), 410–14; Donald Pisani, "Forests and Conservation, 1865–1890," *JAH* 72 (September 1985): 340–59.

23. A precedent for government acquisition of private lands for forest and watershed protection had been established in 1885 when the New York State legislature created the Adirondack Forest Preserve. Gerald W. Williams, "Private Property to Public Property: The Beginnings of the National Forests in the

South," paper prepared for the 2003 American Society for Environmental History conference, Providence, RI, 5; Richard Ely and George Wehrwein, *Land Economics* (New York: Macmillan, 1940), 305; Williams, *Americans and Their Forests*, 406–7.

24. "A Forest Reserve for New England," *Harper's Weekly* (February 13, 1904), 228–29.

25. William W. Ashe was later a secretary of the National Forest Reservation Commission, which after 1911 surveyed and approved purchase units for the national forest system. H. B. Ayres and W. W. Ashe, *The Southern Appalachian Forests,* U.S. Geological Survey Professional Paper No. 37 (Washington, DC: Government Printing Office, 1905), 21; Donald Edward Davis, *Where There Are Mountains* (Athens: University of Georgia Press, 2000), 168; Biography of W. W. Ashe, University of North Carolina Herbarium, http://www.herbarium.unc.edu/Collectors/ashe.htm (accessed on 11 March 2008).

26. Kirby, *Rural Worlds Lost*, 478.

27. Williams, *Americans and Their Forests*, 308, 450.

28. As W. W. Ashe observed, "It essentially restricted the location of forests to rough or mountainous regions where the maintenance of forest growth and the building up of a blanket of absorbent humus and leaf litter beneath the trees would be of value in maintaining the regulation of stream flow." W. W. Ashe, "A National Forest for Vermont," *The Vermonter* 36 (March 1931): 74; Hays, *Conservation and the Gospel of Efficiency,* 32, 48, 205.

29. The Weeks Act also created the National Forest Reservation Commission, which was authorized to recommend lands for purchase as national forest units and set prices for their acquisition. Williams, "Private Property to Public Property," 4–6, 21.

30. Williams, *Americans and Their Forests*, 446–47. See also Gerald Williams, *The USDA Forest Service—The First Century* (Washington, DC: USDA Forest Service, 2000), 37–39. Robert McCullough, *The Landscape of Community* (Hanover, NH: University Press of New England, 1995).

31. William W. Ashe, "The Creation of the Eastern National Forests," *American Forestry* 28 (September 1922): 521; Davis, *Where There Are Mountains,* 173, 205.

32. Ely and Wehrwein, *Land Economics,* 344.

33. This competition began well before the famed 1930s rivalry between Secretary of the Interior Harold Ickes and Secretary of Agriculture Henry Wallace over a federal Department of Conservation. Wallace aid Paul Appleby described the dispute between Ickes and Wallace as rooted in a philosophical dispute over the nature of conservation as in a jurisdictional conflict over power and resources: "a perfectly sincere quarrel based quite simply on two different preoccupations—both functional. Ickes saw land in terms of 'conservation' as a base value around which to organize; Wallace saw 'resource use' as the base value. . . . Agriculture would have said that the problem was to make land *users* take sufficient account of conservation needs; Ickes would

have said that conservation came first and use second." Letter from Paul H. Appleby to William E. Leuchtenburg, 30 August 1950, as cited in William E. Leuchtenburg, *The FDR Years: On Roosevelt and His Legacy* (New York: Columbia University Press, 1995), 168.

34. Henry A. Wallace, "A Personal Report on the National Forests," *Science* 82 (August 1935): 194.

35. According to Stuart Chase, by 1935 an estimated twenty million people visited the recreational facilities of the U.S. Forest Service system, and the national parks had four million visitors. Chase, *Rich Land, Poor Land*, 314, 326.

36. Spencer D. Wood and Jess Gilbert, "Autonomous Policy Expert or 'Power Elite' Member?: Rexford G. Tugwell and the Creation of the U.S. Resettlement Administration in 1935," paper delivered at the Social Science History Association, Chicago, IL, October 1992, 16; Bernard Sternsher, *Rexford Tugwell and the New Deal* (New Brunswick, NJ: Rutgers University Press, 1964), 174–75.

37. See, for instance, Peter Novick, *That Noble Dream: The "Objectivity Question" and the American Historical Profession* (New York: Cambridge University Press, 1988), chapters 3 and 4.

38. John D. Black, *Agricultural Reform in the United States* (Ithaca, NY: Cornell University Press, 1929), 389.

39. L. Dudley Stamp, director of the Land Utilization Survey of Britain, "Planning the Land for the Future," *Science* 80 (7 December 1934): 508.

40. Rural sociologists produced a variety of types of studies of mountain communities during the 1920s and 1930s. For the purposes of this project the most significant are Mandel Sherman and Thomas Henry, *Hollow Folk* (New York: Crowell Books, 1933), which analyzed the mountain hollows of the Blue Ridge, and several studies sponsored by the Vermont Eugenics Survey, particularly Elin Anderson's *Selective Migration from Three Rural Vermont Towns* (Burlington: Eugenics Survey of Vermont, 1931), Genieve Lamson's *A Study of Agricultural Populations in Selected Vermont Towns, 1929–1930* (Burlington: Vermont Commission on Country Life, 1931), and Vermont Commission on Country Life, *Rural Vermont: A Program for the Future, by Two Hundred Vermonters* (Burlington: Vermont Commission on Country Life, 1931). Other famous rural studies that focused on the southern parts of Appalachia include Horace Kephart, *Our Southern Highlanders* (Knoxville: University of Tennessee Press, 1913); Muriel Sheppard, *Cabins in the Laurel* (Chapel Hill: University of North Carolina Press, 1935); John Campbell, *The Southern Highlander and His Homeland* (New York: Russell Sage Foundation, 1921); and Edwin E. White, *Highland Heritage* (New York: Friendship Press, 1937).

41. Harry C. McDean, "Professionalism in the Rural Social Sciences, 1896–1912," *Agricultural History* 58 (1984): 375, 377–78.

42. James Scott, *Seeing Like a State* (New Haven: Yale University Press, 1998), 6.

43. For other examples of this, see Daniel T. Rodgers, "In Search of Progressivism," *Reviews in American History* 10 (December 1982): 126.

44. Thomas Bender, *Intellect and Public Life: Essays on the Social History of Academic Intellectuals in the United States* (Baltimore: Johns Hopkins University Press, 1993), 58–59.

45. Lauren Soth, "Agricultural Economists and Public Policy," *American Journal of Agricultural Economics* 58 (December 1976): 798.

46. Arthur M. Schlesinger, Jr., "Sources of the New Deal," in *Paths of American Thought: American Intellectual History from Colonial Times to the World of Today*, ed. Arthur M. Schlesinger, Jr., and Morton White (Boston: Houghton Mifflin, 1963), 379.

47. Jess Gilbert and Alice O'Connor, "Leaving the Land Behind: Struggles for Land Reform in U.S. Federal Policy, 1933–1965," in *Who Owns America?* ed. Harvey M. Jacobs (Madison: University of Wisconsin Press, 1998), 119; Wood and Gilbert, "Autonomous Policy Expert?" 14; Edward L. Schapsmeier and Frederick H. Schapsmeier, *Henry A. Wallace of Iowa: The Agrarian Years, 1910–1940* (Ames: Iowa State University Press, 1968), 62, 125.

48. Jess Gilbert and Ellen Baker, "Wisconsin Economists and New Deal Agricultural Policy: The Legacy of Progressive Professors," *Wisconsin Magazine of History* 80 (Summer 1997): 287.

49. Ely advised, and brought into the department of political economy, not only Henry C. Taylor, but also John R. Commons. During the early 1920s the BAE also had several other Wisconsin graduates on its staff, including O. E. Baker and O. C. Stine, as well as L. C. Gray and rural sociologist Charles Galpin. Gilbert and Baker, "Wisconsin Economists," 288, 298, 301; David L. Winters, *Henry Cantwell Wallace as Secretary of Agriculture, 1921–1924* (Urbana: University of Illinois Press, 1970), 114, 116; "Henry C. Taylor," obituary in *American Journal of Agricultural Economics* 51 (August 1969):, 733.

50. Kirkendall, *Social Scientists and Farm Politics;* Ely and Wehrwein, *Land Economics.*

51. In 1924 Congress passed the Purnell Act (HR 157), which significantly boosted state expenditures in agricultural research. This legislation appropriated $20,000 a year to each state agricultural experiment station to fund research in agricultural economics, rural sociology, and home economics, with a total of $60,000 granted until 1930. Black, *Agricultural Reform,* 71, 396.

52. Henry C. Taylor, *A Farm Economist in Washington, 1919–1925* (Madison: University of Wisconsin Department of Agricultural Economics, 1992), 65.

53. These are areas that fail to produce a sufficient rent (profit) to sustain the farm according to generally-accepted conditions. As Thomas Robert Malthus described the concept of rent, "The excess of value of the whole produce . . . above what is necessary to pay the wages of labor and the profits of capital employed in cultivation." Ely and Wehrwein, *Land Economics,* 117.

54. L. C. Gray, "Some Ways of Dealing With the Problems of Submarginal Land," in *Proceedings of the National Conference on Land Utilization,* 58.

55. By 1934, the National Resources Planning Board had recommended the retirement of seventy-five million acres of submarginal land, including 450,000 farms with twenty million acres in crops. Ely and Wehrwein, *Land Economics*, 187–88, citing the *National Resources Board Report*, 110–11, 175–84.
56. Thomas P. Cooper, "Extent and Emergency Character of Problems of Submarginal Lands," in *Proceedings of the National Conference on Land Utilization*, 48–50.
57. C. E. Ladd, "New York's Land Utilization Program," in *Proceedings of the National Conference on Land Utilization*, 54; Ely and Wehrwein, *Land Economics*, 190.
58. Cited in Edgar Nixon, ed., *FDR and Conservation*, v. 1 (Hyde Park, NY: General Services Administration and National Archives and Records Administration, 1957), 68, n2.
59. Daniel R. Fusfeld, *The Economic Thought of Franklin D. Roosevelt and the Origins of the New Deal* (New York: Columbia University Press, 1954), 33, 35–36.
60. Minteer, *Landscape of Reform*, 56–66; Maher, *Nature's New Deal*, 189–95; Edward K. Spann, *Designing Modern America: The Regional Planning Association of America and Its Members* (Columbus: Ohio State University Press, 1996), 127–30, 152.
61. Franklin D. Roosevelt, address at Silver Lake, NY, 15 August 1929, *Public Papers of Franklin D. Roosevelt, Forty-eighth Governor of the State of New York, 1929-1932* (Albany, NY: J.B. Lyon, 1930), 726–27.
62. Gertrude Slichter, "Franklin D. Roosevelt's Farm Policy as Governor of New York State, 1928–1932," *Agricultural History* 33 (October 1959): 173.
63. Franklin D. Roosevelt, "The Land Survey of the State of New York, as Outlined by Governor Franklin D. Roosevelt in His Message to the Legislature," Albany, 26 January 1931, in Nixon, *FDR and Conservation*, 78–80.
64. The appropriation began at $1 million in 1932, to increase $200,000 each year, until it reached a total of to $2 million in 1937. Fusfeld, *Economic Thought of Franklin D. Roosevelt*, 131; "Vote 'Yes' on Amendment 3, A Non-Partisan Proposal That Will Benefit Agriculture," *American Agriculturalist* (31 October 1931): 1, 7.
65. Franklin D. Roosevelt, speech at Cornell University Farm and Home Week, Ithaca, NY, 13 February 1931, in Nixon, *FDR and Conservation*, 82–83.
66. By October 1938, 413,688 acres had been purchased or were under contract through this program, and the state was well on its way to a reorganization of the rural landscape. Ely and Wehrwein, *Land Economics*, 190; Ladd, "New York's Land Utilization Program," 56, 57.
67. Message of Franklin D. Roosevelt to New York State Legislature, printed as "Acres Fit and Unfit, State Planning of Land Use for Industry and Agriculture," pamphlet privately printed in Albany, 1931, cited in Nixon, *FDR and Conservation*, 80.
68. Richard T. Ely, "Land Planning and Education," *Journal of Educational Sociology* 4 (September 1930): 10; Roosevelt also worked with foresters from Syra-

cuse University's School of Forestry, using the expertise of Dean Nelson Brown as he crafted a forestry program for his own land at Hyde Park. R. G. Tugwell, "The Fallow Years of Franklin D. Roosevelt," *Ethics* 46 (January 1956): 101; Gertrude Almy Slichter, "Franklin D. Roosevelt and the Farm Problem, 1929–1932," *Mississippi Valley Historical Review* 43 (September 1956): 242.

69. Clifford B. Anderson, "The Metamorphosis of American Agrarian Idealism in the 1920s and 1930s," *Agricultural History* 35 (October 1961): 182, 184.

70. David E. Hamilton, *From New Day to New Deal: American Farm Policy from Hoover to Roosevelt, 1928–1933* (Chapel Hill: University of North Carolina Press, 1991), 20–21.

71. Reports on land utilization are among the best sources for discerning the developing culture of this planning ideology. *Bibliography on Land Utilization, 1918–1936* (Washington, DC: USDA, 1938).

72. Seligman was a close associate of Richard Ely, and they co-founded the American Economic Association. Edwin R. A. Seligman, *Economics of Farm Relief: A Survey of the Agricultural Problem* (New York: Columbia University Press, 1929), 223–24.

73. Few academics have explored the submarginal lands question, although another source on how the submarginal lands question fit into regional planning is James Kates, *Planning a Wilderness: Regenerating the Great Lakes Cutover Region* (Minneapolis: University of Minnesota Press, 2001); Seligman, *Economics of Farm Relief,* 223.

74. Black, *Agricultural Reform,* 401.

75. Arthur M. Hyde, "We're Both Right," *The Country Home Magazine,* July 1930, p. 54.

76. This meeting, cosponsored by the USDA and the state agricultural colleges, responded to the growing interest in land utilization planning. The program of the conference, printed by the USDA, listed meetings entitled "Land Utilization and the Farm Problem," "Land: Its Use and Misuse," "The Place of Forestry in a National Land Utilization Program," "Readjustments in Taxation Made Necessary by Changes in Land Utilization," "Adjustments in Farming in the Better Farming Areas," "Credit Problems in the Readjustment of Land Utilization and Farm Organizations," and "A National Land Utilization Program." See *Proceedings of the National Conference on Land Utilization;* William J. Barber, *From New Era to New Deal: Herbert Hoover, the Economists, and American Economic Policy, 1921–1933* (New York: Cambridge University Press, 1985), 104; Anthony J. Badger, *FDR: The First Hundred Days* (New York: Hill and Wang, 2008), 10.

77. In November 1932, a Special Committee of the Association of Land-Grant Colleges and Universities produced a "Report on the Agricultural Situation," which it submitted at the Association's annual convention in November 1932. The report read: "The National Land Use Planning Committee has made a good beginning in developing coordination among agencies and in unifying

points of view in dealing with national land-use objectives. The time has arrived when there should be national action on these matters. New land-policy legislation is needed at once providing for permanent land-use planning, coordinated research, and a beginning of the retirement of submarginal lands from agricultural use together with provisions for their administration." "Report on the Agricultural Situation," 26, as found in Rexford Tugwell papers, General Correspondence files, container 29, "M. L. Wilson" folder, FDR Presidential Library, Hyde Park (hereafter FDRPL).

78. Kirkendall, *Social Scientists and Farm Politics,* 39, citing William Starr Myers, ed., *The State Papers and Other Public Writings of Herbert Hoover* (Garden City, NY: Doubleday, Doran, 1934), 2:532, 537.

79. USDA Office of Information, "Land Use Committee Announces Cooperative Projects in Two States," press release, 6 October 1932, Herbert Hoover Presidential Library, Cabinet Offices files, Department of Agriculture, box 7, Land Use folder.

80. Slichter, "Roosevelt and the Farm Problem," 243, 251.

81. An account of the Roosevelt campaign's cultivation of advisors is found in Raymond Moley's *After Seven Years* (New York: Harper & Brothers, 1939), 20–21; Kirkendall, *Social Scientists and Farm Politics,* 39, 75–76.

82. Rexford G. Tugwell, *How They Became President: Thirty-Five Ways to the White House* (New York: Simon and Schuster, 1964), 416; Rexford Guy Tugwell, "The New Deal: The Contributions of Herbert Hoover," unpublished manuscript, n.d. (c. 1940s), Tugwell Papers, FDRPL, pp. 30, 36, 61, as cited in Barber, *From New Era to New Deal,* 195.

83. Moley described the principles upon which the campaign was shaped, including "the belief that there was need not only for an extension of the government's regulatory power to prevent abuses . . . but for the development of controls to stimulate and stabilize economic activity ("planning" for agriculture). . . . The former, designed to curb economic power and special privilege, did not depart in principle from the lines of policy laid down in the administrations of Theodore Roosevelt and Woodrow Wilson. But the latter carried us pretty far from ancient moorings." Moley, *After Seven Years,* 23–24.

84. Moley, *After Seven Years,* 12.

85. Franklin Delano Roosevelt, campaign address, Atlanta, Georgia, 24 October 1932, http://teachingamericanhistory.org/library/index.asp?document=85 (accessed 14 January 2010); Fusfeld, *Economic Thought of Franklin D. Roosevelt,* 134, 249.

86. This speech was the result of an extensive collaboration between more than twenty-five people, but the principal authors were soon-to-be New Dealers M. L. Wilson, who wrote the initial draft; Henry A. Wallace; Raymond Moley; Rexford Tugwell; Henry Morgenthau, Jr.; Hugh Johnson; and Franklin Roosevelt. Moley, *After Seven Years,* 43–45; Schapsmeier and Schapsmeier, *Henry A. Wallace of Iowa,* 155.

87. Franklin D. Roosevelt, "Agriculture, What Is Wrong and What To Do About It," speech at Topeka, KS, 14 September 1932 (New York: The Democratic National Committee, 1932), 8–10 (FDRPL, Master Speech Files, #498); Slichter, "Roosevelt and the Farm Problem," 253.
88. I. G. Davis, "The Social Science Fellowships in Agricultural Economics and Rural Sociology," *Journal of Farm Economics* 16 (July 1934): 501, quoted in Kirkendall, *Social Scientists and Farm Politics*, 65.
89. Badger, *FDR*, 157.

CHAPTER 4. DESIGNING THE SHENANDOAH NATIONAL PARK
1. Harold E. Philips, "The Shenandoah National Park," in *Shenandoah National Park: The Official Pictorial Book* (n.p.: National Survey Institute, 1929).
2. See Ethan Carr, *Wilderness by Design* (Lincoln: University of Nebraska Press, 1999); Karl Jacoby, *Crimes Against Nature* (Berkeley: University of California Press, 2001); Linda Flint McClelland, *Building the National Parks* (Baltimore: Johns Hopkins University Press, 1998); Alfred Runte, *National Parks: The American Experience* (Lincoln: University of Nebraska Press, 1979), 117; and Mark David Spence, *Dispossessing the Wilderness* (New York: Oxford University Press, 1999), 5.
3. Benita J. Howell, "Appalachian Culture and Environmental Planning: Expanding the Role of the Cultural Sciences," in *Culture, Environment, and Conservation in the Appalachian South*, ed. Benita J. Howell (Urbana: University of Illinois Press, 2002), 3.
4. Stephen Mather, *Annual Report of the National Park Service*, 1923, cited in United States Department of the Interior, "Final Report of the Southern Appalachian National Park Commission to the Secretary of the Interior," June 30, 1931, pp. 1, 3; Isabelle F. Story, *The National Parks and Emergency Conservation* (Washington, DC: Government Printing Office, 1933), 3.
5. Hubert Work, Secretary of the Interior, address on the subject of "Parks" at the Fifth National Conference on State Parks, Skyland, Virginia, 25 May 1925, NARA, 79/10A/24/1.
6. Department of the Interior, "Final Report," 1; Letter from Hubert Work to Major W. A. Welch, 16 February 1924, NARA RG 79, entry 7, box 23, folder 9; Committee on Public Lands, "Report to accompany H. R. 11980," 68th Congress, 2nd Session, Report No. 1320, 29 January 1925, p. 2; George Freeman Pollock, *Skyland: The Heart of the Shenandoah National Park*, ed. Stuart E. Brown, Jr. (n.p.: Chesapeake Book Company, 1960), 278. The U.S. population in 1920 was 106,021,537, according to the U.S. Census.
7. Department of the Interior, "Final Report," 7.
8. The committee's requirements for the ideal area were that the area possessed: "1) Mountain scenery with inspiring perspectives and delightful details; 2) Areas sufficiently extensive and adaptable so that annually millions of visitors might enjoy the benefits of outdoor life and communion with nature without the confusion of overcrowding; 3) A substantial part to contain

forests, shrubs, and flowers, and mountain streams, with picturesque cascades and waterfalls overhung with foliage, all untouched by the hand of man; 4) Abundant springs and streams available for camps and fishing; 5) Opportunities for protecting and developing the wild life of the area, and the whole to be a natural museum, preserving outstanding features of the southern Appalachians as they appeared in the early pioneer days; 6) Accessibility by rail and road." Department of the Interior, "Final Report," 2, 7.

9. George B. Tindall, "Business Progressivism: Southern Politics in the Twenties," *The South Atlantic Quarterly* 42 (Winter 1963): 93.

10. This proposal was prepared by Skyland owner George Freeman Pollock, regular guest Harold Allen, and cottage owner George H. Judd. Allen had seen an article in the Washington *Evening Star* announcing the creation of the Southern Appalachian National Park Committee, and he pressed Pollock to push the Blue Ridge forward as a contender. The *Evening Star* article was published on February 19, 1924. Pollock, *Skyland (1960)*, 213, 278; "Answer to Government Questionnaire Concerning Proposed Southern Appalachian National Park," SNPA, Zerkel Papers, box 6, folder 1, p. 1.

11. Pollock, *Skyland (1920)*, 8, 10.

12. Pollock, *Skyland (1920)*, 8, 10; "Answer to Government Questionnaire," 1, 3.

13. The *Washington Post* published an account of a 1915 Labor Day bonfire, describing the week's labor of constructing the bonfire and the spectacle of the mountaintop fire, which could be seen from miles away. "Festival at Skyland," *Washington Post*, 12 September 1915; Pollock, *Skyland (1960)*, 275; George Freeman Pollock, "Why Skyland?" *Potomac Appalachian Trail Club Bulletin* 5 (April 1936): 41.

14. NPS Associate Director Arno Cammerer commented on the state of the land around Skyland, observing: "I have gone over the Shenandoah area pretty thoroughly and I believe that it is of national park calibre, even though the area around Skyland is terribly cut up." Letter from Arno Cammerer to George Brown, 7 January 1929, NARA, 79/10A/440/5.

15. "Answer to Government Questionnaire," 3; Pollock, *Skyland (1960)*, 282–83, notes 2, 3, and 12.

16. Department of the Interior, "Final Report," 7.

17. Historians of the Park Service have acknowledged the conflict inherent within the preservationist-utilitarian nature of park development, and how the recreational agenda of tourism often conflicted with the other rationale, nature preservation. Richard West Sellers, *Preserving Nature in the National Parks: A History* (New Haven: Yale University Press, 1997), 16; SANPC, report to Secretary Work, 12 December 1924, as cited in Department of the Interior, "Final Report," 2, 6.

18. Department of the Interior, "Final Report," 7; *Annual Report of the Director of the National Park Service* (Washington, DC: Government Printing Office, 1925), 2–3.

19. An Act *To provide for the securing of lands in the southern Appalachian Mountains and in the Mammoth Cave regions of Kentucky for perpetual preservation as national parks*, Public Law 437, 68th Congress (21 February 1925).

20. The committee appointed in February 1924 had been reappointed by Secretary Work as a commission, with the new responsibility of facilitating park creation, following the passage of enabling legislation for the parks on February 21, 1925 (Public Act 437, 68th Congress). Department of the Interior, "Memorandum for the Press," 14 April 1926, NARA, 79/10A/24/7; Department of the Interior, "Final Report," 9; Hubert Work, "Memorandum for the Press," 26 January 1925, p. 3, NARA, CP 79/10A/24/6.

21. Address by Col. H. J. Benchoff at Afton Inn, Front Royal, VA, 6 December 1924, University of Virginia Special Collections, Charlottesville, VA; Northern Virginia Park Association, "A National Park Near the Nation's Capital, Information Bulletin on the Proposed Location of the New Southern Appalachian National Park in the Beautiful Blue Ridge Mountains of Virginia," 11–12.

22. Memorandum for Colonel Smith, from G. A. Mosley, Assistant Attorney, National Park Service, NARA, 79/10A/24/1; Letter from Glenn Smith to H. W. Temple, 10 April 1925, NARA, 79/10A/24/6; Letter from Henry Temple to Col. H. J. Benchoff, President, Shenandoah National Park Association, 25 May 1925, NARA, 79/10A/25/11; Department of the Interior, "Memorandum for the Press," 14 April 1926, p. 11; Letter from John Paul, Chairman SNPA and former Congressman, to every citizen of three counties, August 1925, NARA, 79/10A/25/11; Harry Flood Byrd, "Foreword," in Pollock, *Skyland*, xi. Byrd was given the cottage by his father as a wedding gift in 1913 but apparently sold it in 1921: Ronald Heinemann, *Harry Byrd of Virginia* (Charlottesville: University Press of Virginia, 1996), 88, cites *Culpeper (VA) Exponent*, 8 December 1927, in Carson scrapbooks, I, 23, Virginia State Library, Richmond, VA.

23. The development and maintenance of Virginia's road network was coordinated by a state highway commission after 1919. Tindall, "Business Progressivism," 101–2; "Virginia Byrds Again to Fore: Long Scattered and Dormant, the Family of Richmond's Founder Develops a Governor of the State and an Arctic Flier," *New York Times*, 14 February 1926; Works Projects Administration Writers Program, *Virginia: A Guide to the Old Dominion* (New York: Oxford University Press, 1940), 96; Raymond Pulley, *Old Virginia Restored: An Interpretation of the Progressive Impulse* (Charlottesville: University Press of Virginia, 1968), 177–81; Allen Moger, *Virginia: Bourbonism to Byrd* (Charlottesville: University Press of Virginia, 1968), 340–42.

24. William Joseph Showalter, "Virginia—A Commonwealth That Has Come Back," *The National Geographic Magazine* 55 (April 1929): 414–15; H. I. Brock, "Governor Byrd Conducts a Revolution," *New York Times*, 4 March 1928.

25. Harry Flood Byrd, "Program of Progress," Senate Doc. No. 5, *Journal of the Senate of Virginia, 1928*, p.5, as cited in John F. Horan, Jr., "Will Carson and

the Virginia Conservation Commission, 1926–1934," *The Virginia Magazine of History and Biography* 92 (October 1984): 396.

26. Carson appointed the commission's other members: Blue Ridge landowner and former opponent of the Shenandoah National Park "Lee Long of Dante; Coleman Wortham, affiliated with a stockbroker in Richmond; Rufus G. Roberts, owner of the *Culpeper Star;* Thomas L. Farrar, vice president of a Charlottesville bank; Edward Griffith Dodson, a Norfolk bank officer; and Junius P. Fishburn, editor of the *Roanoke World-News* and a former president of the state chamber of commerce." *The Inaugural Address of Harry Flood Byrd, Governor, to the General Assembly and the People of Virginia, Monday, February 1, 1926* (Richmond: Davis Bottom, Superintendent of Public Printing, 1926), 12; Heinemann, *Harry Byrd of Virginia,* 59; Horan, "Will Carson and the Virginia Conservation Commission," 394–96, 400.

27. The Virginia pledges totaled $1,249,154 by April 1. Darwin Lambert, *The Undying Past of the Shenandoah National Park* (Boulder, CO: Roberts Rinehart, 1989), 204; Harold Ickes, speech at dedication of the Shenandoah National Park, 3 July 1936, NARA College Park, 79/10A/1635/8; Editorial, "Buy an Acre!" *Washington Star,* 1 April 1926; "Urges Virginians to Buy Park Land," *Washington Post,* 26 May 1925; "Shenandoah Park Project Boosted with $30,000 Here," *Washington Post,* 30 March 1926; *An Act To provide for the establishment of the Shenandoah National Park in the State of Virginia and the Great Smoky Mountain National Park in the States of North Carolina and Tennessee, and for other purposes,* Public Act 268, 69th Congress (22 May 1926).

28. Acreages from "Hearings for Interior Department Appropriation Bill," 1928, p. 1014, NARA, 79/10A/440/6.

29. According to a May 1927 SCDC press release, almost two-thirds of the original pledges remained unpaid, and a significant amount had already been expended on administrative expenses, which raised the total fundraising goal. Press release, prepared at the suggestion of Governor Byrd and the Commission on Conservation and Development, "The Status of the Shenandoah National Park Movement," for release 20 May 1927, NARA, 79/10A/26/4.

30. Durwood Dunn, *Cades Cove* (Knoxville: University of Tennessee, 1988), 246; Letter from Mason Manghum, Managing Director of the Richmond Chamber of Commerce, to Glenn Smith, Appalachian National Park Commission, 4 January 1928, NARA, 79/10A/24/1; Letter from Glenn Smith to Coleman Wortham, Care Davenport and Company, 25 January 1928, NARA, 79/10A/24/1.

31. Horan, "Will Carson and the Virginia Conservation Commission," 399; An Act Providing for the Condemnation of Lands and Buildings for use as a Public Park or for Public Park Purposes (23 March 1928), *Acts of Assembly (VA),* chapter 410, Acts 1928. Judge Philip Williams decided the *Rudacille* case in favor of the SCDC on October 1, 1929: *Thomas Jackson Rudacille vs. State Commission on Conservation and Development,* 1 October 1929, NARA, 79/10A/440/5. Dennis E. Simmons, "Conservation, Cooperation, and Con-

troversy: The Establishment of Shenandoah National Park, 1924–1936," *The Virginia Magazine of History and Biography* 89 (October 1981): 397.

32. The 1924 report is cited in Department of the Interior, "Final Report," 9; "Byrd Recommends $1,000,000 Tax Cut Taking Effect . . ." *Richmond Times-Dispatch,* 6 December 1927. This article cites $1,011,798 to date in subscriptions by the people of Virginia (it is unclear whether this includes Washington, DC), with $296,194 remaining uncollected. March 1926 articles in the *Washington Star* suggest that $1.2 million was subscribed by Virginia citizens in March 1926. "Shenandoah Park Success Assured," *Washington Star,* 16 March 1926.

33. Showalter, "Virginia," 419.

34. Hoover reportedly invested $114,000 in developing the area, although the value of his donation of the land and its buildings to the SCDC was placed at $26,861.80. He and his wife also supervised the establishment of a school in the mountains above Rapidan Camp, and funded the maintenance of the school and its teacher for years. Darwin Lambert, *Herbert Hoover's Hideaway* (Luray, VA: Shenandoah Natural History Association, 1971), 82–100, 124; Letter from Herbert Hoover to W. E. Carson, 7 August 1929, in John T. Woolley and Gerhard Peters, *The American Presidency Project,* http://www.presidency.ucsb.edu/ws/?pid=21885 (accessed 2 May 2008); Carson scrapbook I, 235, 4 May 1929,Virginia State Library, Richmond, VA, as cited in Horan, "Will Carson and the Virginia Conservation Commission," 400.

35. Virginia acquired this land through eminent domain. Congress appropriated money for the Shenandoah road project, with the first $696,425 allocated out of funds allotted to the construction of trails and roads in the national parks and monuments. Letter from Glenn S. Smith to W. E. Carson, 21 September 1929, NARA, 79/10A/26/1; William J. Showalter, "In the Shenandoah Valley of Virginia," *The Sunday Star* (Washington, DC), 10 July 1932; Horan, "Will Carson and the Virginia Conservation Commission," 402; Horace M. Albright and Robert Cahn, *The Birth of the National Park Service: The Founding Years, 1913–1933* (Salt Lake City: Howe Brothers, 1985), 267.

36. Pamphlets advertising the opening from October 22 to November 30, 1932, in "Blue Print," Records of the National Park Service, NARA College Park, 79/10B/1647/1; Simmons, "Conservation, Cooperation, and Controversy," 398.

37. The evolution of the purchase area was described in a memorandum from Horace Albright to Secretary of the Interior Wilbur, 10 December 1929, in NARA, 79/10A/440/5. The boundaries were changed by Public Law 33, 70th Congress, approved February 16, 1928. Letter from Arno Cammerer to W. E. Carson, 15 January 1934, and reply from W. E. Carson to Arno Cammerer, 16 January 1934, NARA, 79/10B/1654/1.

38. The Park Service acknowledged that Virginia's condemnation process had the potential to limit the amounts paid for park area land. While a benefit to the Commonwealth, that frugal approach to acquisition came at a significant

price to park area landowners. Cammerer, in an internal memorandum, remarked: "It was hoped that the cost under the appraisal system used by the State of Virginia could be brought down to about $3,000,000." A. B. Cammerer, confidential memorandum for the files, 14 October 1931, NARA, 79/10A/441/8. G. A. Moskey, Assistant Director, National Park Service, Memorandum for Mr. Cramton, 7 March 1932, NARA, 79/10A/443/14.

39. Letter from Miriam Sizer to Herbert L. Brooks, 21 August 1932, NARA, 79/10A/442/4.

40. "In the Circuit Court of Warren County, at Front Royal, Virginia, The State Commission on Conservation and Development, of the State of Virginia, Petitioner, vs. Virginia Atwood and Others, and Thirty Thousand (30,000) Acres, More or Less, of Land in Warren County, Virginia, Defendants," *The Warren Sentinel*, 7 November 1929.

41. Letter from George Freeman Pollock to Ferdinand Zerkel, 5 January 1925, SNPA, L. Ferdinand Zerkel Papers, box 6, folder 3.

42. The memo was directed to the attention of George A. Moskey, assistant director and the Park Service's legal counsel, and Conrad Wirth, assistant director in charge of the Branch of Land Planning. Arno Cammerer, memorandum for Mr. Moskey and Mr. Wirth, 15 August 1931, NARA, 79/10B/1649/9.

43. In a memo about Sizer's work facilitating the integration of the mountain residents into other communities, NPS official Herbert Brooks wrote: "In this contact work she will be representing herself in the same category of a missionary and it will not be disclosed that she is in any way connected with the Government or the National Park Service." Memorandum for Mr. Cammerer from Herbert Brooks, 22 August 1932, NARA, 79/10A/442/1.

44. Arno B. Cammerer, memorandum for Mr. Albright, 28 March 1932, NARA, 79/10A/443/8.

45. T. H. Watkins, *Righteous Pilgrim: The Life and Times of Harold L. Ickes* (New York: Henry Holt, 1990), 552–53.

46. Arno Cammerer, memorandum for the files, 31 October 1933, NARA, 79/10B/1654/1.

47. Cammerer, memorandum for the files, 31 October 1933; Albright and Cahn, *Birth of the National Park Service,* 294.

48. Horan, "Will Carson and the Virginia Conservation Commission," 405, citing Virginia Conservation Commission, *Conserving and Developing Virginia* (Richmond: Virginia Conservation Commission, 1935), 32, 33, 99; Reed L. Engle, *Everything Was Wonderful: A Pictorial History of the CCC in Shenandoah National Park* (Luray, VA: Shenandoah National History Association, 1999), 10; Lambert, *Herbert Hoover's Hideaway*, 124–26; Albright and Cahn, *Birth of the National Park Service*, 290; Lambert, *Undying Past*, 222–23.

49. Harlan Kelsey to Arno Cammerer, 14 July 1936, NARA 79/10B/1638/20.

50. According to Maher, the expansion of the CCC's mandate from a focus on restoring natural resources to restoring human resources as well through the

development of recreational facilities first occurred in the summer of 1935. However, evidence from both Virginia and Vermont pushes this date back to 1933. Neil Maher, *Nature's New Deal* (New York: Oxford University Press, 2008), 70–71, 117, 146; Engle, *Everything Was Wonderful*, 88.

51. Camp cooks served both the president and enrollees: fried steak with gravy and string beans, mashed potatoes, tomato and lettuce salad, iced tea, and apple cobbler. "President Inspects 5 Forest Camps: He Is Pleased By Conditions found in 180-Mile Trip—Eats Steak with Men," *New York Times*, 13 August 1933.

52. Maher, in *Nature's New Deal*, contextualizes the conflicts over CCC conservation and recreation projects and the move to add wildlife biologists to CCC projects (p. 168).

53. Aldo Leopold adroitly described the problem with these aggressive forms of conservation in "Conservation Economics," in *The River of the Mother of God*, ed. Susan L. Flader and J. Baird Caldicott (Madison: University of Wisconsin Press, 1991), 197. Letter from Charles E. Peterson, Chief of Eastern Division, NPS, to J. R. Lassiter, Acting Superintendent, SNP, 24 January 1934, NARA, 79/10B/1657/2. For information on the extent of the forest cleanup and landscape "manipulation," see Engle, *Everything Was Wonderful*, 80–81. Letter from Verne Chatelain, Acting Assistant Director, Branch of Research and Education, NPS, to J. R. Lassiter, 23 May 1934, NARA, 79/10B/1670/3. Maurice Sullivan, Naturalist Assistant, "Let us Give the People a Maximum Opportunity to Observe our Wild Life," unpublished essay, NARA, 79/10B/1641/1. Maurice Sullivan, Naturalist's Report #4, 9/5–10/15/1934, pp. 2–3, NARA, 79/10B/1641/1. Maher, *Nature's New Deal*, 157, 161, 178.

54. Benton MacKaye, the originator of the idea of a hiking trail along the mountain chain, which developed into the Appalachian Trail, wrote in June of 1934 that the idea of a skyline road, though inspiring and promotable, was less desirable and far less scenic than a comparable "flankline" road that followed the contours at the sides of the mountains, venturing only periodically up to the crests. Benton MacKaye, "Flankline vs. Skyline," *Appalachia: The Bulletin of the Appalachian Mountain Club* 20 (June 1934): 104–8.

55. Harold C. Anderson, "What Price Skyline Drives," *Appalachia* 21 (November 1935): 412.

56. Harold P. Ickes, "Wildernesses and Skyline Drives," *The Living Wilderness* 1 (September 1935): 12; Watkins, *Righteous Pilgrim*, 550; Lambert, *Undying Past*, 214–15; Letter from Myron H. Avery to Honorable Harold L. Ickes, Secretary, Department of the Interior, 9 January 1936, NARA, 79/10A/506/8. For the best treatment of the debate over park roads, see Paul Sutter, *Driven Wild: How the Fight Against Automobiles Launched the Modern Wilderness Movement* (Seattle: University of Washington Press, 2002). Letter from W. T. Stephens, acting superintendent, to Mr. Norman G. Keig, 7 October 1941, answering several questions about Warren County, SNPA, RMR, Series I, box 6, folder 7, "Park Lands—Part I to 1929–1944."

57. The case went directly into the federal court as a suit in diversity (filed in federal court because the citizens of two states were involved). Filing for *Via v. Virginia Commission on Conservation and Development*, Docket # Equity 91-NC, Motion to Quiet Title, 10 November 1934, SNPA, SCCD Records, box 8, folder 12.

58. It followed, therefore, that since Via had been granted access to adequate remedy at law, he had no right to sue at equity, which could have enabled him to force an injunction that would reverse the condemnation process and trigger the termination of the project of park creation.

59. *Via v. State Commission on Conservation and Development*, 9 F. Supp. 556 (W.D. Va. 1935); "Shenandoah Park Case is Dismissed," *The Evening Star* (Washington, DC), 26 November 1935.

60. Carson, who had overseen the fundraising and collection of pledges, facilitated the construction of the Skyline Drive and nurtured the park almost to completion. Shortly thereafter, in November 1934, he stepped down from the SCDC after a disagreement with Senator Byrd. Horan, "Will Carson and the Virginia Conservation Commission," 413. Of the total sum of the park purchase, $1,859,909.72 was paid out to landowners, and the balance of roughly $400,000 went toward administrative costs, "what might be termed overhead expenses." Funds allocated through ECW projects were used to buy an additional 12,823.81 acres for the park, with a total cost of $152,592.25 as of July 1, 1936. "Some Park Figures," newspaper clipping without date or newspaper name, SNPA, Zerkel Papers, box 13, folder 4. Lambert, *Undying Past*, 225. Letter from Charles West, Acting Secretary of the Interior, to Acting Comptroller General of the United States, 11 September 1937, NARA, 79/10B/1649/8. G. A. Moskey, Memorandum for Mr. Tolson, 1 July 1936, NARA, 79/10B/1649/8.

61. "Shenandoah National Park Reality as Deeds Are Filed; Scenic Area Open to Public," *Christian Science Monitor*, 23 January 1936; "National Park Condemnation Act To Be Carried To U.S. Supreme Court," *Harrisonburg Record*, 8 April 1935; "A Marvelous Playground," *Richmond Times-Dispatch*, 28 December 1935; Letter from J. R. Lassiter to Wilbur Hall, 23 August 1935 (reporting that there were still 300 families living within park area under special use permits, 69 families without permits), SNPA, Resource Management Records.

62. Katrina M. Powell's *The Anguish of Dispossession* focuses on a small collection of letters in the Shenandoah National Park archives, concerning the management of park-area resources. Concerned primarily with the "politics of literacy" and the use of rhetoric in this correspondence, the book captures the needs and frustrations of a group of articulate correspondents—but do not include those cited in this chapter. Katrina M. Powell, *The Anguish of Displacement: The Politics of Literacy in the Letters of the Mountain Families in the Shenandoah National Park* (Charlottesville: University of Virginia Press, 2007), 25, 119, 132.

63. "Park Land Owners Organize," *Page News and Courier,* 25 February 1929; Letter from Lewis Willis to Hon. R. L. Wilbur, 13 April 1931, NARA, 79/10A/443/15; Letter from Lewis Willis to Hon. Horace M. Albright, 27 April 1931, NARA, 79/10A/443/15; Letter from Lewis Willis to His Excellency, Herbert Hoover, 22 June 1932, NARA, 79/10A/443/15.

64. Willis lived below the landmark Mary's Rock, within half a mile of the road crossing through the central section of the park, the Lee Highway, and so unlike the research subjects of Sherman and Henry's *Hollow Folk* he had enjoyed easy access to town and markets. Willis owned fifty acres of valuable bluegrass pasture in addition to the small fields in which he grew corn and other grains; the rest of his land was in forest. His farm consisted of 229 acres and contained flower and vegetable gardens and an orchard, as well as a barn, a meat house, and shelters for hogs and chickens. The property was originally assessed by the condemnation commission at $4,650, although Willis ultimately received $6,890 in recognition of the worth of his improvements and the timber and, probably, because of his articulate complaint. "A Database of Shenandoah National Park Land Records," prepared by Reed Engle and Caroline Janney, 1997, SNPA; Lambert, *Undying Past,* 230; Letter from Willis to Hoover, 22 June 1932.

65. The presence of businesses like Cliser's near the entrances to the park concerned SANPC officials, because they detracted from the intended beauty of the park. Minutes from the meeting of the Southern Appalachian National Park Commission, 30 December 1930, at the Department of the Interior, NARA, 79/10A/24/9. Letter from H. M. Cliser to E. O. Flippin, 18 August 1926, Records of the Department of Conservation and Economic Development, Virginia State Archives, Richmond, VA, RG 18. Letter from H. M. Cliser to the Secretary of the Interior, 3 September 1929, NARA 79/10A/440/5. "Hall Declares U.S. Officials Asked Eviction of Cliser," *Washington Star,* 4 October 1995. "Cliser's Eviction Stirs State-U.S. Controversy" (newspaper clipping, no publication information), 8 October 1935, NARA, 79/10B/1653/16. The Great Smoky Mountains National Park also sought to expel "undesirable" commercial developments from the margins of the park. See Jane Becker, *Selling Tradition* (Chapel Hill: University of North Carolina Press, 1998), and Margaret Brown, *The Wild East* (Gainesville: University Press of Florida, 2001).

66. Letter from H. M. Cliser to Hon. H. F. Byrd, U.S. Senator, 13 February 1937, NARA, 79/10B/1653/16; Transcribed letter from Melanchthon Cliser to Hon. Burr P. Harrison, M. C., 21 March 1947, NARA, 79/10B/1653/16.

67. This area consisted of lands already purchased and for which the deeds had been prepared and submitted to the National Park Service, although the last people had not been resettled by the end of the calendar year. "Herring on Trial for Firing House in National Park," *Harrisonburg News-Record,* 27 October 1936. Jack Temple Kirby, "Retro Frontiersmen," chapter 2 in *The Countercultural South* (Athens: University of Georgia Press, 1995), 34–35. For April

1936, Shenandoah officials examined fire statistics more carefully: six fires occurred within the park, four of which were suspected of being incendiary. "Forester's Monthly Report, April 1936," part of the Report to the Chief Forester on Emergency Conservation Work, April 1936, NARA, 79/42/32/5.

68. Justin Reich, "Recreating the Wilderness: Shaping Narratives and Landscapes in Shenandoah National Park," *Environmental History* 6 (January 2001), 109.

69. Memo for Regional Director, Region 1, from Hillory Tolson, Acting Director of the National Park Service, responding to the Forest Protection Requirements Report for the Shenandoah National Park, 10 August 1944, NARA, 79/10B/1669/13.

70. W. E. Carson, "Shenandoah National Park," in *Shenandoah National Park: Official Pictorial Book* (Harrisonburg, VA: Shenandoah National Park Tourist Bureau, 1929).

71. "In every part of the country, local and State and Federal authorities are engaged in preserving and developing our heritage of natural resources; and in this work they are also conserving our priceless heritage of human values by giving to hundreds of thousands of men the opportunity of making an honest living." Franklin D. Roosevelt's Address at Dedication of Shenandoah National Park, 3 July 1936, in SNPA, Resource Management Records, box 2, folder 1.

72. Felix Bruner, "CCC Honored By Roosevelt As He Opens Virginia Park," *Washington Post*, 4 July 1936; text of Roosevelt's Address at Dedication of Shenandoah National Park, NARA, 79/10B/1635/2.

73. L. F. Schmeckebier and Harold Allen, "Shenandoah National Park, The Skyline Drive and the Appalachian Trail," *Appalachia* (1936): 81.

74. Shenandoah National Park Superintendent's Monthly Report, September 1940, NARA, 79/10B/1639/2.

CHAPTER 5. CULTIVATING THE VERMONT FOREST

1. John A. Douglass, "Final Draft, History of the Green Mountain N. F., Vermont," May 1981, unpublished manuscript, p. 44, U.S. Forest Service, GMNF.

2. John M. Thomas, "The Conservation Movement," in *Report of the Commission on the Conservation of the Natural Resources of the State of Vermont, 1911–1912* (Rutland: The Tuttle Company, 1912), 9.

3. "The Abandoned Farm Problem," *Green Mountain State Forest News*, v. 6, n. 4 (September 1930): 1 (reprinted from the *Burlington Free Press*).

4. From a statewide high of 35,522 farms in 1880, the number of farms declined steadily. In 1900 only 32,890 farms were still operating, while by 1920 the number had dropped to 29,075; as of 1940, by the time the pall of the Depression began to lift, only 23,582 farms remained in Vermont. Harold Fisher Wilson, *The Hill Country of Northern New England: Its Social and Economic History in the 19th and 20th Centuries* (Montpelier: Vermont Historical Society, 1947), 346–47.

5. Vermont Forest Service, "Proposed Northern Extension of National Forest Purchase Unit in Vermont," unpublished report, 1933, p. 10, GMNF.

6. Vermont Commission on Country Life, *Rural Vermont: A Program for the Future, by Two Hundred Vermonters* (Burlington: Free Press, 1931), 113.

7. H. P. Young, "Cash Crops for Vermont Farms and Towns," *Green Mountain State Forest News* v. 1, n. 5 (April 1925): 12–13; *Green Mountain State Forest News*, v. 1, n. 1 (December 1924): 8–9; Richard McCullough, *The Landscape of Community: A History of Communal Forest in New England* (Hanover: University Press of New England, 1995), 128, 155.

8. E. H. Jones, Commissioner of Agriculture, "Abandoned Farm Problem and Forestry," *The Green Mountain State Forest News*, v. 2, n. 1 (January 1926): 2.

9. C. F. Morgan, "Address in the Report of the Vermont Maple Sugar Makers' Association," in *Vermont Department of Agriculture Report, 1922–1924* (1924), 5, as cited in Wilson, *Hill Country*, 237; McCullough, *Landscape of Community*, 157, 159.

10. K. R. B. Flint, "Forestry as a Municipal Undertaking," *The Vermont Review* (July–August 1927): 43.

11. [Elin Anderson], *Selective Migration from Three Rural Vermont Towns and Its Significance*, Fifth Annual Report of the Eugenics Survey of Vermont (Burlington: University of Vermont, 1931), 69–70.

12. Sheffield's population was 543 in 1930. This type of land utilization program was described by L. C. Gray, "Some Ways of Dealing With the Problems of Submarginal Land," in *Proceedings of the National Conference on Land Utilization*, Chicago, IL, November 19–21, 1931, called by the Secretary of Agriculture and the Executive Committee of the Association of Land-Grant Colleges and Universities (Washington, DC: Government Printing Office, 1932), 62.

13. Gray, "Problems of Submarginal Land," 62; Flint, "Forestry as a Municipal Undertaking," 42–43.

14. "Municipal Forests," *Green Mountain State Forest News* v. 1, n. 12 (November 1925): 5–6.

15. Wilson, *Hill Country*, 244; McCullough, *Landscape of Community*, 156.

16. Act 14 of the Vermont State Legislature in 1929 permitted the state government to accept donations of land for state forest parks, or to purchase land to be developed for a new system of recreational parks. The state forest park system included a number of sites better suited to recreation than forest management. Perry H. Merrill, *The Making of a Forester: An Autobiographical History* (Montpelier: Perry H. Merrill, 1984), 62.

17. Wallace Nutting, *Vermont Beautiful* (New York: Garden City, 1922), 96.

18. Of the total forest acreage, 3,780 acres were donated, and another 30,837 acres purchased, costing $83,947.14, for an average of $2.72 per acre. "Value of State Forests," *Green Mountain State Forest News*, v. 5, n. 3 (December 1929): 2.

19. By 1931, the state owned nineteen state forests, with 39,000 acres, purchased for an average of $2.83 per acre. Vermont Commission on Country Life, *Rural Vermont*, 114.

20. McCullough, *Landscape of Community*, 159–62; Merrill, *Making of a Forester*, 62.

21. Richard Munson Judd, *The New Deal in Vermont* (New York: Garland Publishing, 1979), 33.

22. *Biennial Report of the Commissioner of Forestry of the State of Vermont for the Term Ending June 30, 1932* (Springfield, VT: Springfield Printing Corp., 1932), 46.

23. James P. Taylor, "The Blazing," in *A Footpath in the Wilderness: The Long Trail in the Green Mountains of Vermont* (Middlebury: Middlebury College Press, 1941), 11; Louis J. Paris, "The Green Mountain Club," *The Vermonter* 16 (May 1911): 170.

24. Blake Harrison, *The View from Vermont: Tourism and the Making of an American Rural Landscape* (Burlington: University of Vermont Press, 2006), 113; "Address of Governor Stanley C. Wilson of Vermont on The Long Trail," pamphlet reproducing broadcast from Station WBZ, 26 September 1931 (Montpelier: Vermont Bureau of Publicity, 1931), 3.

25. Paul M. Searls, *Two Vermonts: Geography and Identity, 1865–1910* (Hanover: University of New Hampshire Press, 2006), 88; Hal Barron, *Mixed Harvest: The Second Great Transformation in the Rural North, 1870–1930* (Chapel Hill: University of North Carolina Press, 1997), 37–38.

26. In fact, the 1870 toll road climbing Vermont's highest peak, Mount Mansfield, was rebuilt to serve motor traffic in 1923, thus allowing auto tourists the most expansive vista in the state. Nutting, *Vermont Beautiful*, 13–14; Earle Newton, *The Vermont Story: A History of the People of the Green Mountain State, 1749–1949* (Montpelier: Vermont Historical Society, 1949), 218.

27. Vermont supplemented town and federal contributions to road maintenance with a user fee beginning in 1923, a gasoline tax of one cent per gallon. The tax rate increased to four cents per gallon by 1929. Wilson, *Hill Country*, 283–84; Arthur F. Stone, *The Vermont of Today: With Its Historic Background, Attractions and People* (New York: Lewis Historical Publishing Company, 1929), 696–99; Deborah Pickman Clifford and Nicholas R. Clifford, *"The Troubled Roar of the Waters": Vermont in Flood and Recovery, 1927–1931* (Hanover, NH: University Press of New Hampshire, 2007), 37–40.

28. Stone, *Vermont of Today*, 161–62.

29. Stone, *Vermont of Today*, 161.

30. Clifford and Clifford, *Troubled Roar of the Waters*, 32.

31. Wilson, *Hill Country*, 356; Stone, *Vermont of Today*, 190.

32. "Flood Area Races Against Winter, Stricken Towns Speed Efforts to Repair Damage Before Ice Holds Sway," *New York Times*, 10 November 1927.

33. From Weeks' message to the special session, 30 November 1927, as cited in Samuel B. Hand, *The Star That Set: The Vermont Republican Party, 1854–1974* (New York: Lexington Books, 2002), 124.

34. Weeks' message: *Journal of the Senate of the State of Vermont*, Special Session, 1927 Biennial Session (Montpelier: Capital City, 1929), 33–36; Clifford and Clifford, *"Troubled Roar of the Waters,"* 84–85.

35. Leon S. Gay, "Keeping Unspoiled Vermont Unspoiled," *The Vermonter* 40 (August 1935): 161.

36. Clifford and Clifford, *"Troubled Roar of the Waters,"* 168.

37. That same year, the state spent $4.5 million on road construction and improvement, almost double the $2.6 million expended in 1926, before the ravages of the flood. "Educational Facilities for Rural People," in Vermont Commission on Country Life, *Rural Vermont*, 234; John Nolen, Philip Shutler, Albert La Fleur, and Dana M. Doten, "Graphic Survey: A First Step in State Planning for Vermont," report submitted to the Vermont State Planning Board and National Resources Board, p. 56, UVMSC; Wilson, *Hill Country,* 284.

38. Judd, *New Deal in Vermont,* 33, cites the Brattleboro *Reformer,* 29 August 1932; Hand, *Star That Set,* 134–35.

39. Nolen, et al., "Graphic Survey," 18.

40. Clifford and Clifford, *"Troubled Roar of the Waters,"* 169, cites *Burlington Free Press,* 3 November 1932, p. 2; 3 November 1937, p. 6; 4 November 1937, p. 6.

41. Clifford and Clifford, *"Troubled Roar of the Waters,"* 153, citing letters from Perkins to Brigham, 2 April 1928, Brigham Papers, Congress File 1928, Pa-Pl.; Perkins to Weeks, 24 February 1928, VCCL PRA 23, "Executive Committee Correspondence" folder; Perkins to "Dear Friend," 23 May 1927.

42. Vermont Commission on Country Life, *Rural Vermont,* 131.

43. E. D. Fletcher, "Supplemental Report on Proposed Purchase Under the Weeks Law in the State of Vermont," September 1920, pp. 1, 3, 5, GMNF.

44. Letter from W. B. Greeley to Hon. Frank L. Greene, 19 March, 1928, p. 4, in "Work Up on Creation of the Green Mountain National Forest" folder, GMNF.

45. *Clarke-McNary Act,* 16 *U.S.C.* 570 (1924), sec. 8.

46. Public Act 1 (H. 56). Approved 17 February 1925. *Acts and Resolves Passed by the General Assembly of the State of Vermont at the Twenty-Eighth Biennial Session, 1925* (Bellows Falls, VT, 1925), 1.

47. Vermont State Forest Service, "A National Forest for Vermont," *Vermont State Forest News* v. 1, nn. 9 and 10 (August and September 1925): 7.

48. Vermont State Forest Service, "A National Forest for Vermont," 4, 7.

49. Vermont Forest Service, "Proposed National Forest Purchase Units in Vermont," report transmitted to the President, National Forest Reservation Commission, 5 December 1928, pp. 7–8, GMNF.

50. From 1919 to 1930, the number of partially operated farms increased 144 percent, and the number of abandoned farms increased 180 percent. Clayton and Peet, *Land Utilization,* 33–36; Wilson, *Hill Country,* 362.

51. C. F. Clayton and L. J. Peet, *Land Utilization as a Basis of Rural Economic Organization, Based on a Study of Land Utilization and Related Problems in 13 Hill Towns of Vermont* (Burlington: University of Vermont Agricultural Experiment Station, 1933), 133.

52. Vermont Forest Service, "Proposed National Forest Purchase Units," 15–16.

53. Stone, *Vermont of Today,* 335; "Resolution of the Vermont Commission on Conservation and Development," 5 December 1928, attached to "Proposed National Forest Purchase Units."

54. Vermont State Chamber of Commerce, "Resolution," 6 December 1928, attached to "Proposed National Forest Purchase Units."

55. The National Forest Reservation Commission recommended the creation of a national forest in the southern part of the state. Federal forest surveyors examined this land, estimating that 10 percent remained in virgin timber, 50 percent in "culled lands," and 30 percent in cutover areas, with another 10 percent in cleared or farmed land. C. E. Beaumont, "Reconnaissance Report of the Green Mountain Purchase Area (Southern Unit) Containing 370,000 Acres in Bennington, Windham, Rutland and Windsor Counties, Vermont," December 1928, p. 3, Boundaries folder, GMNF.

56. Beaumont, "Reconnaissance Report," 6.

57. Beaumont, "Reconnaissance Report," 9.

58. Louis M. Prindle, "Geologic Reconnaissance of the Green Mountain Purchase Area Vermont (Southern Unit) For the Forest Service," United States Geological Survey report No. 50 (27 August 1929), pp. 2, 15., "Cooperation-Geological Survey" folder, GMNF.

59. "The Green Mountain National Forest," *Green Mountain State Forest News,* v. 7, n. 2 (April 1931): 2.

60. Of the 30 towns, 23, or 76.6 percent, were characterized by the "development of economic and social conditions associated with isolation and the utilization of meager physical resources." Clayton and Peet, *Land Utilization,* 4–6; *Acts and Resolves Passed by the General Assembly of the State of Vermont at the Thirty-Third Biennial Session, 1935* (Montpelier: Capital City Press, 1935) 4; Merrill, *Making of a Forester,* 73.

61. Stuart Chase, *Rich Land, Poor Land* (New York: Whittlesey House, 1936), 304.

62. Edgar Nixon, ed. *Franklin Delano Roosevelt and Conservation* (Washington, DC: Government Printing Office, 1957): 537; Christopher McGrory Klyza and Stephen Trombulak, *The Story of Vermont* (Hanover, NH: Middlebury College Press, 1999), 100; Merrill, *Making of a Forester,* 74.

63. R. M. Evans, "National Forests in Vermont," 6 February 1935, p. 5, "Publicity" folder, GMNF.

64. Vermont Forest Service, "Proposed Northern Extension," 1–3.

65. Green Mountain Club, "Resolution Favoring Extension of Green Mountain National Forest in Vermont," 25 June 1933, attached to Vermont Forest Service, "Proposed Northern Extension."

66. Historians who have examined the New Deal years in Vermont have offered a variety of explanations for the state's ambivalence about federal aid. Richard Munson Judd observed, "The history of the New Deal in Vermont is, in large measure, a record of the triumph of progressive planning over provincial inertia. . . . The future looked dismal in 1930. Dwindling resources and incomes, reactionary provincial attitudes, an inhospitable rugged land and a severe climate all seemed to preclude any kind of new deal for most Vermonters." However, the evidence from the early 1930s does not bear out this argument, since in 1930 the Vermont Commission on Country Life report, tinged with persistent optimism, was about to come out; economic crisis had not yet struck the state, and so many small businessmen and farmers still felt smug about economic conditions. Furthermore, the groundwork for cooperation between the state and town governments, and between the state and federal governments, had been established and had begun to expand. Judd, *The New Deal in Vermont*, 24.

67. E. H. Jones, "Personal Report of the Commissioner of Agriculture," in *Agriculture of Vermont: Eighteenth Biennial Report of the Commissioner of Agriculture of the State of Vermont, 1935–1936* (Montpelier, 1936), 5; Report of the Brookmire Economic Service, 7 June 1932, quoted in the *Burlington Free Press*, 4 July 1932, as quoted in Wilson, *Hill Country*, 377n.

68. Message of Stanley C. Wilson, Governor of the State of Vermont, to the General Assembly, 19 July 1933, in *Radio Addresses of Governor Stanley Wilson* (Montpelier: Vermont Bureau of Publicity, 1933); "Retirement of Land Studied," *Brattleboro Daily Reformer*, 10 July 1934.

69. Nolen, et al., "Graphic Survey," i–iv.

70. Nolen, et al., "Graphic Survey," xiii–xiv.

71. Vermont's first CCC camp, Camp Danby in Mt. Tabor, opened on June 18, 1933. Perry H. Merrill, *Roosevelt's Forest Army: A History of the Civilian Conservation Corps, 1933–1942* (Montpelier: Perry H. Merrill, 1981), 194; Judd, *The New Deal in Vermont*, 37.

72. By 1934, there were eighteen forestry CCC camps in Vermont: two in the Green Mountain National Forest (400 men); five in state forest parks (1,000 men); eleven in state forests (2,200 men). Perry H. Merrill, *Biennial Report of the Commissioner of Forestry of the State of Vermont for the term ending June 30, 1934* (Rutland: Marble City, 1934), 46–47.

73. Merrill, *Roosevelt's Forest Army*, 183, 194; Otto G. Koenig, "Green Mountain National Forest in Vt.," *The Vermonter* 44 (November 1939): 264.

74. *Biennial Report of the Commissioner of Forestry, 1934*, 49–50.

75. The CCC employed 11,243 Vermonters, while a total of 40,868 enrollees worked in Vermont, a disproportionately high number given the size of the state. Judd, *The New Deal in Vermont*, 39–40; *Biennial Report of the Commissioner of Forestry, 1934*, 50; Merrill, *Roosevelt's Forest Army*, 180.

76. Judd, *The New Deal in Vermont*, 56.

77. The apt term "provincial progressive" is found in Arthur Schmidt, Jr., "Aiken and the Hillside Mentality: The Early Political Career of George David Aiken of Vermont" (senior thesis, Princeton University, n.d.), 1.

78. George D. Aiken, *Speaking from Vermont* (New York: Frederick A. Stokes, 1938), 164.

79. From the *Burlington Free Press*, quoting "Forest Control," *Rutland Herald*, 4 September 1934.

80. "Notes on the History of Green Mountain National Forest," dated 19 August 1964, signed "OGK," p. 3. "GMNF History—Narratives" folder, GMNF.

81. Figures are from Forestry Service estimates: Nolen, et al., "Graphic Survey," 9.

82. "Col. William J. Wilgus Explains Proposed Green Mt. Parkway," *Burlington Free Press*, 26 August 1933; Autobiography of William J. Wilgus, "Activities in Retirement, 1931–1947," 240–41, UVMSC, Wilgus Reference File; "Special Meeting of the Trustees," *The Long Trail News* 7 (September 1933): 1; William Wilgus, *Vermont's Opportunity* (Burlington: Vermont State Chamber of Commerce, 1933), 2, cited in Hal Goldman, "James Taylor's Progressive Vision: The Green Mountain Parkway," *Vermont History* 63 (Summer 1995): 160.

83. *Green Mountain Parkway Reconnaissance Survey, 1934* (Burlington: Vermont State Chamber of Commerce, 1934), 2, 4, 6.

84. *Green Mountain Parkway Reconnaissance Survey*, 6.

85. Ernest H. Bancroft, "Why People Should Favor Green Mountain Parkway," *The Vermonter* 41 (January–February 1936), 5–8; "Interpreted," clipped from the *Burlington Daily News*, in *Rutland Herald*, 6 March 1936.

86. Arthur Wallace Peach, "Proposed Parkway a Threat to the State's Well Being," *The Vermonter* 41 (January–February 1936), 9–13; Gay, "Keeping Unspoiled Vermont Unspoiled," 154.

87. "Special Meeting of the Trustees," 2.

88. "An All-Vermont Plan," in *Journal of the House, Biennial Session, 1935* (Montpelier: Capital City Press, 1935), 232–34.

89. George D. Aiken, *Pioneering with Fruits and Berries* (New York: Stephen Daye, 1936), ix–x; Aiken, *Speaking from Vermont*, 20.

90. Laurie Davidson Cox, "The Green Mountain Parkway, 'The Greatest Single Artistic Opportunity Presented to the People of New England,'" *Informational Bulletins on State Problems: Bulletin No. 7* (Burlington: Vermont State Chamber of Commerce, 1934), 2.

91. *The Long Trail News* 8 (April 1935): 2.

92. Letter from George D. Aiken to S. G. Brown, Newfane, 24 February 1936, Aiken Papers, 60-3-5, UVMSC.

93. Letter from George D. Aiken to Birney L. Hall, Montpelier, 18 February 1936, Aiken Papers, 60-3-5, UVMSC.

94. George D. Aiken to C. K. Johnson, Burlington, 28 February 1936, UVMSC, Aiken Papers, 60-3-5.

95. "A Hideous Joke," *Rutland Daily Herald*, 4 September 1934.

96. Peter S. Jennison, *Roadside History of Vermont* (Missoula, MT: Mountain Press, 1989), 246.

97. Frank M. Bryan and Kenneth Bruno, "Black-Topping the Green Mountains: Socio-Economic and Political Correlates of Ecological Decision-Making," *Vermont History* 41 (1973): 224–35; Goldman, "James Taylor's Progressive Vision," 158–79; Hannah Silverstein, "No Parking: Vermont Rejects the Green Mountain Parkway," *Vermont History* 63, n. 3 (Summer 1995): 133–57.

98. M. A. Mattoon, "Memorandum for the Regional Forester," 29 December 1934.

99. R. M. Evans, Memorandum for the Record, 19 January 1935, "GMNF Enabling Legislation" folder, GMNF.

100. Evans, "National Forests in Vermont," 6 February 1935, pp. 12–14.

101. "Legislators Start Drive to Block Further Federal Land Acquisition in State," *Rutland Herald*, 31 January 1935.

102. The officials on the National Forest Board were the governor, lieutenant governor, attorney general, state forester, and commissioner of agriculture. *Acts and Resolves, 1935*, 3–4; M. A. Mattoon, Memorandum for the Files, 8 May 1935, "GMNF Enabling Legislation" folder, GMNF; Letter from Otto Koenig to Regional Forester, WDC, 21 June 1937, "GMNF Enabling Legislation" folder, GMNF.

103. Evans, "Memorandum for the Record," 19 January 1935; Minutes from the committee formed by H. 365, 7 May 1935, Governor Smith Papers, reel S-3196, "Submarginal Lands," Vermont State Archives, Montpelier, VT.. According to Regional Forester Evans, "The half-million acres ultimately destined for National Forest ownership, in accordance with this program, are between 8 and 9 percent of the total land area of the State." Evans, "National Forests in Vermont," 6; Mattoon, Memorandum for the Files, 8 May 1935.

104. Douglass, "Final Draft, History of the Green Mountain N. F.," 94.

105. This practice dates back to the passage of the Weeks Act in 1911, Section 13 of which provided 5 percent of total receipts from timber sales in a given national forest to "the State in which such national forest is situated, to be expended as the state legislature may prescribe for the benefit of the public schools and the public roads of the county or counties in which such national forest is situated." The payment was later raised to 25 percent of sales. Perry Merrill, *History of Forestry in Vermont, 1909–1959* (Montpelier: State Board of Forests and Parks, 1959), 51; Gerald W. Williams, "Private Property to Public Property: The Beginnings of the National Forests in the South," paper prepared for the 2003 American Society for Environmental History conference, Providence, RI, pp. 6, 22; "Towns Receive Share of Nat'l Forest Receipts," *Manchester Journal*, 23 March 1944.

106. In 1941, the state legislature drafted a joint resolution that requested federal reimbursement to towns for the lost revenues due to national forest lands. Although the Forest Service did not comply with this request, citing the Weeks Act formula for reimbursement, the state did thus demonstrate its

frustration with the current state of forest management. By 1964, however, the thirty-three towns with land in the national forest earned revenues from forest harvest equivalent to thirty cents per acre, although the amount varied by harvest year. Evans, "National Forest in Vermont," 11; Andrew E. Nuquist, *Town Government in Vermont* (Burlington: University of Vermont Government Research Center, 1964), 193–94; Douglass, "Final Draft, History of the Green Mountain N. F.," 92, 99.

107. Letter from A. C. Van Nort to Otto G. Koenig, Acting Forest Supervisor, to Regional Forester, Washington, DC, 13 February 1936, GMNF.

108. Letter from Otto G. Koenig to Regional Forester, Washington, DC, 2 March 1936, "L-Boundaries, Green Mountain" folder, GMNF.

109. Letter from Otto G. Koenig, Acting Forest Supervisor, to Regional Forester, Washington, DC, 2 March 1936. GMNF.

CHAPTER 6. REFORMING SUBMARGINAL LANDS, 1933–1938

1. L. C. Gray, "The Resettlement Land Program," *American Forests* (August 1936): 3.

2. Gray, "Resettlement Land Program," 1.

3. "Resettlement Administration," brochure (Washington, DC: Government Printing Office, 1936), SNPA, Zerkel Papers, box 12, folder 3, p. 4.

4. Paul Mertz, *New Deal Policy and Southern Rural Poverty* (Baton Rouge: Louisiana State University, 1978); Grant McConnell, *The Decline of Agrarian Democracy* (Berkeley: University of California, 1959), 96.

5. Jess Gilbert, "Rural Sociology and Democratic Planning in the Third New Deal," *Agricultural History* 82 (Fall 2008): 424, 434; Jess Gilbert and Alice O'Connor, "Leaving the Land Behind: Struggles for Land Reform in U.S. Federal Policy, 1933–1965," in *Who Owns America: Social Conflict Over Property Rights,* ed. Harvey M. Jacobs (Madison: University of Wisconsin Press, 1998), 114.

6. The major New Deal policy histories to consider land use are Sidney Baldwin, *Poverty and Politics: The Rise and Decline of the Farm Security Administration* (Chapel Hill: University of North Carolina Press, 1968); Marion Clawson, *New Deal Planning: The National Resources Planning Board* (Baltimore: Johns Hopkins University Press, 1981); Paul Conkin, *Tomorrow a New World* (New York: Da Capo, 1976); Kirkendall, *Social Scientists and Farm Politics*; and Bernard Sternsher, *Rexford Tugwell and the New Deal* (New Brunswick, NJ: Rutgers University Press, 1964).

7. For an assessment of the compromised vision of the TVA, see Michael J. McDonald and John Muldowny, *TVA and the Dispossessed: The Resettlement of Population in the Norris Dam Area* (Knoxville: University of Tennessee Press, 1982); see also James Scott, "High Modernist Social Engineering: The Case of the Tennessee Valley Authority," in *Experiencing the State,* ed. Lloyd I. Rudolph and John Kurt Jacobsen (New York: Oxford University Press, 2006), 19–20; Sarah T. Phillips, *This Land, This Nation* (New York: Cambridge

University Press, 2007), 83–107; Neil Maher, *Nature's New Deal* (New York: Oxford University Press, 2008), 191–200.

8. Among the best accounts of this period are David Hamilton, *From New Day to New Deal* (Chapel Hill: University of North Carolina Press, 1991); David Kennedy, *Freedom From Fear* (New York: Oxford University Press, 1999); and William Leuchtenburg, *Franklin D. Roosevelt and the New Deal* (New York: Harper and Row, 1963).

9. The Land Policy Section was headed by H. R. Tolley, a native of Indiana and graduate of Indiana University, who moved to the BAE in 1923 and helped to shape its research program. From 1933 to 1935 Tolley served as chief of AAA Program Planning Division, before returning to the BAE as its chief from 1938 to 1946. Richard Kirkendall, *Social Scientists and Farm Politics in the Age of Roosevelt* (Columbia: University of Missouri Press, 1966), 15–17, 70–74.

10. "Resettlement Administration," 1, 13.

11. L. C. Gray, "Some Ways of Dealing With the Problems of Submarginal Land," in *Proceedings of the National Conference on Land Utilization*, Chicago, IL, November 19–21, 1931 (Washington, DC: Government Printing Office, 1932), 58.

12. Kirkendall, *Social Scientists and Farm Politics*; Baldwin, *Poverty and Politics*.

13. The functions of the Land Policy Section of the AAA were defined as follows: "To determine the total area of land needed for production of the various agricultural commodities and forest products in the US; to work with other agencies in designating areas which need to be withdrawn from agricultural production and areas which should be restricted to extensive use, and in determining utilization of areas withdrawn from farming; in general to coordinate the program of the AAA with the government land utilization program." The Surplus Relief Corporation appointed the AAA as the administrator of the planning and development of specific submarginal land acquisition projects. "Retirement of Land Studied, Vermont Committee Prepares to Join Federal Project," *Brattleboro Daily Reformer*, 10 July 1934; letter from L. C. Gray to J. E. Carrigan, 25 May 1934, Governor Wilson Papers, reel S-3192, "Submarginal Lands," Vermont State Archives (hereafter referred to as the VSA); Spencer D. Wood and Jess Gilbert, "Autonomous Policy Expert or 'Power Elite' Member?: Rexford G. Tugwell and the Creation of the U.S. Resettlement Administration in 1935," paper delivered at the Social Science History Association, Chicago, IL, October 1992, 25; Henry A. Wallace, *New Frontiers* (New York: Reynal and Hitchcock, 1934), 242–43.

14. "Niagara County Man Doing Colossal Job for the Government," *The Evening* [illegible], in Rexford Tugwell papers, Clippings: 1933–34, container 111, at FDR Library, Hyde Park, NY; Rexford G. Tugwell, "Resettling America: A Vast Land Program," *New York Times*, 14 January 1934.

15. The committee members were Commissioner of Agriculture E. H. Jones, State Forester Perry Merrill, Commissioner of Fish and Game James Brown, and J. A. Hitchcock, agricultural economist at the University of Vermont. "Retirement of Land Studied."

16. The location of this committee report in the governor's papers indicates that it came into his files during the early summer of 1934. It is probably the document referred to by a letter on 8 June from E. H. Jones to Governor Wilson. "A Proposal for the Withdrawal From Cultivation of Poor Farm Lands in Vermont Under the Federal Submarginal Land Acquisition Program," Governor Wilson Papers, reel S-3192, "Submarginal Lands," VSA.

17. The report also suggested that two or three towns be eliminated, though it did not indicate which ones; it argued that significant savings could be achieved from this consolidation. "Proposal for the Withdrawal From Cultivation."

18. It is worth noting that the first proposal had suggested 86,000 acres for immediate federal purchase and the relocation of 295 families, while the August proposal was less expansive in its description of 20,000 acres for purchase and 250 families for resettlement. E. H. Jones, *Agriculture of Vermont: Seventeenth Biennial Report of the Commissioner of Agriculture of the State of Vermont, 1932–1934* (Montpelier, 1934); Submarginal Land Committee, "A Proposal for the Purchase of Submarginal Lands in Vermont," 14 August 1934, Governor Wilson Papers, reel S-3192, "Submarginal Lands," VSA; letter from Governor Stanley Wilson to the Submarginal Land Committee, 14 September 1934, Governor Wilson Papers, reel S-3192, "Submarginal Lands," VSA.

19. George D. Aiken, *Speaking from Vermont* (New York: Frederick A. Stokes, 1938), 10; D. Gregory Sanford, "The Presidential Boomlet for Governor George D. Aiken, 1937–1939; or, You Can't Get There from Here" (master's thesis, University of Vermont, 1977), 69.

20. Untitled memo, SNPA, L. Ferdinand Zerkel Papers, box 5, folder 3; L. Ferdinand Zerkel to Hon. Wm. E. Carson, 5 December 1930, NARA, 79/10A/445/6.

21. Section 208 of the National Industrial Relations Act (NIRA) allotted money for the creation of communities of subsistence homesteads that would serve the needs of "stranded" urbanites. The NIRA funded the subsistence homesteads project, allocating twenty-five million dollars to "provide for aiding in the redistribution of the overbalance of population in industrial centers," combining jobs and farm homes for underemployed workers. John H. Bankhead, "The One Way to Permanent National Recovery," *Liberty* 10 (July 22, 1933): 18. Conkin, *Tomorrow a New World*, 87–88, 102.

22. United States Department of the Interior, Division of Subsistence Homesteads, "General Information Concerning the Purposes and Policies of the Division of Subsistence Homesteads," circular 1 (Washington, DC: Government Printing Office, 1933), 5.

23. "Park Subsistence Homes Are Set Up," *The Evening Star* (Washington, DC), 21 April 1934.

24. Twenty-one men and women spread through the mountains investigating the 465 families who still remained within the park boundaries, and the Shenandoah Homesteads office subsequently developed a projection of the prospective homesteaders' requirements for assistance. The survey reported that,

although there had once been 511 families resident within the park boundaries, 84 had moved by September 1935. "Names of Park Area Families," SNPA, Resource Management Records, box 100, folder 1; "Summary of Preliminary Information for Proposed Subsistence Homestead Project for the Shenandoah Park Families," SNPA, Resource Management Records, box 99, folder 7.

25. "Reasons for Small Communities," SNPA, Zerkel Papers, box 5, folder 3, p.2; "Plan of Cooperation between Subsistence Homesteads and Federal Emergency Relief Administration in Shenandoah Park Project," SNPA, Resource Management Records, Moving Schedules, 1934–1940, box 101, folder 5.

26. The Division of Subsistence Homesteads purchased a total of 6,889 acres surrounding the park for an average price of forty-six dollars per acre. The committee convened in 1934 was composed of B. L. Hummel, director of the Virginia Agricultural Extension Service; M. M. Kelso, chief of the Planning Section, Division of Subsistence Homesteads; L. Ferdinand Zerkel, supervisor of the Subsistence Homesteads project; and two clerks from Zerkel's staff, Vincent R. Rhodes and Robert F. Strickler. The committee reviewed sites from June 6 to June 8, 1934. "Copy of Report of Dr. S. S. Obenshain, Soils Specialist, VPI and State Department of Agriculture," in Resource Management Records, Moving Schedules, 1934–1940, box 101, folder 5; Letter from G. H. Clark, County Agent, to L. F. Zerkel, 28 September 1935, SNPA, Zerkel Papers, box 5, folder 3. An untitled press release from the FSA notes the expectation that approximately 175 of the 250 families remaining in the park would be resettled to the homestead communities: 5 May 1937, SNPA, Zerkel Papers, box 6, folder 4.

27. Wallace, *New Frontiers*, 240–41.

28. Wallace, *New Frontiers*, 248.

29. William E. Leuchtenburg, *Flood Control Politics: The Connecticut River Valley Problem, 1927–1950* (Cambridge, MA: Harvard University Press, 1953), 37–38.

30. A retrospective on the Subsistence Homesteads program cautioned critical observers to acknowledge the emergency that faced the nation in 1933, and to recognize the tremendous needs of the moment. "We must constantly remind ourselves, as we look at these projects today, that they were established at a time when haste had to be a watchword, when pressures were coming from all sides, and when there was no experience in such matters that could be taken as a guide." Russell Lord and Paul H. Johnstone, *A Place on Earth: A Critical Appraisal of Subsistence Homesteads* (Washington, DC: USDA, 1942), 3; Conkin, *Tomorrow a New World*, 128.

31. FERA rural rehabilitation communities were all planned for relief clients, so they resembled most the stranded communities of Subsistence Homesteads. Prospective settlers did most of the work for the communities. Conkin, *Tomorrow a New World*, 136–37.

32. "Reasons for Small Communities," notes by Zerkel on Shenandoah Homesteads project, SNPA, L. Ferdinand Zerkel papers, box 5, folder 3; Zerkel, "Em-

ployment History and Notes of Personal Comments upon L. Ferdinand Zerkel, Project Manager, Shenandoah Park Homesteads," compiled by Zerkel on 22 February 1937, SNPA, Zerkel Papers. Text included in collection finding aid.

33. "Reasons for Small Communities"; "Employment History and Notes of Personal Comments"; "Mountain People," undated notes from L. Ferdinand Zerkel to Director of the National Park Service, Arno Cammerer, and Secretary of the Interior Harold Ickes, received by the Department of the Interior, 10 April 1935, NARA, 79/10B/1654/1.

34. Around Lake Bomoseen, between 3,000 and 8,000 acres were under option in Hubbardton, Pittsford, Castleton, and environs. Minutes from meeting of legislative board mandated by H. 365, 7 May 1935, Governor Smith Papers, reel S-3196, "Submarginal Lands," VSA; Perry H. Merrill, *The Making of a Forester: An Autobiographical History* (Montpelier: Perry H. Merrill, 1984), 70; Richard West Sellers, *Preserving Nature in the National Parks: A History* (New Haven: Yale University Press, 1997), 135–36.

35. In his autobiography, Merrill alludes to the resettlement program in conjunction with the possibility of National Park Service–sponsored recreational demonstration projects in the area around Lake Bomoseen. But he never discussed the significance of the RA program, or his appointment as an agent of the federal government in the State of Vermont. This omission seems noteworthy, and it suggests Bradder's early appointment as project manager, because Merrill's text tends to list every honor, award, appointment, or project he received or was involved with. Or, perhaps the politics of the RA caused him some political discomfort and he attempted to distance himself from the program. Letter from Perry Merrill to Hon. Stanley C. Wilson, 25 September 1934, Governor Wilson Papers, reel S-3192, "Submarginal Lands," VSA; Letter from A. W. Manchester to Perry Merrill, 24 September 1934, Governor Wilson Papers, reel S-3192, "Submarginal Lands," VSA.

36. The motto of Aiken Nurseries, the lieutenant governor's business, was: "Grown in Vermont, It's Hardy." Letter from Aiken Nurseries re. Beck order for plants, 25 November 1936, National Archives and Records Administration, Waltham, MA (hereafter National Archives, Waltham), 96/32/127/VT-723-05.

37. Samuel B. Hand and D. Gregory Sanford, "Carrying Water on Both Shoulders: George D. Aiken's 1936 Gubernatorial Campaign in Vermont," *Vermont History* 43 (1975): 292–306; Michael Sherman, ed., *The Political Legacy of George D. Aiken, Wise Old Owl of the U. S. Senate* (Woodstock, VT: The Countryman Press, 1995).

38. Aiken, *Speaking from Vermont,* 22.

39. Aiken, *Speaking from Vermont,* 17, 30; "One Phase of the Submarginal Land Problem and its Relation to Proposed Purchase and Retirement by A.A.A.," Governor Smith Papers, reel S-3196, "Submarginal Lands," VSA.

40. In 1929, Byrd traveled to Vermont to give a talk on his signature economic program, "pay as you go." Ronald Heinemann, *Harry Byrd of Virginia*

(Charlottesville: University of Virginia Press, 1996); Leuchtenburg, *Flood Control Politics*. George Aiken cited in Sanford, "Presidential Boomlet," 69, 77.

41. "The idea for this agency was my own, and I was made its administrator. President Roosevelt was, however, immediately interested because it touched matters he cared about a great deal." Rexford G. Tugwell, "The Resettlement Idea," *Agricultural History* 33 (October 1959): 159; Conkin, *Tomorrow a New World*, 153.

42. Roosevelt's decision to establish the agency in the executive branch, which protected the purity of its mission, also eventually undermined the agency because of its lack of legislative sanction. Like other emergency agencies, the RA was thus freed from the precedents in the USDA, and allowed to shape its mission to solve the "new and complex problems" of the age. This was Roosevelt's frequent response to the problems of the day, and one which backfired as often as it succeeded. William E. Leuchtenburg, *The FDR Years: On Roosevelt and His Legacy* (New York: Columbia University Press, 1995), 23; Baldwin, *Poverty and Politics*, 91.

43. Tugwell, "Resettlement Idea," 159.

44. Tugwell, "Resettlement Idea," 160.

45. Gray, "Resettlement Land Program," 1.

46. Baldwin, *Poverty and Politics*, 93.

47. Baldwin, *Poverty and Politics*, 91–94.

48. Roosevelt directed the RA: "(*a*) To administer approved projects involving resettlement of destitute or low-income families from rural and urban areas, including the establishment, maintenance, and operation, in such connection, of communities in rural and suburban areas. (*b*) To initiate and administer a program of approved projects with respect to soil erosion, stream pollution, seacoast erosion, reforestation, forestation, and flood control. . . . To the extent necessary to carry out the provisions of this Executive Order the Administrator is authorized to acquire, by purchase or the power of eminent domain, any real property or any interest therein and improve, develop, grant, sell, lease (with our without the privilege of purchasing), or otherwise dispose of any such property or interest therein." Telegram from Carl C. Taylor, Director of the Division of Resettlement and Rural Rehabilitation, to Governor Charles Smith, 22 June 1935, Governor Smith Papers, reel S-3195, "Rural Rehabilitation," VSA; Franklin D. Roosevelt, Executive Order for the Establishment of the Resettlement Administration (No. 7027), 30 April 1935, amended 26 September 1935.

49. "Rehabilitation Gives a Man a Break," *Vermont Farm Bureau News* (October 1935): 8ff.

50. John Nolen, Philip Shutler, Albert La Fleur, and Dana M. Doten, "Graphic Survey: A First Step in State Planning," report submitted to the Vermont State Planning Board and National Resources Board, p. 15, UVMSC.

51. H. 365 of 1935 (Act 3), reported by the Committee on Conservation and Development, "An Act Giving Consent to the Acquisition by the United States by Purchase or Gift of Certain Lands Under Certain Conditions" signed by Governor Smith on 10 April 1935, *Senate Journal, 1935* (Montpelier: Capital City Press, 1935), 718; Aiken, *Speaking from Vermont*, 10.

52. Act 3 of 1935; Christopher McGrory Klyza and Stephen Trombulak, *The Story of Vermont* (Hanover, NH: Middlebury College Press, 1999), 100; Minutes from meeting of legislative board mandated by H. 365, 3 October 1935, Governor Smith Papers, reel S-3196, "Submarginal Lands," VSA.

53. This board consisted of the lieutenant governor, speaker of the house, auditor of accounts, and attorney general. Also present at this meeting were the governor and the commissioner of forestry. Minutes from the committee formed by H. 365, 7 May 1935, Governor Smith Papers, reel S-3196, "Submarginal Lands," VSA.

54. Letter from W. E. Bradder to Governor Charles Smith, 17 August 1935, Governor Smith Papers, reel S-3196, "Submarginal Lands," VSA; Minutes from the committee formed by H. 365, 7 May 1935.

55. Letter from George Gercke to Kenneth Clark, 13 December 1935, National Archives, Waltham, 96/32/50/163

56. Letter from George Gercke to Frederick R. Soule, Regional Information Officer, RA, San Francisco, 28 May 1937, National Archives, Waltham, 96/32/50/163.

57. Minutes from meeting of legislative board mandated by H. 365, 3 October 1935, VSA, Smith Papers.

58. Aiken, *Speaking from Vermont*, 11.

59. Arthur Schmidt, Jr., "Aiken and the Hillside Mentality: The Early Political Career of George David Aiken of Vermont" (senior thesis, Princeton University, nd.), 60, cites *Brattleboro Reformer*, 15 October 1936.

60. Letter from A. W. Manchester to Attorney General Lawrence Jones, n.d., Governor Smith Papers, reel S-3196, "Submarginal Lands," VSA; Letter from Aiken to Hon. Ernest E. Moore, 6 February 1936, Aiken Papers, UVMSC, crate 60, box 3, folder 5.

61. Address of Governor Charles M. Smith to the Joint Assembly, Special Session, Tuesday, December 10, 1935, *Journal of the Joint Assembly, Special Session, 1935–1936* (Montpelier: Capital City Press, 1936), 121; letter from Charles Kraus to Rexford Tugwell, 24 January 1936, National Archives, Waltham, 96/32/46/LE-VT-142.

62. Letter from George D. Aiken, Lieutenant Governor, to J. W. T. Wettleson, Managing Editor, *The Rutland Daily Herald*, 7 January 1936, Aiken papers, UVMSC, crate 60, box 3, folder 4.

63. As Tugwell observed retrospectively, during the controversy over the expansion of the Supreme Court, "President Roosevelt was defeated in that engagement in a peculiarly humiliating way. But less spectacularly he began to lose battles for the continuation of the New Deal agencies. During the next few

years many of them were either disallowed or emasculated in the continuing Executive-Legislative struggle. And Resettlement Administration was one of the first to go." Tugwell, "Resettlement Idea," 163.

64. Letter from Aiken to Wettleson, 7 January 1936.

65. *House Journal, Special Session 1935–1936* (Montpelier: Capital City Press, 1936): 1264, 1301–2, 1336–39, 1341–43, 1379.

66. Although eventually Bomoseen State Park was dedicated in 1959, Merrill recalled that this project was made possible only through a large gift of land from the estate of a local landowner, and it cost the state far more than the original recreational demonstration project would have. Ultimately, more than twenty years had passed since the RA program fizzled, during which generations of children had been denied the pleasure of a local lakefront park. Merrill, *Making of a Forester,* 70; Letter from Dorothy M. Beck to Governor Smith, 10 April 1936, Governor Smith Papers, reel S-3194, "Rural Rehabilitation," VSA.

67. Report from John O. Walker, Director, Resettlement Division, to C. B. Baldwin, Assistant Administrator, RA, on the "Brief Study of the Social and Economic Status of Families on LP-VA-7 and the Adjoining Shenandoah Park Area Proper," 8 June 1937, NARA 96/4A/492/1.

68. Darwin Lambert, *The Undying Past of the Shenandoah National Park* (Boulder, CO: Roberts Rinehart, 1989), 252; Letter from John Fischer, Acting Director, FSA Division of Information, to Miss Nora E. Crickenberger, 10 March 1938, NARA, 79/10A/491/1; Letter from Walter E. Packard, Director, Rural Resettlement Division, RA, to Arno Cammerer, Director, NPS, 10 December 1936, SNPA, Resource Management Records, box 101, folder 9; Untitled memo, 5 May 1937, SNPA, Zerkel papers, box 6, folder 4; B. L. Hummel, "Summary Statement Concerning Families in the Shenandoah Park Area," SNPA, Resource Management Records, box 99, folder 7.

69. The tools were enumerated in project documents: two hoes, a hand plow, a combination seeder, a rake, a pruning shear, a grub axe, a pick, an axe, a carpenter's saw, a hatchet, a milk pail, and a strand of cable. Outline of Shenandoah Homesteads Project, Schedule Xva, "Estimated Cost per Homestead (200 Families)," SNPA, Moving Schedules, 1934–1940, Resource Management Records, box 101, folder 5, p. 2; Letter from Fischer to Crickenberger, 10 March 1938.

70. Outline of Shenandoah Homesteads Project, Schedule Xva, p. 1.

71. See Paul Conkin, *Tomorrow a New World,* for a similar face-off between Ickes and Eleanor Roosevelt over provisions for the Subsistence Homesteads community in Red House/Arthurdale, WV. Conkin, *Tomorrow a New World,* 171.

72. USDA, FSA, "Shenandoah Homesteads: Final Report of Project Costs to June 30, 1939," as cited in Conkin. Conkin set the cost at $6,626 for 160 units, for a total expenditure of $1,060,125.49. See the chart in Conkin, *Tomorrow a New World,* p. 333, which conflicts with his figures on p. 164.

73. Conkin, *Tomorrow a New World,* 164; Ronald L. Heinemann, *Depression and New Deal in Virginia: The Enduring Dominion* (Charlottesville: University Press of Virginia, 1983), 124.

74. Thomas R. Henry, "200 Years of Calm in Blue Ridge Hollow Broken as Resettlement Workmen Erect New Village," *Washington Post,* undated clipping (1936), SNPA, Resource Management Records, box 131, folder 7; Letter from Mable B. Humrickhouse to R. Taylor Hoskins, 18 March 1938, SNPA Resource Management Records, box 101, folder 4.

75. "Resettlement," *Baltimore Sun,* 10 June 1936.

76. Conkin, *Tomorrow a New World,* 127; "To Pay $5 A Month Rental," *Page News and Courier,* 28 December 1937.

77. "Park Settlement Opens Next Week," Harrisonburg *Daily News-Record,* 17 September 1935; Lambert, *Undying Past,* 252; Superintendent's Monthly Reports, October and November, 1937, January 1938, March 1938, NARA, 79/10B/1639/3; Letter from Fischer to Crickenberger.

78. In spite of the enthusiasm generated among planners and some farmers over the programs of the Resettlement Administration, only 4,441 families were moved nationwide—only a sliver of the 500,000 projected in early estimates. "Resettlement Administration," in *The Historical Dictionary of the New Deal,* ed. James S. Olson (Westport, CT: Greenwood Press, 1985), 419; Donald Holley, *Uncle Sam's Farmers: The New Deal Communities in the Lower Mississippi Valley* (Urbana: University of Illinois Press, 1975).

79. Anthony J. Badger, *The New Deal: The Depression Years* (Chicago: Ivan R. Dee, 2002), 148.

80. Leuchtenburg, *Franklin D. Roosevelt and the New Deal,* 140.

81. Aiken, *Speaking from Vermont,* 9.

82. Benjamin Gates, Auditor of Accounts, at meeting of Submarginal Land Board, 7 May 1935, Submarginal Lands Board minutes, p. 2. Governor Smith Papers, reel S-3196, "Submarginal Lands," VSA..

83. Rexford G. Tugwell, "Resettlement Administration," *The Democratic Book, 1936* (Philadelphia: Democratic National Convention, 1936), 249; Luther A. Huston, "Resettlement Agency Expects to Carry On," *New York Times,* 21 November 1936.

EPILOGUE

1. According to a list from December 31, 1934, a total of thirty-six households (typically of one to two people, of ages ranging from 58 to 89 years) were approved by the Secretary of the Interior to retain their homes in the park until their deaths. The number of Old Age Exemptions fluctuated during the park development, but there were originally around forty houses that remained occupied after the park removals. "Aged Residence [sic] Residing in Park Area," n.d., but with note reading "List approved by Sec'y Dec 31, 1934 to remain in park for balance of life," NARA, 79/10B/1652/3.

2. James Risser, "The Forest Service and its Critics," *The Living Wilderness* 37 (Summer 1973): 9; The Wilderness Society editorial updates, "Eastern Front," *The Living Wilderness* 36 (Spring 1972): 6.

3. Bill Richards, "Wilderness Battle Rages: Residents See U.S. Designation as Intrusion," *Washington Post,* 16 November 1975.

4. Press Release, "Forest Service to Implement New Wilderness Law," December 4, 2006, p. 2.

5. As Richard W. Judd and Christopher S. Beach explain in *Natural States: The Environmental Imagination in Maine, Oregon, and the Nation* (Washington: RFF Press, 2003), this concern was part of a larger national awakening of environmental consciousness. See also Harold A. Meeks, *Vermont's Land and Resources* (Shelburne, VT: The New England Press, 1986), 283; Blake Harrison, *The View From Vermont: Tourism and the Making of an American Rural Landscape* (Lebanon, NH: University of Vermont Press, 2006), 217–20.

6. State of Vermont, *Governor's Commission on Environmental Control, Reports to Governor,* January 19, 1970, May 18, 1970, 1–3.

7. The Commission was popularly referred to as the Gibb Commission, after its chair Arthur Gibb. Meeks, *Vermont's Land and Resources,* 288; Harrison, *View From Vermont,* 220–23.

8. Meeks, *Vermont's Land and Resources,* 289; Harrison, *View From Vermont,* 223–24.

9. In 1975 George Aiken retired from the Senate, and Harry Flood Byrd, Jr., was gearing up to run for reelection to his father's Senate seat.

10. Green Mountain Club, *Long Trail Guide* (Waterbury Center, VT: Green Mountain Club, 2000), 1–2.

11. Blake Harrison, *The View from Vermont* (Burlington: University of Vermont Press, 2006) 216, cites Vermont Agency of Environmental Conservation, *Vermont Vacation Home Inventory, 1973* (Montpelier: The Agency, 1974), 3, 6.

"Citizenry and the State in the Shaping of Environmental Policy"
Susan L. Flader : Environmental History Vol. 3 (Jan 1998) 8-24

· "As a people, we don't really appreciate the extent to which our
centuries-long skepticism of governmental authority — our preference
for a limited state — has necessitated a concomitantly strong tradition
of civic involvement in the affairs of our communities and our nation. 8

· I would like to encourage more attention to the relationship of citizens
and the state in our own historical tradition, 10

· I think that a tension has persisted throughout our American environmental
experience between the claims of the community and the self-interest
of individuals. 11

· As conflicts over competing visions of society increasingly found
resolution in the courts rather than legislatures, dynamic, development-
oriented uses of property tended to win out over traditional or static
uses, as Ted Steinberg demonstrates in "Nature Incorporated." 11

· When Alexis de Tocqueville observed democracy in America in the
1830s, he marveled at the ability of our "incomplete national gov't"
to hold in dynamic tension the power of a centralized state and
the security of a small republic. The security resulted from what
Tocqueville called the "principle of association", 12 ... In
Tocqueville's view, the extreme atomism of democratic society made
the possibility of voluntary association a virtual necessity.

· "One of the first lessons we learned at Hull-House," wrote Jane Addams,
" was that private beneficence is totally inadequate to deal with
the vast numbers of the city's disinherited." She and her coworkers
were always ready to hand over their activities to willing governments, 15